MW01061443

SISTERS OF THE ACADEMY

SISTERS OF THE ACADEMY

Emergent Black Women Scholars in Higher Education

Reitumetse Obakeng Mabokela and Anna L. Green, Editors

STERLING, VIRGINIA

Published in 2001 by

Stylus Publishing, LLC
22883 Quicksilver Drive
Sterling, Virginia 20166

Copyright © 2001 by Stylus Publishing, LLC

All rights reserved. No part of this book may be reprinted or reproduced in any form or by any electronic, mechanical or other means, now known or hereafter invented, including photocopying, recording and information storage and retrieval, without permission in writing from the publishers.

Library of Congress Cataloging-in-Publication Data

Sisters of the academy : emergent Black women scholars in higher education / edited by Reitumetse Obakeng Mabokela and Anna L. Green.—1st. ed.
    p. cm.
  Includes bibliographical references and index
   ISBN 1-57922-038-X (alk. paper)—ISBN 1-57922-039-8 (pbk. : alk. paper)
    1. Afro-American women college teachers—Social conditions—20th century. 2. Discrimination in higher education—United States. 3. Sex discrimination in higher education—United States. I. Mabokela, Reitumetse Obakeng. II. Green, Anna L. (Anna Lucille), 1970–

LC2781.5 .S57 2001
378'.0082—dc21

00-066131

First edition, 2001
ISBN: hardcover 1-57922-038-X
ISBN: paperback 1-57922-039-8

Printed in the United States of America

All first editions printed on acid-free paper

10 9 8 7 6 5 4 3 2 1

CONTENTS

PREFACE
Lee Jones

As I read through the pages of this long awaited book, I was reminded of the paradox of our time. Africans in America have made significant accomplishments through turbulent times but yet have so far to go. As the editor of *Brothers of the Academy* (a volume that chronicles the experiences of African American men in the academy), I have received hundreds of inquiries from scholars around the country who ask, "What about the sisters of the academy?" This is a critical question. While African American men and women scholars share similar concerns in the academy, there are issues that speak directly to the experience of sisters. *Sisters of the Academy* is both a response to these inquiries and a reflection of a particular experience within the academy as seen through the eyes of African American scholars.

In the pages that follow, scholarship, research, and personal testimonies take us on a journey through the lives of fifteen African American women whose stories may otherwise not be told. The substance of the chapters shared by these women is timely and extremely relevant for all scholars of higher education.

It has been an honor to serve as the consulting editor of this book because I saw firsthand the hard work and dedication of the co-editors, Reitumetse Obakeng Mabokela and Anna L. Green. This exciting and substantive book holds special meaning for me as an African American man and scholar for a number of reasons: First, it reflects the hopes and visions of African America women, such as Mary McLeod Bethune, Toni Morrison, and Johnetta Betsch Cole, who preceded us. Second, while it highlights the scholarship of a few African American women, it speaks volumes about the broader experience of other women in the academy. Finally, it is written by and about African American women.

Stories of African American women scholars have often been written and told by those who have never experienced what I believe to be the tri-consciousness of African American women's experiences. The first level of consciousness emerges from being an African woman in America. Given the racialized history of this country, women of African descent have not been provided with the comfort of living their dreams and aspirations based on their own concepts of reality. For the most part, their lives have been defined by other people's perception of reality. History has shown us that those women who dared to live and guide their lives using their own perspectives have become misplaced, marginalized, and dispossessed.

The second level of consciousness relats to being a woman in a male-dominated society, including the higher education sector. Despite the fact that there are more female college students than there are males, there is still a disproportionately high number of men who occupy major leadership positions in higher education. Women continue to be critically under-represented in the upper echelons of the higher education hierarchy. For African American women, the numbers are more dismal.

The third level of consciousness, so real to many African American women with whom I have communicated, is almost too taboo to discuss, that is, inequities *within* the African American community of scholars. Despite the fact that the struggles of African American men and women are inextricably intertwined, there are continuing disparities that compromise the accomplishments of African American women. As an African American male scholar, this is a reality that must be acknowledged and addressed.

As I read through the pages of this book, I found myself, quietly and sometimes very loudly, crying. Crying because the narratives in this volume took me on an emotional roller coaster. On one hand, I was intellectually stimulated by the thought-provoking discussions; while on the other hand, I was moved by the painful truth of some of the experiences shared. The chapters left me drained because, in many ways, they reflect how far we still have to go to truly humanize the academy. Many of the chapters re-educated me about the struggles African American women face in higher education. As scholars, understanding the content of this book places a tremendous responsibility on our shoulders to do our part to make the academy more accountable to African American women and others who choose higher education as a viable career option.

Finally, I applaud the efforts of Reitumetse Obakeng Mabokela and Anna L. Green for undertaking the important task of co-editing this book. Each of them will continue to play an important role in shaping the culture of higher education institutions to be more responsive to the needs of African American women. I acknowledge the hard work and commitment of the other contributing authors whose tenacity saw this project to its completion. I am humbled and honored to have played a small role in such a significant book. I am positive that the scholarly contributions of these women will impact the lives of all who are serious about equity, equality, and true academic freedom.

ACKNOWLEDGMENTS

We sincerely thank the thirteen sisters who contributed to this volume. *Sisters of the Academy* would not have seen the light of day without your contributions. Many thanks to Lee Jones for his feedback and insight, from the beginning to the end of this process. We express our appreciation to our publisher, John von Knorring, and the staff at Stylus Publishing who worked diligently with us to produce this book. We thank Yvonne Weems for her administrative support and Sarah Wiseman for her prompt and thorough assistance with the proofreading. Our greatest appreciation goes to our family members for their continued love, support, and encouragement in our various professional pursuits.

Dr. Reitumetse Obakeng Mabokela

Dr. Reitumetse Obakeng Mabokela is currently an assistant professor in the Higher, Adult, and Lifelong Education (HALE) program in the Department of Educational Administration at Michigan State University. She received her doctorate in the Department of Educational Policy Studies at the University of Illinois at Urbana-Champaign and her masters degree in labor and industrial relations from the same institution. She received her bachelor of arts degree in economics (*magna cum laude*) from Ohio Wesleyan University, where she was inducted into the Phi Beta Kappa honor society.

Dr. Mabokela maintains an active research agenda in South Africa and the United States. Her research interests include an examination of race, ethnicity, and gender issues in postsecondary education; leadership issues among Black female faculty and administrators; and organizational culture and its impact on historically marginalized groups. Dr. Mabokela is the author of the recently released *Voices of Conflict: Desegregating South African Universities,* which examines how academic programs and structures at historically White South African universities have been affected by, and have responded to, changes in their undergraduate student populations. She is the co-editor of the forthcoming *Apartheid No More: Case Studies of Southern African Universities in the Process of Transformation,* which chronicles the divergent transformation experiences of institutions of higher education in South Africa and Namibia. As an emergent scholar, she has published articles in *Comparative Education, American Educational Research Journal,* the *Journal of Negro Education, Education as Change,* and other academic journals.

Dr. Mabokela is a member of various professional organizations: the Comparative and International Education Society (CIES), the Association for the Study of Higher Education (ASHE), and the American Educational Research Association (AERA), where she has presented scholarly papers.

INTRODUCTION

SOARING BEYOND BOUNDARIES

Reitumetse Obakeng Mabokela

As a young girl growing up in South Africa under apartheid policies of the former National Party government, I was not completely aware of the far-reaching and detrimental implications of these discriminatory policies. Growing up in a small town in the heart of the Free State province, life looked pretty good. I was surrounded by my parents, extended family members, friends, and community members who loved and cared about me and nurtured my unwounded spirit so that I could soar beyond the trappings of the apartheid system.

As I grew older and spread my wings beyond the protective cocoon of my family and community, I began to experience and understand the insidious nature of apartheid, especially its impact on the education of Black children. This is a system that branded all Black people as inferior and underclass in their own country. It was peculiar that even though Black South Africans comprised 85 percent of the total population of this country, their (our) lives were confined to barren, economically unsustainable homelands comparable to Indian reservations in the United States. The government at that time passed a plethora of stringent laws that virtually dictated and criminalized the most normal activities of their (our) lives, from where we could live, work, and attend school or university, to where we could be buried. These government initiatives sought to marginalize the productive engagement of Blacks in the political, economic, social, and cultural life of South African society.

The education system of this country did not escape the atrocious aims of apartheid. In fact, the government took great care to establish a racially divided system of education, which provided White students with the best resources, facilities, teachers, and opportunities. The curriculum was used as a tool to imbue Black students with negative images of their culture; a weapon to decimate the very core of their identity; a mechanism to reinforce the subservient position that the government had reserved for Blacks in the social hierarchy of this society; and a way to perpetuate the inflated position of White/European culture as superior. As an example, the history curriculum rarely discussed positive contributions of Black South Africans. Although our parents told us stories about powerful African leaders like Chief Moroka of the Barolong, Chief Moshoeshoe of the Basotho, and King Shaka of the Zulu, they rarely made it into the history books. If there were any discussions of Africans, they were frequently presented as "savages and pagans" who had to be "christianized" and inculcated with the morals and values of "civilized" culture, or as stupid, lazy, and untrustworthy. We had to read about European settlers who "discovered" South Africa and brought "civilization" to this part of the world. Needless to say, there were indigenous African peoples who occupied this part of the African continent. It is in this system riddled with racial disparities that I found the foundations of my early education.

In the midst of this turbulence that sought to assault the very essence of our existence, there were teachers who quietly defied the goals of apartheid and created a space where Black students could dream and envision a future full of hope and success. These teachers were our parents at home, instructors in the schools, and other adults (elders) in the broader community who inculcated us with life lessons that would fortify us against the daily assaults of inequitable treatment. They created a space where they could nurture our spirit so we could ascend beyond the potentially devastating effects of deeply entrenched discrimination.

My unwounded spirit (and access to certain opportunities) carried me thousands of miles across the Atlantic ocean to pursue my postsecondary studies in the United States. I was struck by the similarities that I observed in these two societies. With each passing year, I noted how the system of education privileged some groups while chronically failing to provide adequate academic preparation for other groups. I was particularly unnerved by pervasive inequities, which seemed to systematically jeopardize the academic success of students of color, students in urban environments, women, students in poor rural communities, and other groups of students who were (are) seen as invasive "Others." Once again I found (and find) myself reliving parts of a reality I thought I had left behind in apartheid South Africa.

The Context

In the United States, women of African descent[1] are confronted with many of the same challenges that limit access to opportunities and threaten their (our)

---

1. In this introduction, I use the terms Black women, African American women, and women of African descent interchangeably.

success in the education sector. Pervasive representations of Black women in the popular media type them (us) as "welfare queens," "over-sexed," "manipulative," "lazy," "exotic," and other such morbid labels. In cases where women of African descent are presented in a less negative light, images of success have been limited to those in the entertainment industry. While we cannot negate the contributions of entertainers, they represent a small fraction of Black women. *Sisters of the Academy* does not dwell on these negative portrayals of women of African descent but rather highlights and celebrates their contributions and successes in academic environments that are not always supportive. The fifteen women scholars who contributed to this volume trace the trajectory of Black women in education, with a particular interest in higher education. These scholars combine research and personal narratives to explore educational issues ranging from historical accounts of Black female teachers in the nineteenth century to challenges and triumphs of being an activist researcher at the turn of the twenty-first century. The chapters in this volume address specific historical, social, cultural, political, and academic issues that affect Black women in the academy, and provide readers with tangible examples of how these scholars have transcended some of the challenges in their pursuit of academic excellence. While these chapters do not claim to provide the "magic solution" or a "how-to-guide" to success, they do raise thought-provoking issues that are critical to the success of Black women in higher education. Further, it is important to note that these women represent only a small proportion of emergent scholars of African descent. Therefore, their accounts are not intended to serve as "the universal voice" for all Black women in higher education.

It is important to understand the current status of African Americans in higher education, and to provide a context within which to locate the issues that are addressed in the forthcoming chapters. There are disturbing trends in the continuing under-representation of African Americans in higher education. According to Jones (2000), during the 1997 academic year, there were 27,668 terminal degrees awarded in higher education. Of these terminal degrees, only 4.8 percent or 1,335 degrees were awarded to African Americans. When these data are disaggregated by gender, an even more disconcerting pattern emerges; that is, the proportion of African American doctorate recipients remained stagnant, and in some cases, dropped over the three-year period between 1995–1997. In 1995, 1.8 percent or 490 African American men received doctoral degrees. In 1996 there were 535 or 1.9 percent, and in 1997 there were 527 or 1.9 percent. While the proportion of African American women who were awarded terminal degrees in the same period is somewhat higher than that of their male counterparts, their representation is far from satisfactory. For example, in 1995, 819 or 2.9 percent of terminal degrees were awarded to

African American women, in 1996, 780 or 2.8 percent and in 1997, 808 or 2.9 percent (Jones, 2000).

Access and entry of African American women to higher education is an important factor, but even more critical is the quality of the educational and professional experiences that these women receive once they gain admission to the academy. These experiences are what influence the success and retention of African American women once they have been admitted. There are a number of scholars who have examined the experiences of women of color in the United States as well as other parts of the world. What is striking about these earlier studies are the common experiences that resonate among women scholars across different geographical and cultural divides.

Brooks's (1997) research on women in the United Kingdom and New Zealand revealed concerns about promotion and tenure issues, lack of support and mentorship, and hostility in the work place. In her examination of South African women in higher education, Mabokela (2000) revealed similar concerns about institutional policies, practices, and a culture that does not support the professional and academic pursuits of African women scholars. Similarly, in the United States, Fleming (1984), Welch (1992), Lindsay (1994), Gregory (1999), Turner and Myers (2000), among others, highlight the "chilly" environment that women of color experience within the academy. These works clearly demonstrate that despite the cultural, social, and political particularities of each society, there are common threads that transcend the experiences of women of color in academic institutions.

Despite the challenges that women of African descent experience within the academy, there are victories and success stories; however, stories of success are often overshadowed by a negativity that pervades the experiences of these scholars. It is thus imperative to emphasize these beacons of success and pave the road for future generations of Black women scholars. To this end, *Sisters of the Academy* celebrates fifteen emergent scholars of African descent who have used the challenges they encountered in their journeys through the academy to create opportunities for success.

Organization of the Book

Sisters of the Academy begins with two historical chapters that contextualize the position and role of Black women in education. In chapter 1, Adah Ward Randolph's chapter assesses the effects of politics, race, class, and gender on the educational experiences of Black women educators in Ohio at the turn of the twentieth century. This historical inquiry illuminates the experiences of these early educators in a societal context where racism and sexism prevailed, and sheds light on how they achieved success in a sociopolitical context that did not value their contributions. The author's conclusion that "the 'problem' with Black female teachers was their race and gender" compels us to think about the ways in which race and gender continue to impact the experiences of Black female educators today.

In the history presented in chapter 2, Alicia C. Collins explores how education was used as a tool of socialization and liberation after the emancipation of enslaved Africans. The chapter highlights the role of historically Black women's colleges, such as Spelman and Bennet, in the education of women of African descent. The author notes that while these early institutions of higher education were influenced by the Puritan values of the missionaries who founded them and were created to reinforce the social place of women under the principles of the "cult of true womanhood" (Perkins, 1988), they also created a space where Black women could work together to uplift the race.

In chapter 3, "In Search of a Theoretical Framework," Jennifer E. Obidah explores the limitation of existing theoretical frameworks, which tend to represent the development of African Americans in deficit terms. Her discussion focuses on the *making* of theories, that is, why they were written and why they continue to influence educational research. More specifically, this chapter examines how the construct of race in American society influences the development and maintenance of deficit theories. The chapter concludes with an analysis of the usefulness of postmodern theoretical concepts as alternative explanations to those posited by deficit theories of African American underachievement, and provides avenues by which African American and other scholars can enter and redefine elements of the theoretical discourse.

Chapter 4 examines the professional development experiences of tenured Black faculty members at a major research university, especially those conditions that have contributed to their success in White male-dominated academic institutions. The author, Mary V. Alfred, discusses a number of strategies that the faculty in her study identified as central to their successful navigation through the academy: the power of self-definition, knowledge, voice, visibility, and a fluid life structure. While this chapter does not claim to have a "one-size-fits-all formula for success" in the academy, it does provide thought-provoking alternatives to issues that plague so many women in higher education.

Chapter 5 offers another perspective from tenured faculty at a major research university. In this chapter, Gloria D. Thomas illuminates the dual role of scholar and social agent that tenured African American and Latina faculty have to assume. The author suggests that these scholars see social change, that is, changing social structures in and out of the academy, as a fundamental part of their professional responsibility. This commitment to social change drives *some* African American and Latina faculty to persevere in academic environments that are not always supportive and hospitable.

Lisa D. Williams's chapter offers a poignant reflection of how race and gender continue to inform and influence the position of Black faculty. In chapter 6, the author presents several examples from her teaching that illustrate the continued stereotyping of Black women and a resistance to view them as scholars, researchers, and active participants within the system of higher education. For a young Black scholar to have to justify her worth everyday can sometimes be exhausting; however, the author asserts that the presence of Black scholars is critical to create a space to transform and challenge misconceptions about African American women in higher education.

Invisible Women is Rochelle L. Woods's characterization of the position of Black female graduate students at a major research university. Chapter 7 highlights the quest of female graduate students to succeed, despite being denied important aspects of graduate training such as mentoring. The author portrays these graduate students as *survivors* because they have achieved doctoral candidacy and are well on their way to obtaining their doctoral degrees. This chapter paints a disturbing picture of the institutional practice of recruiting highly qualified candidates while failing to provide the requisite support systems to ensure their academic success once on campus.

In chapter 8, Dionne A. Blue explores some of those same difficulties in the context of the racial identity and schooling experiences of African American women. By examining the stories of four collegiate African American women in the context of her story as a African American woman scholar and researcher, the author hopes to provide insights into the particular realities and the broader requirements of social living, complete with the conflicts and struggles that define our individual interpretations of lived experiences (Dillard, 1996). Among these conflicts and struggles is the ability to negotiate racial incidents in and out of school, and to understand the effects of marginalization on self-perception and academic achievement.

Cynthia A. Tyson explains how her multiple roles as teacher, researcher, and activist inform her practice as a scholar in the academy. The author provides examples of how her engagement in activist pedagogy and research serves as a catalyst for transformation of the education system and the emancipation of those who have been traditionally underserved by the system. Chapter 9 illuminates the struggles and triumphs and the sacrifices and rewards that allow activism to find its place in the academy.

In chapter 10, Melanie Carter employs personal narratives to capture and relay varied accounts of schooling. She contends that African American scholars have a responsibility to not only tell their stories but to use them as a means to demonstrate the centrality of their experience in any interpretation of the American schooling system. The author presents two challenges: First, as scholars of African descent, how do we unearth those accounts that remain hidden under the illusory veil of the common schooling experience? Second and more importantly, how do we employ the knowledge gathered through narratives to inform our work as scholars in the academy?

In chapter 11, "Sufficiently Challenged: A Family's Pursuit of the Ph.D.," Lesa M. Covington Clarkson invites readers to join her through her family's journey to obtain a doctoral degree. The chapter presents a heartfelt account of the last thirty-six months of Clarkson's life with her three children and the lessons they learned in their pursuit of this degree. The author emphasizes that while her family's narrative can in no way be assumed to be typical or representative of every family's experiences, it illuminates the survival strategies that helped the Clarksons live to tell their tale of the Ph.D.

In chapter 12, Brenda Jarmon presents a poignant account of her journey to the academy, specifically highlighting the critical role of mentors at various junctures. The author draws from personal narratives to illustrate the significance of mentorship, or lack thereof, in the early professional lives of academics.

In chapter 13, Thandeka Joyce Kirk presents a moving account of her experiences as a researcher during the days of apartheid in South Africa. Kirk's narrative demonstrates the integral relationship between the sociopolitical context of one's research and the direction of one's research agenda. She further demonstrates how her identity, beliefs, and values as scholar informed and influenced her approach to research.

This volume raises important issues about the experiences and contributions of Black women scholars. In the epilogue, co-editor Anna L. Green invites readers to reflect about other significant ways in which scholars of African descent can claim their place within the academy.

Bibliography and Suggested Readings

Brooks, A. (1997). *Academic women*. Bristol, UK: Society for Research Into Higher Education and Open University Press.

Curry, B. (2000). *Women in power: Pathways to leadership in education*. New York: Teachers College Press.

Dillard, C. B. (1996). Engaging pedagogy: Writing and reflecting in multicultural teacher education. *Teaching Education, 8*(1), 13–21.

Eggins, H. (Ed.). (1997). *Women as leaders and managers in higher education*. Buckingham: Society for Research Into Higher Education and Open University Press.

Fleming, J. (1984). *Blacks in college: A comparative study of students' success in black and in white institutions*. San Francisco Jossey-Bass Publishers.

Gregory, S. T. (1999). *Black women in the academy: The secrets to success and achievement*. Lanham, MD: University Press of America.

Jones, L. (Ed.). (2000). *Brothers of the academy: Up and coming black scholars earning our way in higher education*. Sterling: Stylus Publishing.

Kanter, R. M. (1977). Some effects of proportions on group life: Skewed sex ratios and responses to token women. *American Journal of Sociology, 82 (5)*, 965–990.

Lindsay, B. (1994). African American women and *Brown:* A lingering twilight or emerging dawn? *The Journal of Negro Education 63(3)*, pp. 430–442.

Mabokela, R. O. (2000). *Voices of conflict: Desegregating South African universities*. New York: Garland Press.

Perkins, L. M. (1988). The impact of the "cult of true womanhood" on the education of black women. In L. F. Goodchild & H. S. Wechsler (Eds.), *The history of higher education* (pp. 183–190). Needham Heights: Simon and Schuster.

Turner, C. S. V. & Myers, S. L. (2000). *Faculty of color in academe: Bittersweet success*. Needham Heights, MA: Allyn and Bacon.

Welch, L. B. (1992). *Perspectives on minority women in higher education*. New York: Praeger.

Dr. Adah Ward Randolph

Dr. Adah Ward Randolph received her doctorate in August 1996 from The Ohio State University in educational policy and leadership. Her dissertation, a historical case study of an all-Black school, Champion Avenue School, received Honorable Mention for Best Dissertation at the 1997 American Educational Research Association Annual Meeting in Division K. Dr. Ward Randolph's first publication, "Difference to Synchronization: A Model of an Urban Teacher's Transformation, Implications for Teacher Education," was published by *Teacher Education and Practice* in 1996. Her most recent work is "Race, Class and Gender: Black Women in Academia" in *HUArchivesNet* (May, 2000).

Dr. Ward Randolph has presented her research to the American Educational Research Association, the History of Education Society, the Holmes Partnership, the National Women Studies Association, the Association for the Study of Afro-American Life and History, and at many other conferences. Dr. Ward Randolph is currently co-editing a special issue of *The Journal of Critical Inquiry into Curriculum and Instruction* and a book tentatively titled *Just Like Home: Black Education in an All-Black Northern Urban School: 1921–1959.*

Dr. Ward Randolph is currently an assistant professor at Ohio University in the Department of Educational Studies in the Cultural Studies Program. Her research interests include African American education history with an emphasis on the northern urban experience; African American women educators during the late nineteenth and early twentieth century; urban education; multicultural education and history; curriculum history, theory, and development; and race, class, and gender in education.

Dr. Ward Randolph earned her bachelors' degree in physical education and dance from the University of Iowa. She obtained a masters degree in history, a masters degree in curriculum, and finally her doctorate, all from The Ohio State University. She is the first person in her family to earn a doctoral degree.

I

FEAR OF MISCEGENATION

BLACK WOMEN EDUCATORS IN COLUMBUS, OHIO (1898–1909)

Adah Ward Randolph

Introduction

In the nineteenth century, educated Black women were primarily teachers (Perkins, 1987). Some of them we know because of their role beyond the classroom as activists, school founders, and reformers. Recent texts such as *Charlotte Hawkins Brown and Palmer Memorial Institute: What One Young African American Woman Could Do* (Wadelington & Knapp, 1999), *Mary McLeod Bethune: Building a Better World* (McCluskey & Smith, 1999), and *The Voice of Anna Julia Cooper* (Lemert & Bhan, 1998) capture the lives and experiences of three Black women educators. Anna Julia Cooper argued that teachers were "ministers of the Gospel of Intelligence" (Lemert & Bhan, 1998, p. 250) and that "woman's strongest vindication for speaking [was] that the world needs to hear her voice" (Lemert & Bhan, 1998, p. 107). Cooper and her contemporaries taught in all-Black schools in the South (Carby, 1987; Lemert & Bhan, 1998; Shaw, 1996; Wadelington & Knapp, 1999). But what about women who were teachers but not activists? What about Black women who taught in the urban North? What possibilities did their lives hold, particularly during the later half of the nineteenth and the early twentieth century?

Linda M. Perkins's *Fannie Jackson Coppin and the Institute for Colored Youth* (1987) captures the educational history, life's work, and contributions of a Black woman. A graduate of Oberlin, Coppin not only taught in the urban North, but was the principal of an all-Black school in Philadelphia

(Perkins, 1987). Like Perkins's work, this research aims to further our understanding of the public and possibly the private lives of African American educators in the later half of the nineteenth century.

This chapter assesses the effects of politics, context, race, class, and gender on the educational practices and possibilities of Black women educators in Columbus, Ohio from 1898–1909. Whereas Coppin taught in an all-Black school, Black women teachers in Columbus taught in racially mixed schools where they were often unwanted because their very presence incited fears of miscegenation. Hazel Carby (1987) posits that the "links between black women and illicit sexuality consolidated during the antebellum years had powerful ideological consequences for the next hundred and fifty years" (p. 37). These teachers were educated; they were not viewed only as educated women, but as educated Black women.

"It is imperative to understand the objective reality of racism and sexism and at the same time to distinguish it from the subjective experiences of individuals who lived in a racist and sexist society" (Shaw, 1996, p. 5). This essay attempts to discover how and what these Black women educators "could and did do as much as what they could not do" (Shaw, 1996, p. 5). As an historical inquiry, the essay analyzes how these women fared and poses several questions: Why were Black women teachers viewed as a problem? How did Black women teachers fight back and defend themselves? Were they successful? And finally, how do their experiences speak to Black women teachers today in primary, secondary, or higher educational institutions? This is an essay that attempts to further our understanding of the complexity of Black women educators' lives in the urban North during the late nineteenth and early twentieth century.

Possibilities: Black Life in Columbus: 1863–1896

> Parents of colored youth, like parents of white youth, demand that those appointed to teach their children shall have the requisite educational qualifications; be pure in their lives; orderly in deportment; devoted to their work, and successful (Reverend James Preston Poindexter, 1878, as cited in Ward, 1993, p. 67).

Between 1860 and 1910, the African-American population in Ohio increased by seventy-five percent, doubling from one and six-tenths to two and three-fourths percent of the state's total population. Outside of Philadelphia and New York, Columbus had the largest percentage of Blacks in the urban

North (Gerber, 1976). During this period, Blacks in Ohio, and in Columbus in particular, increased their access to educational, political, and social avenues. In Ohio, Blacks succeeded in acquiring equal access to public facilities and repealing the last vestiges of the Black Codes when *de jure* segregated schools were outlawed and the ban against interracial marriages was lifted in 1887. Blacks' gains, however, were short lived.

In the 1890s, Blacks experienced greater racial discrimination primarily because of the popularization and spread of so-called "scientific" racial theories associated with Darwinism, because increased numbers of blacks migrated to Columbus, and because of the economic recessions of the 1890's (Gerber, 1976). Nevertheless, by 1900, African Americans in Columbus could boast of a larger and younger class of professionals (Gerber, 1976). Black teachers were among them.

In 1882, prior to the statewide demise of *de jure* educational law and hence, segregated facilities in the State, Columbus had closed its all-Black Loving School. The Loving School was closed as a result of protests by Black parents and leaders, such as the Reverend James Preston Poindexter, as well as political and economic forces such as the recession of the 1870s. When the all-Black Loving School was closed, Black teachers were dismissed from the system. From 1882 on, Poindexter (the first Black appointed to the City Council in 1881 and the first Black Board of Education (BOE) member in 1884) supported the employment of "qualified" Black teachers for the racially mixed students of Columbus. By the close of the nineteenth century, Columbus employed seven Black teachers in its mixed system.

After the separate-but-equal doctrine instituted by *Plessy vs. Ferguson* in 1896, Black gains faltered amidst increased racial intolerance. Blacks' political, social, economic, and educational advances began to erode (Gerber, 1976; Hines & Thompson, 1998). Poindexter's position as the first Black on the City Council and later the school board, represented one of the advances made by Blacks in Columbus. Black access was first challenged in educational settings. Poindexter and others had secured the repeal of the Black Codes that permitted segregated educational institutions; the close of the century, however, would find some members of the school board seeking to subvert the recently altered school law by seeking to re-institute segregated schooling. In 1898, two primary incidents occurred involving Black students and a Black teacher that spearheaded the resegregation of Columbus schools. Consequently, Black students and teachers were eventually viewed as "problems."

The "Negro Problem" in Columbus Schools: Protests and Petitions

As noted earlier, in 1882 Columbus ended its dual system of racially segregated education because of social, economic, and political changes. Racially mixed schools became the norm in Columbus. These schools, however, did not immediately employ Black teachers.

Black Teachers Return

In 1882, the BOE Committee on Teachers required new teachers to attain an additional year of training beyond high school. New standards for teachers were implemented. The Normal school later changed its policies and teaching curriculum (Annual Report of Columbus Board of Education, 1893–1894). The Committee also recommended that teachers be selected from abroad except when qualified candidates existed in the city. In this atmosphere of changing standards and increasing professionalization of education, African American teachers sought employment in Columbus.

From 1882 forward, Columbus Normal School graduated eligible African American educators. From this pool of candidates, the BOE found eligible African American educators for the mixed schools in Columbus. In 1886, Jennie A. Lee became the first Black teacher hired in Columbus since the closure of Loving. Lee was a graduate of the High School and had five years of teaching experience. Although Black teachers encountered difficulties in the school system, their numbers continued to increase (Annual Report of Columbus BOE, 1881–1882; Columbus City Directory, 1899–1900).[1] The employment of Lee and others as teachers was primarily due to the efforts of Poindexter, who was succeeded by the second Black BOE member, the Reverend Joshua Jones in 1894. Because of their powerful position on the board and in the community, both men were influential in securing teaching positions for Black teachers (Seifert, 1978).[2]

Poindexter, and later Jones, challenged BOE opposition to Black teachers. Both men combated the impact of Darwinian science on the education profession, particularly "integrated" educational facilities. For example, "Influences

1. Jennie Lee is the first documented black teacher in the *Annual Report Columbus BOE, 1890–1891* report. She probably was on the reserve list of teachers after 1886. Reserve teachers had been hired by the BOE, not as full-time teachers, but as assistants and substitutes.
2. On June 10, 1878, Poindexter wrote a letter to *The Ohio State Journal* stating that "since there is no colored man on the Board of Education to find out and keep before the Board the true inwardness of colored people and present truly what is regarded the moral status of any colored applicant for the position of teacher."

of Race Upon Educational Methods," published in *Education,* blamed integration for the problems in education. The article called for teachers to study *Races of Man* and to acquire in their preparation "at least a knowledge of the different demands made by different race types upon the teacher" (Crehore, 1887, pp. 402–403).

Whites' belief in their supremacy underpinned the social sciences. In education, this belief deemed African Americans as mentally deficient and incapable of learning. In the urban North, and in Columbus, White students and teachers were educated to believe in their own supremacy. Hence, most European Americans, regardless of region, held negative opinions about African Americans. Those prejudices were translated into institutional law and sometimes action, particularly after the passage of *Plessy* (Hines & Thompson, 1998). In Columbus, White racism manifested itself in protests. Within three years of his appointment, Jones would encounter racism directed at Black students and eventually, Black teachers.

Protests against Colored Students

European Americans' disapproval of Black students in the public school system in Columbus occurred in 1898. Their protests came on the heels of increased migration of Blacks from the South and European immigrants. Additionally, the compulsory school law of 1893 increased the enrollment of all children. The result was school overcrowding, coupled with the belief that Black migrant children were intellectually inferior to northern Blacks. In turn, patrons of the Twenty-third Street school protested the increased enrollment of Black students by transferring their children from the district, and by filing a resolution with the BOE seeking to alter contact between the races (*The Black Negro,* 1904).[3] The Twenty-third Street school in the Eighth ward, where most African Americans lived, became the scene of the first White protests against integration (Seifert, 1978).[4] Jones contended that the patrons' agitation would "have a tendency to stir up race prejudice" (Board of Education Minutes, Record 11, p. 61).[5] Jones's foreboding about increased "race prejudice" was right.

---

3. *The Black Negro: A Social Study Of The Columbus Negro* (1904) text provides information about the social sentiment white and black Columbusonians held on the Negro condition and progress in all social areas.

4. According to Seifert (1978), in 1883, a Mr. O. T. Gunning of the Douglas School Committee tried unsuccessfully to pass a resolution for the "readoption of separate schools for colored children." See *The Ohio State Journal,* March 22, 1883 for details; BOE Minutes, Record 11, 56.

5. The Licking county schools celebrated the work of a black teacher named Miss Mary Wood Roberts. She was a prior student of the Twenty-third Street school and attests to the quality of blacks in that area.

Whereas the school board did not address the petitioners' request regarding the increase of "colored" students at the Twenty-third Street school by
altering Black students' attendance at the school, they did change the boundaries of the school the following year. During that same year, 1898–1899,
increased racism would account for a protest against a Black teacher.

We Don't Want No Colored Teacher

In 1898, some White citizens perceived the one Black teacher in the Medary
school district as a "problem." At that time, Columbus employed seven
African American female teachers: Jennie A. Lee, Dickie Joyce, Maud Baker,
Abbie McFarland, Ruby Roney, Nellie B. Moffitt, and Celia Bell Davis. These
Black women were educated in Columbus schools and trained at Columbus
Normal (BOE Minutes, June 1900; Annual Report Columbus BOE, 1890).
Celia Bell Davis had graduated from the North High School in June of 1895
after attaining an excellent standing. Davis then earned a Class A three-year
teaching certificate from the Board of Examiners on June 21, 1898. It was the
highest qualification a teacher could attain from the Normal school (*The Ohio
State Journal,* July 20, 1898; Annual Report Columbus BOE, 1899–1900). At
Medary, however, Davis was unwanted.

During this era, most educated Black women educators were involved in
"racial uplift" activities. Moreover, they organized institutions such as the
National Association of Colored Women (NACW) whose motto was "uplifting as we climb" (Giddings, 1984; Hines, 1994). According to Perkins, "the
threads that held together the organizational as well as the individual pursuits
of black women were those of 'duty' and 'obligation' to the race. The concept
of racial obligation was intimately linked with the concept of racial 'uplift' and
'elevation'" (Hines, 1994, p. 83).

On the 5th of October in 1898, Superintendent J. A. Shawan presented a
petition to the BOE from concerned White parents in the Medary district
(Annual Report Columbus BOES, 1897–1898; *The Ohio State Journal,* October 6, 1898). The three primary speakers for the petition, J. F. Manion,
E. McVey, and J. G. Galbraith, along with 366 other "concerned" citizens,
requested that Davis be transferred from Medary where she was the only
Black teacher (BOE Minutes, Record 11). The October 7th edition of *The
Ohio State Journal* reported the result of the Medary patrons' meeting with
the BOE.

> The residents of the Medary Avenue School district, who are opposed
> to the teaching of their school by a colored instructor, are indignant
> that their request for the transfer of the teacher was not granted by

the board of education. They now promise to organize a school of their own. A number of these dissatisfied citizens said that if the board would not heed their protests, then they would band together, rent a room, employ a teacher and conduct a school of their own. They say that as there are but three colored pupils in the school, they feel that a white teacher should be assigned there, and the colored teacher sent to a school where the proportion of colored scholars is greater (*The Ohio State Journal,* October 7, 1898, p. 2).

Medary property owners were motivated by financial concerns because "renters in the school district threaten to move away if a white teacher is not secured," and classroom attendance had fallen since Davis's appointment (*The Ohio State Journal,* October 7, 1898, p. 2).[6]

On November 1, Conrad A. Howell presented a petition charging Miss Celia Davis with not maintaining,

The discipline necessary to the perfectly carrying out her duties as teacher at the Medary Avenue School, and Whereas, The entire school district has and is suffering on account of her holding present position. Moved, that the teachers committee be authorized to transfer Miss Davis to such other school as they think she can possibly conduct (BOE Minutes, Record 11, pp. 325–326).

Jones utilized his power as a BOE member and requested a special meeting of the committee of the whole to consider the Medary petition. Even though the Medary petitioners had secured an attorney, the effort to transfer Davis failed. They tried to remove Davis because of her race (BOE Minutes, Record 11; BOE Minutes, Record 12). If Davis had been incompetent, the protesters would have sought her resignation. Still, the Board elected to keep her at Medary—at least for that year, but employing Black teachers was perceived as a "problem" (Annual Report Columbus BOE, 1900–1901; BOE Minutes, Record 13).[7]

At an all-Black school in the South, Davis's presence would have been unmemorable. But at Medary, because of her race within the racially mixed

---

6. *The Ohio State Journal,* October 7, 1898, 2; In the September 13, 1898 issue of *The Ohio State Journal,* the Superintendent reported an attendance of 264 students; In the October 11, 1898 issue of *The Ohio State Journal,* the Medary residents posted a notice of their "Indignation Meeting" to be held that evening. The members of the district vowed to agitate until the Board heard and complied with their demands.

7. Miss Davis was moved to the Front Street school in 1900. She died on September 17, 1904. Before her death, she had written to the BOE to explain her tardiness due to a leg injury. She graduated from North High School in 1895 and entered the Normal School.

student and teacher population, Davis was unpopular with White parents. Even though Davis earned a three-year certificate and acquired "proper recognition of merit against which no one can justly complain" (Annual Report Columbus BOE, 1897–1898, p. 113), her credentials did not bestow equality. In the urban North, Blacks were provided access but not necessarily acceptance. Medary parents were "opposed to the teaching of their [white] school by a colored instructor . . . and feel that a white teacher should be assigned" (*The Ohio State Journal,* October 7, 1892, p. 2).

At the close of the nineteenth century, Black educated women such as Fannie Barrier Williams, Mary Church Terrell, Mary McLeod Bethune, and others had organized to fight against the negative perception of their womanhood.

> In the late nineteenth century, America moved inexorably toward a society best characterized as "biracial dualism." While white Americans, north and south, accepted black subordination as representing the Darwinian natural order, black leaders of the race focused almost completely on winning educational, political and economic rights. Black women, on the other hand, focused on eradicating negative images of their sexuality (Hines, 1994, p. 16).

On November 2, 1898, the White Medary protestors explicitly questioned the moral as well as educational fortitude of Davis because of her race and gender.

> Celia Davis has been unable to maintain the discipline necessary to the perfectly carrying out of the duties as teacher at the Medary Avenue School. . . . the said school on account of *her inability* to maintain this discipline has become *badly demoralized . . .* and the entire school district has and *is suffering* on account of her holding her present position (BOE Minutes, Record 11, p. 329).

They viewed her as suitable to teach "colored scholars." As a Black woman, she was viewed as *the problem* when the problem was the beliefs of the White patrons. Davis was out of place in their predominately White school. On one hand, the racial uplift ideology of the period supported Black women who were educated to uplift the race. On the other, as evidenced by the Medary case, where they could use their talents was limited. From this time forward, Black women teachers were subject to continual scrutiny by the BOE in the mixed school system.

Davis was not moved by the BOE until the following year. The records do not indicate her opinion or position on the matter. Davis only replied to the BOE once concerning her lateness due to an injury that required her to take a taxi to school. Davis's experience represented the beginning of the shift from mixed schools to segregated schools. Additionally, the passage of the 1899 U.S. Supreme Court's *Cummings vs. County Board of Education* decision extended the "separate but equal" doctrine to education and eventually increased racial discrimination in schools (Annual Report Columbus BOE, 1892–1893; Annual Report Columbus BOE, 1893–1894; West, 1972).

Black Teachers for Black Students: Back to the Past

The President of the Board of Education, Charles E. Morris, addressed the problem of "colored" teachers in the *1898–1899 Annual Report:* "The Abolishment several years ago of schools for the colored youth has had the effect of keeping out of employment many intelligent colored people who were fully competent to manage and instruct any school" (pp. 20–21). Yet the Board had not hired qualified Black female teachers in proportion to the number who passed the required examinations. From 1881–1891, sixteen Blacks (including one man) had taken the required city examiner's test (Annual Reports Columbus BOE, 1898–1899). For the previous ten years, the BOE, according to Morris, "employed as teachers 5 or 6 ladies of African descent noted for their scholarship, refinement, and skill in management" (Annual Reports Columbus BOE, 1898–1899, pp. 20–21). There were only six full-time Black teachers in Columbus in 1898–1899.

Morris indicated a few reasons why Black teachers were not employed in Columbus, such as racial prejudice and the absence of a separate Black school. He did not directly state that the BOE limited the employment of Black teachers, but that the "conditions" of Columbus did. Morris recognized the "deep seated prejudice" against Black female teachers. Davis' experience confirmed his assertion of racism. Morris, however, did not challenge the system, but hinted at a needed change. He viewed "separate" classes and even schools as the solution to the "problem" of Black women teachers. He wrote:

> It occurs to me that in buildings where the numbers will justify it, that the colored children could be given their own rooms and enjoy the instruction of their own teachers. Such an arrangement would be mutually beneficial, and would give employment to a large number of colored teachers . . . Now, if they could have their own teachers, and, where no hardship is involved, their own schools (Annual Reports Columbus BOE, 1898–1899, p. 21).

Morris advocated "separate" schools for Black teachers and students. Lastly, the President of the Board argued that only people of the same race, class, and experience were truly capable of teaching their own kind.

Their [colored] teachers understand their habits of thought better and can enter more fully into sympathy with their conditions and purposes than white teachers can ever hope to do. A few colored teachers with the spirit of Booker Washington would accomplish wonders for their people in this city. I believe that a majority of the colored people would themselves prefer such an arrangement. They have their own churches, their own societies, and their own organizations, and would not thank any one who would attempt to abolish them. Now, they could have their own teachers, and where no hardship is involved, their own schools, they would be able to work out their own problems in a manner more satisfactory to themselves than any one else is able to work them out for them (Annual Reports Columbus BOE, 1898–1899, pp. 21–22).

Since Morris believed that White teachers could not educate Black children, he also probably believed that Black teachers could not effectively teach White children. Therefore, Morris, and probably the majority of the BOE, indirectly limited the number of Black teachers. Morris' ideas supported the popular sentiment regarding segregation of the races in social spheres. Finally, Morris' agreement with Booker T. Washington's philosophy was a subtle way to affirm his belief in segregated schools for Black children and teachers.

Washington's philosophy of Industrial Education appealed to Morris and like-minded Whites because it did not promote social equality between the races. In the North, Whites used Washington's ideals to negate Black demands for reforms such as integration (Washington, 1986). "Washington's conservatism went beyond educational theory into all aspects of black life, and it appealed mightily to white America" (Hines & Thompson, 1998, p. 197). Morris desired teachers such as Washington, who were not integrationists in orientation and not revolutionaries. Morris' position conflicted with Ohio law, with Black leaders such as Poindexter, and with educational theorists such as DuBois.

Several years later in *The Souls of Black Folk* (1903), DuBois rejected the accommodationist view of Washington and his supporters and viewed Washington as "a compromiser between the South, the North, and the Negro" (pp. 170–171). DuBois warned that Washington wanted Black people to give up what they needed to become full citizens in America: the right to vote, civic equality, and the education of youth according to ability. In practice, however, Tuskegee's curriculum provided opportunities for female students, such as a program in nursing (Dubois, 1903). Although Washington gathered financial and political support from northern White industrialists, DuBoisian classical liberal philosophy had a greater influence in Black teacher training institutions

(Anderson, 1988; McCluskey & Smith, 1999; Shaw, 1996; Wadelington & Knapp, 1999). In them, Black teachers were trained to be leaders of their race. Morris would presumably agree with this philosophy as long as they were teaching Black children.

Racism, increased northern migration of Southern Blacks, and court decisions such as *Cummings* increased racial hostility toward Black teachers and students. When the Board refused to transfer Davis in 1898, many White parents withdrew their children from Medary and established a private school. In 1899, BOE member H. B. Herron presented a resolution authorizing Davis's transfer. Herron was motivated because "the feeling of opposition to her [Davis] in that district has not abated" and because White parents no longer wanted to incur the cost of a private school (BOE Minutes, Record 12, pp. 21–22). The BOE's subcommittee, the Teachers Committee, did not transfer Davis and closed the matter. Whites continued their private school.

As African Americans approached the new century, they were increasingly aware of the racist sentiment against their inclusion in education and society in general (Gerber, 1976). African Americans in Columbus had worked hard to overcome *de jure* segregated schools. Blacks in Columbus, particularly Black women teachers, would encounter increased racism in the next century (Andrews, 1886; Chapman, 1899; Gerber, 1976; Frederickson, 1971).

The Twentieth Century

In 1898, the United States fought and won the Spanish American War, and in 1901, Theodore Roosevelt, a veteran and a hero of that war, became President. The United States had begun its imperialist surge, and adopted the "White Man's Burden" philosophy of colonization in order to control Third World countries. Racism towards Black Americans in social, political, and educational institutions continued to surge. As the debate escalated over which educational curriculum would be adopted for the majority Black population in the South, the Columbus School Board began implementing policies designed to segregate Black teachers and students.

By 1900, most southern teachers of Black children were Blacks educated at Spellman, Hampton, Fisk, Tuskegee, and other historically Black teaching institutions (West, 1972; Neverdon-Morton, 1989; Anderson, 1988). Black teacher training was critical in the South where ninety percent of African Americans still lived. Policymakers' decisions to train Blacks as "drawers and hewers," or intellectual leaders, would affect the progress of African Americans for centuries. Changing teacher certification standards and increased professionalization of education affected all teachers, regardless of race (Young, 1901).

In 1900, six Black teachers were employed full-time in Columbus's schools, which had been integrated for more than a decade. Black teachers were minimally included in the schools, and they taught Black and White children. Columbus's Black teachers were trained primarily at northern educational institutions such as Oberlin and Wilberforce and later the Normal School in Columbus (BOE Minutes, Record 11; Neverdon-Morton, 1989; Anderson, 1988; West, 1972). The socialization process in these schools was very different from that practiced at Black teacher training institutions.

Stephanie Shaw argues that formal and informal Black education prepared Black women to be not just professionals, but exemplars of their race. Educational institutions, such as Oberlin and even Tuskegee, exemplified the "abolitionist legacy." She attests "many of these women knew when they left their home [or school] they were on a mission. The mission involved self-development and racial advancement. . . . Therefore the graduates represented the future and the hope of the race" (Shaw, 1996, p. 102). Consequently, Black teachers who came to Columbus from these institutions intended to uplift their race through their leadership in the Black community.

Black teachers trained in the Normal School in Columbus were probably socialized by the larger Black community and their families to serve the greater good as representatives within the mixed system to prevent "social persecution of men on account of color" (Shaw, 1996, p. 70). However, this outlook did not prevent persecution "on the account of color" as experienced by Celia Davis. Thus, socialization of Black teachers in Columbus probably only occurred outside of the schools by their families, churches, and communities.

Poindexter believed that Black teachers within the mixed system represented the acceptance of Blacks by Whites as social and intellectual equals. Hence, Black teachers in the system meant the advancement of the race and a general decrease in negative sentiment towards Blacks. This was not, however, the philosophical underpinning of the Normal School.

The movement to professionalize education affected the training and employment of all teachers in Columbus. The BOE required teachers to matriculate from one of the developing Normal Schools in Ohio (BOE Minutes, Record 12). Black students who attended them were prepared to serve White society and not particularly Blacks. They were not educated to be "hewers or drawers," or the "talented tenth" leaders of their people, but dedicated teachers. Black candidates who received Normal school certification were on par with their White contemporaries in education, and when employed in Columbus, earned the same pay. African American women who were educated in all-Black institutions were inculcated, however, with racial uplift ideology in their formal and informal education (Gaines, 1996).

In Columbus, Black teachers were expected to have equal competency with their White counterparts because they were teaching White and Black children. Black teachers were scrutinized more because they were educating Whites and Blacks. Davis's case alludes to the dominant assumptions within society at the time concerning the morality and competency of Black women because of their race and gender (Hines & Thompson, 1998; Giddings, 1984). Columbus's Black teachers were daughters of the developing Black professional class in Columbus. Their class status and standing were secure within the Black community, but their race and gender continued to create problems for them in the school system.

Black Teachers and the Powers That Be

In 1900, the six full-time Black teachers in Columbus were: Dickie Joyce, Maud C. Baker, Nellie Moffitt, Celia Davis, Jennie Lee, and Abbie McFarland. Four other Black teachers were on the reserve list: Ruby Roney, Cordella Bowles, Rennetta Monmouth, and Maud Patterson (BOE Minutes, Record 12). All were women from middle-class backgrounds where education was woman's primary professional vocation. The position conferred high status and responsibility within the Black community (Laney, 1899). Outside of the community, they were not just individuals, but representatives of their race. As a group, they would become targets of racism.

The first attempt to segregate Black teachers was in June of 1900. H. B. Herron offered an amendment to the election of teachers for the coming year. Herron addressed the "large proportion of colored children living in the vicinity of the Twenty-third Street school building" and resolved that

> A district composed of the territory contained in the present Twenty-third street district and territory contiguous thereto . . . which all colored children shall be required to attend such Twenty-third St. building; [and the] Twenty-third Street building when such districts are so established shall be equipped with a colored principal and colored teachers and that the Superintendent and Teachers Committee be instructed to so assign such colored teachers when the same are elected by the Board (BOE Minutes, Record 12, pp. 194–195).

Moreover, Herron sought a sub-division that would "best provide school facilities for the white children residing" in the area. Herron's "special" district for the education of Black students, and the employment of Black teachers, was not legal. The rationale behind the decision was White supremacy. The "great experiment" of mixed schools had existed for eighteen years, but there was no longer any Black on the BOE.

Columbus's few Black teachers were graduates of its Normal School. Nellie Moffitt, for instance, had graduated from the general literary course at Central High School in 1894 when she gave a presentation entitled, "Three Writers of Today." Abbie McFarland graduated from the Normal School in 1894. Maud Baker began teaching in Columbus in 1893 at the Stevenson School, having first been on the reserve list of teachers in September 1892. Dickie Joyce began teaching in 1893 at the Garfield School. Rennetta Monmouth graduated from Sullivant Elementary School in 1893 and from the Normal School in June of 1899 and obtained a three-year certificate. Ruby Roney graduated from Garfield Elementary in 1892. Celia Davis had not only taught in the regular elementary schools, but was also an evening school teacher. Maud Patterson was on the reserve list of teachers with Ruby Roney in November 1898. Both had two-year certificates at that time. Maud Patterson, however, received her three-year certificate in August of 1899, and Cordella Bowles had attained a three-year certificate by 1900. Jennie Lee began teaching in Columbus in 1886 (Annual Reports Columbus BOE, 1891–1894; 1897–1899; BOE minutes, Record 11). The six regular teachers taught at the Mound, Medary, Garfield, Spring, and Rich schools. The new board policy sought to place them in an all-Black school.

With their 400 White Columbus colleagues, Black teachers shared qualifications, dedication, and exemplary service, but Black teachers were bound by an additional criteria of service: uplift ideology. Black teachers particularly believed in the National Association of Colored Women's motto "Lifting As We Climb." Like their Southern sisters, these Columbus teachers probably viewed education as a means of advancing the race (Neverdon-Morton, 1989). They also gained advancement into the larger White society, but the social status of these Black women was just what the anti-Black faction questioned. The BOE ultimately limited Black participation as either students or teachers in the Columbus system of education.

Fear of Miscegenation: Board Actions

It was not what the fathers of 30 years ago had done on the color line, but what would be the effect 30 years in the future. If the children are taught by colored teachers, the influence would be such that in years to come there shall be inter-marrying (Conrad A. Howell, Columbus BOE, June, 1900).

By 1900, the BOE was completely White. Individual board members actively sought to exclude or separate Black teachers and students from White teachers and students. Most of the nineteen member board remained neutral, but there was a pro-Black faction of Theodore E. Glenn, Edward L. McCune, and John J. Stoddart, and an anti-Black faction of August Brandes, Fred J. Heer, Henry Holterman, Pinckney D. Shriner, Charles E. Morris, Conrad A. Howell, and H. B. Herron. There were no Black males on the BOE. As noted earlier, Herron was a leader of the anti-black movement, but the pro-Black faction blocked passage of his solution. But Herron and his cohorts continued their efforts to segregate Black female teachers (BOE Minutes, Record 12). The anti-Black faction presented resolution after resolution proposing to dismiss all Black teachers, to hire no more Black teachers, to limit their placement to certain schools, and to limit their number in any particular school. During heated debates in June of 1900, fears of miscegenation were first expressed.

The pro-Black board members supported the hiring of Black teachers, protected the legal rights of the Black teachers, and spoke to the "general satisfaction" of services provided by Black teachers (BOE Minutes, Record 12). Leonard asserted that dismissing Black teachers "would be exceedingly unjust, because the colored teachers had given general satisfaction" and that "under the laws of Ohio . . . there is no such distinction, and the Board had no right to go beyond the law and their own powers (p. 195)." Yet Howell contended that Black teachers should not teach White children because "it was not what the fathers of 30 years ago had done on the color line, but what would be the effect 30 years in the future. If the children are taught by colored teachers, the influence would be such that in years to come there shall be inter-marrying" (p. 195). Miscegenation was unacceptable to him. McCune charged the BOE anti-Black faction with racism and cowardice. If a teacher was inefficient in one district, she would be in another, but he had heard no complaint of incapacity against any colored teacher. The sole purpose of raising the question was to eliminate the colored teachers from the schools. If so [then] the members should be manly enough to say so.

Stoddart argued that "the question was a dead issue; the rights of the colored people were precisely the same as those of the white people." Again, Howell feigned that "he wanted to put them [black teachers] where they could do the most good" (Seifert, 1978, pp. 53–55). Howell and others advocated Black teachers for Black students, not for White students. He thought that their purpose was to educate their own race, just as Morris had contended in his 1898 Presidential Address. The anti-Black faction questioned the placement of Black women as equals with White women and children. Black female teachers perceived themselves as equals because of their socialization in their communities and families, but the anti-Black faction wanted to remove them from positions of power and influence among Whites.

BOE actions and ideas lead one to assess the position of Black teachers in the mixed system. Were they perceived as leaders of strong moral standing, and were they viewed as leaders only of Black students? Subsequent BOE actions reveal and reflect divided conceptions on the importance, place, and contributions of Black women teachers in Columbus at the turn of the century.

As noted earlier, BOE member Leonard emphasized to the board that their attempts to segregate Black teachers were beyond the power granted to them by the state of Ohio. As a result, the Columbus BOE sought to acquire such power (BOE Minutes, Record 12). At each subsequent meeting, some board members attempted to limit the participation of Black teachers in the schools (BOE Record 12; Annual Reports Columbus BOE, 1897–1898, 1898–1899). Black female teachers were employed in the Fifth, Eighth, Ninth, and Nineteenth wards; the majority taught in central downtown schools (Annual Report Columbus BOE, 1898–1899, 1900–1901). Black teachers were teaching in two wards represented by the growing anti-Black faction which spearheaded the separate school movement to stop "race mixing." Howell researched the proposition for a Black district (BOE Minutes, Record 12). By 1903, the movement to segregate Black teachers had grown. The 1903–1904 school year would be a critical year in Columbus.

On August 11, 1903, Shriner protested "the assignment of so many [two] colored teachers to the Mound Street school" (Boe Minutes, Record 13, p. 365) in the Fifth ward central district. During the September meeting, Shriner proposed "that not more than one colored teacher be employed to teach in any Public School of this city in any one ward" (Boe Minutes, Record 13, p. 390). His proposal reveals a movement to establish a *de jure* Black teacher quota system. Shriner was incited by the placement of two Black teachers at Mound Street school and by four Black teachers in the central city schools. At this time, Black teachers taught in the Fourth, Sixth, Seventh, Eighth, and Eleventh wards. Shriner's goal was to transfer the two Black teachers at Mound Street school. His motion was defeated, but tabled. Shriner was steadfast. In September, he petitioned "the School Board of the City of Columbus [shall] employ no more colored teachers" (Boe Minutes, Record 13, pp. 390–391). Shriner proposed many resolutions, but the only one that passed instituted a *de jure* quota system limiting the hiring and placement of Black teachers.

At the next meeting, the BOE reconsidered the proposal of a separate Black school in the Twenty-third Street school district where the majority of students were Black (*The Black Negro,* 1904). Black teachers taught at the Garfield and Spring Street schools, which had few Black students, but the Twenty-third Street school had no Black teachers. Consequently, the Superintendent was "authorized and directed" to transfer the seven Black teachers (Lee, Davis, Joyce, Baker, Moffitt, McFarland, and Roney) from their respective schools (First Avenue, Front Street, Garfield, Mound Street, Spring Street, and Fieser Street) to the Twenty-third Street school. In addition, Shriner required the Superintendent to "transfer any [White] pupils from the Twenty-third Street school to any other school upon application" (BOE Minutes, Record 14, p. 398; *The Black Negro,* 1904, pp. 20–23). The motions failed, but a special committee consisting of Glenn, Morris, Heinrich, Herr, and Shriner was appointed to investigate the legality of a "separate school for colored children" with the State Attorney General (BOE Minutes, Record 14).

When the employment list for the next year came before the board in June of 1904, BOE president Shriner voted for all teachers, "except the colored teachers" (BOE Minutes, Record 13). In the *1903–1904 Annual Report,* Shriner summarized the role of Black teachers and students in Columbus.

> Many years ago, the State Legislature repealed the law providing for the maintenance of separate schools for colored pupils. . . . As a result of this system, young women of color, educated in our schools and graduates of our Normal schools have been employed as teachers in the schools. These women have been competent and faithful and are capable instructors, but their employment as teachers for white children, meets with most strenuous objection in almost every school where they are located. If schools were maintained especially for colored pupils governed by colored teachers, it would give employment to many more colored teachers. . . . If these children were provided with colored teachers [state wide] it would require about twenty-four hundred colored teachers, probably a hundred times as many as are now employed. Columbus is the only city in Ohio that employs colored teachers for white children, in spite of the fact that it has enough colored pupils to employ many colored teachers profitably. A very prominent colored gentlemen who [B. T. Washington?] is at the head of one of the great colored institutions of learning in this country, recently informed me that of the seventy-five or eighty graduates annually from that institution, much the larger number could secure no employment as teachers in the north, . . . That opportunity would be largely increased if colored schools were maintained as above recommended (Annual Report Columbus BOE, 1903–1904; pp. 25–26; BOE Minutes, Record 13, p. 535).

Shriner and past BOE president Morris (1898) perceived Black teachers and students as "problems." Additionally, new board member, Dr. William Oxley Thompson, President of The Ohio State University agreed with the anti-Black faction (BOE Minutes, Record 13; BOE Minutes, Record 14; BOE Minutes, Record 15). Their drive for resegregation was supported by petitions from the White community. The BOE pursued legal ways to continue and began to purchase a building site for the future Hawthorne Avenue school, later renamed Champion Avenue School. The Black community mobilized belatedly and ineffectively (BOE Minutes, Record 14; BOE Minutes, Record 15).

Black Protest: Too Little Too Late

Three years later in 1907, Columbus Blacks organized to oppose building the Champion Avenue school. They had learned about the proposed school for Black children and teachers from a press report covering the September 16th meeting of the BOE. At that meeting, Thompson wanted legally "the power . . . to establish separate schools for the white and black races and to compel the children . . . to attend" (BOE Minutes, Record 15, p. 295). In response, on September 24, 1907, a mass meeting of 800 Black citizens resolved to send the BOE a resolution. Historically, the Black community in Columbus had been divided over the role of segregated schools. Nonetheless, a delegation of professional Black men presented their concerns to the BOE on September 30.

> Whereas, such a separation, we deem, would mitigate against and subject the colored children to undue disadvantages; and Whereas, The boundary lines of certain school districts in the city having been drawn so as to separate colored children, was an act of injustice committed against the many, both white and colored, to satisfy the prejudices of a few; and . . . selfish, narrow and not in accord with the board Christian spirit . . . we, the colored citizens of Columbus . . . condemn any action of the School Board having for its object, either directly or indirectly the establishment of separate schools for the education of colored children, and that we are unalterably opposed to class legislation of any kind under any conditions . . . be it further resolved, that the condition of our people objectionable or otherwise, is due largely to the treatment which we have received at the hands of the American white people, therefore, we feel that the white citizens of our city, owe it to us to give us that benefit which accrues as a result of education by contact and association in the public schools, as they now are (BOE Minutes, Record 15, p. 306; Seifert, 1978, pp. 59–60).

The Black community adopted arguments utilized by earlier integrationists such as Poindexter. However, Poindexter was deceased; and sentiment towards the social, political, and economic advancement of Blacks in Columbus had changed. The Black men argued against the "separate" school on religious and legal grounds, on the detrimental psychological effect on racial relations of creating separate schools for Black and White children, and on the importance of social contact between the races needed to diminish racism. As if they were not at the center of the issue, their many arguments failed to address the importance of Black women teachers. The board did not respond and continued its course of action (BOE Minutes, Record 15).

Even though the BOE did not respond, the Black community continued to present resolutions. However, their efforts failed. In fact, Thompson, in one meeting, indicated that the Black community "was laboring under a misapprehension regarding the conditions pertaining to the erection of such building" (BOE Minutes, Record 15, p. 481). The board never identified the school as a "colored" school because legally the board did not possess the power "to compel colored and white children to attend separate schools" due to *Board of Education vs. State* (450.s.555) which ruled against such provisions. The BOE did have the power to establish educational conditions under Section 4013 that "best promote the interest of education in their districts, [although] such power cannot be exercised with reference to race or color of the youth" (BOE Minutes, Record 15, pp. 310–311). Therefore, the BOE continued gerrymandering. They believed they were making progress when they created the newly renamed Champion Avenue. By doing so, they were affirming White supremacy as "the the natural and desirable order of things. To interfere with it was to stand in the way of progress" (Hines & Thompson, 1998, p. 194).

While the pastor and members of the Hawthorne Street Methodist Episcopal Church endorsed the idea of a district Black school, the rest of the African American community continued their effort to stop it. In June of 1908, the Black community told the BOE that the "separation of the races . . . always results ultimately in inferior school equipment for colored children. Moreover, it tends to set the races further and further apart, so to hinder that mutual sympathy and better understanding which close personal contact in the plastic years of childhood helps to cultivate" (BOE Minutes, Record 15, pp. 496–497). Poindexter had been more direct in his argument that the "white child imbibes the false idea that the *color of his skin* makes him the colored child's *superior*" (Ward, 1993, p. 67). The BOE's goal was to ensure the primacy of White children. They would succeed.

The Black protest, including a lawsuit filed by Charles T. Smith, failed, and the BOE moved forward with its plan to prevent "race-mixing" in the schools by ignoring the lawsuit. In 1909, Champion Avenue School, an all-Black school staffed by a Black principal and teachers, opened (BOE Minutes, Record 17).

After 1909, Black teachers were not employed in Columbus schools except at Champion. Dr. W. O. Thompson responded to an African American teacher who sought employment in Columbus that it was "not true that the Board of Education of Columbus is establishing a school for colored youth. It is true, however, that the Champion Avenue School will have more than 90% of colored children in it. All the teachers will be colored teachers" (The Ohio State University Archives, 3/e/12/37). After, most, but not all, Black students on the East side of Columbus were educated at Champion. Columbus schools were *de facto* segregated schools. The BOE, now led by Thompson, had installed a "segregated" school in a supposedly "integrated" system through gerrymandered districts (BOE Minutes, Record 17). The establishment of Champion had achieved a goal that had been more than ten years in the making. Fears of miscegenation were quelled by creating a school of all-Black teachers.

Champion Teachers

Champion's teachers matriculated from Columbus public schools, Columbus Normal School, Cheyney Institute, and Columbia University. While Champion was one of the best buildings provided for Blacks in Columbus, it was from the beginning *de facto* segregated. But an all-Black faculty in a single building produced unintended benefits for the larger Black community.

> The education process [in Black contexts] went beyond simple schooling—it imparted an orientation toward achievement. Family members supplemented formal schooling by encouraging these daughters to believe that regardless of the limitation others might impose on them because of their race, class, or sex, none of those conditions determined their abilities and neither could race, class, or sex inhibit their aspirations (Shaw, 1996, p. 1).

Consequently, the now all-Black teaching force at Champion was propelled to achieve the same aims for Black children in spite of the segregated setting. Black women educators, and now a Black male, were propelled like their Southern contemporaries to organize for the good of the race. The Board intended to limit their influence, but at Champion Avenue School they were empowered by a great call-to-service, the prevalent racial uplift ideology of the Black middle-class community (Gaines, 1996). Their efforts would directly better Blacks.

Champion's Black teachers included Maud Baker, Mary Cardwell, Alma Isabel, Abbie McFarland, Nell Moffitt, Nella Stewart, Pitman M. Smith, Frances Smith, Mable Scott, Renetta Monmouth, and Minnie Patterson

(Annual Report Columbus BOE, 1909–1910; BOE Minutes, Record 17).[8] Six of these teachers had previously worked in Columbus: Maud Baker, Nellie Moffitt, Renetta Monmouth, Abbie McFarland, Frances Smith, and Alma Isabel. The segregation of Champion did not significantly increase the number of Black teachers in Columbus, a previous rationale provided for the action.

The BOE sought to control what was actually taught at Champion. As noted earlier, former BOE president Morris contended that Black "teachers understand their [Black children] habits of thought better and can enter more fully into sympathy with their conditions and purposes than white teachers can ever hope to do" (Annual Report Columbus BOE, 1898–1899, pp. 21–22). But the BOE believed that those habits should be fashioned toward industrial education. Thus, they instituted an industrial education program at Champion staffed with Black teachers from traditionally Black institutions. Pitman Smith and Nella Stewart were both educated at Cheyney Institute, a classical industrial education school in the B. T. Washington mode. But, as Anderson and others have pointed out, these schools did not train their teachers to limit Black education but to reach their highest potential (BOE Minutes, Record 18). To the board, Smith and Stewart represented a southern approach to education for Blacks and further suggests that the BOE had built Champion not just to segregate Blacks, but also to train Black children to accept *de facto* segregation.

Over the next several years, the teachers at Champion worked as leaders of the Black community. Champion aided in the acculturation of adult Blacks, particularly those who migrated from the South. They opened an Evening School and a kindergarten (BOE Minutes, Record 17). Champion, under the leadership of principal Maud Baker, became an important organization within the Black community. Additionally, Champion's teachers, particularly Moffitt and Baker, became leaders within and outside the Black community. Their segregation in an all-Black school only reinforced "family and community values regarding what a woman ought to be and do" (Shaw, 1996, p. 75).

8. Abbie McFarland was assigned as needed for substitution. Viola I. Dorsey was also hired as a teacher for Champion; however, she is not listed in the list of teachers. The Committee on Finance credited Mabel Scott with one year of experience on January 24, 1911 even though she had three years of teaching experience before employment in Columbus. Where she taught before is unknown, 243. Nella Campbell [Stewart] was confirmed as Domestic Science teacher as early as 1908. Nellie M. Whitaker and Nettie A. Innis were also hired as teachers for Champion in 1909, but were not found on the list after that date, 190. Monmouth, Smith, McFarland, Moffitt, Baker, Whitaker, and Innis were all hired for Champion in 1909, 189–191.

Conclusion

> No accurate social or cultural history of black America is possible without a detailed examination of the institutions crafted by still unrecognized local black women (Hines, 1994, p. 16).

At the turn of the century and beyond, Black teachers in Columbus schools educated Black and White children. Columbus had eradicated its *de jure* segregated educational system prior to legal mandates, but White supremacy and fears of miscegenation did not disappear. Black teachers and students were the objects of progressive reforms attempted by the changing BOE.

This essay concludes that the "problem" with Black female teachers was their race and gender. Even though Columbus's Black teachers matriculated from such institutions as Wilberforce, Oberlin, and even Columbus Normal, they were not viewed as equal to their peers. Before racially mixed schools, within Columbus schools, Black educators taught Black children in prescribed segregated schools. The BOE had received no complaints regarding that policy and practice from Whites. In the mixed system, the crux of the issue became what influence Black teachers would have with White children.

In the view of Columbus's Black community, Black teachers were the best and brightest who would alter the perception of their race. They represented Black achievement and advancement. In the perception of the White community, however, they were not equals and should not be afforded status as Blacks or as Black women.

> Negative images, racial stereotypes, and biased perceptions serve specific functions in a capitalistic patriarchal society . . . black women activists and club organizers well understood the power of images to determine the treatment of black girls and women by the larger society (Hines, 1994, p. 126).

The establishment of racially segregated Champion Avenue School severed contact between Black teachers and White children and limited the social access of Black students and teachers to the White community. Black teachers in Columbus were challenged by the changing Northern urban context, changing laws, changing ideologies, changing leadership, and changing goals in both the White and Black communities. *Charlotte Hawkins Brown and Palmer Memorial Institute: What One Young African American Woman Could Do* (Wadelington & Knapp, 1999), *Mary McLeod Bethune: Building a Better World* (McCluskey &

Smith, 1999), and *The Voice of Anna Julia Cooper* (Lamert & Bhan, 1998) capture the lives and experiences of southern Black women educators. Like the teachers in Columbus, they were limited by their contexts, but they defended their name through their work. They told their stories through their lives. In spite of segregation, they achieved not just for themselves, but to better the race and the world. Champion's teachers were in the same situation as their southern contemporaries—teaching in all-Black schools.

From 1898 to 1909 in Columbus, Black educators were the frontline of racial stigmatization. The Columbus BOE denied equality to Black teachers, who were viewed as competent, but inferior. Black teachers were placed where Whites believed "they could do the most good." Black women were viewed from the position of race, more than of gender or class. Their legacy speaks to the role of Black women educators.

Bibliography and Suggested Readings

Anderson, J. D. (1988). *The education of blacks in the south, 1865–1935.* Chapel Hill, NC: University of North Carolina Press.

Anderson, J. D. & Franklin, V. P. (1978). *New perspectives on black educational history.* Boston: G. K. Hall & Company.

Andrews, Rev. C. G. (1886). The education of the colored race: Its importance, its methods, its limitations. *Education, 6,* 221–232.

Carby, H. V. (1987). *Reconstructing womanhood: The emergence of the Afro-American woman novelist.* New York: Oxford University Press.

Chapman, F. W. (1899). The European and Non-European: Or, The relation of the white to the colored race. *Education, 20,* pp. 3–7.

Columbus Board of Education. Annual report Columbus public schools: 1871–1915. Columbus.

Columbus Board of Education. Board of Education minutes, records 11–18: 1871–1913. Columbus.

Columbus Board of Education (1978). Education in Columbus before 1889. Columbus.

Columbus City Directory. 1871–1910. Columbus.

Crehore, C. F. (1887). Influences of race upon educational methods. *Education, 7,* 403.

Dubois, W. E. B. (1969[1903]). *The souls of black folk.* New York: New American.

Fredrickson, G. M. (1971). *The black image in the white mind.* Middletown: Wesleyan University Press.

Gaines, K. A. (1996). *Uplifting the race: Black leadership, politics and culture in the twentieth century.* Chapel Hill, NC: University of North Carolina Press.

General Assembly of Ohio (1842). *School officers guide for the state of Ohio laws*. Columbus.

Gerber, D. A. (1976). *Black Ohio and the color line, 1960–1915*. Urbana, IL: University of Illinois.

Giddings, P. (1984). *When and where I enter: The impact of black women on race and sex in America*. New York: Bantam Books.

Hickok, C. T. (1975[1896]). *The negro in Ohio: 1802–1870*. New York: Ames Press.

Himes, J. S. (1942). Forty years of negro life in Columbus, Ohio. *Journal of Negro History, 27*, 133–154.

Hines, D. C. (1994). *Hine sight: black women and the re-construction of American history*. New York: Carolson.

Hines, D. C. (1993). *Black women in America: An historical encyclopedia*. New York: Carlson.

Hines, D. C. & Thompson, K. (1998). *A shining thread of hope: The history of black women in America*. New York: Broadway Books.

Laney, L. C. (1899). The burden of the educated colored woman. *Southern Workman*, Volume 27, 341–346.

Laws of Ohio. V 32, 37.

Lee, A. E. (1919). *A history of the city of Columbus*. Columbus, OH: Memorial Publishing.

Lemert, C. & Bhan, E. (1998). *The voice of Anna Julia Cooper: Including a voice from the south and other important essays, papers, and letters*. Lanham, MD: Rowman & Littlefield.

McCluskey, A. T. & Smith, E. M. (1999). *Mary McLeod Bethune: Building a better world*. Bloomington: Indiana University Press.

Minor, R. C. (1947). *James Preston Poindexter elder statesman of Columbus*. Columbus: The Ohio State Archaeological and Historical Quarterly.

Neverdon-Morton, C. (1989). *Afro-American women of the south and the advancement of the race 1895–1925*. Knoxville, TN: The University of Tennessee Press.

Perkins, L. M. (1982). Heed life's demands: The educational philosophy of Fanny Jackson Coppin. *Journal of Negro History, 51*, 181–190.

Perkins, L. M. (1987). *Fanny Jackson Coppin and the institute for colored youth, 1865–1902*. New York: Garland Publishing.

Quillin, F. (1969). *The color line In Ohio*. New York: Negro Universities Press.

Seifert, M. T. (1978). *Early black history in the Columbus public schools*. Columbus.

Shaw, S. J. (1996). *What a woman ought to be and to do: Black professional women workers during the Jim Crow era*. Chicago: University of Chicago Press.

State of Ohio Laws. 1842, 3.

The black negro: A social study of the Columbus negro. (1904). Columbus: Privately printed.

The National Union Catalog: Pre-1956. 7, 51.

The Ohio State Archives. 3/e/12/37; RG/3/e/7.

The Ohio State Journal. 1829–1913.

U.S. Government. (1918). *Negro population in U.S., 1790–1915.*

Wadelington, C. W. & Knapp, R. F. (1999). *Charlotte Hawkins Brown and Palmer Memorial Institute: What one young African American woman could do.* Chapel Hill, NC: University of North Carolina Press.

Ward, A. L. (2000). *Race, class, and gender: Black women in academia.* http://HUArchives. Net

Ward, A. L. (1993). *The African American struggle for education in Columbus, Ohio: 1803–1909.* M.A. Thesis: The Ohio State University.

Washington, B. T. (1986). *Up from slavery.* New York: Penguin.

West, E. H. (1972). *Black American and education.* Columbus, OH: Merrill.

Young, N. B. (1901). The training of the negro teacher. *Education, 21,* 359–364.

Ms. Alicia C. Collins

Ms. Alicia C. Collins is currently a doctoral candidate in the Department of Administrative and Policy Studies at the University of Pittsburgh. Ms. Collins holds a bachelor of arts degree in political science from Central State University in Wilberforce, Ohio. She also has a Masters of Public Administration (M.P.A) from Ohio University. Her research interests include socialization in higher education, women's studies, and minority issues in higher education. Alicia's dissertation examines the socialization of undergraduates at the two remaining Black Women's Colleges: Bennett College and Spelman College.

Ms. Collins was born in Buffalo, New York. As a child, she lived in a number of different places because of her mother's occupation. Her mother, the Reverend Carrie Nobles, is the pastor of Carter Community A.M.E. Church in Queens, NY. Ms. Collins credits her mother for leading her to Christ, and for always reminding her where all her blessings come from. Ms. Collins is a member of the National Council of Negro Women, the American Educational Research Association, and the American Educational Studies Association. She is also active in her local church. She lives by Psalm 34: 1: "I will bless the Lord at all times: his praise shall continually be in my mouth."

2

BLACK WOMEN
IN THE ACADEMY
AN HISTORICAL OVERVIEW

Alicia C. Collins

At the intersection of race and gender stand women of color, torn by the lines of bias that currently divide white from non white in our society, and male from female. The worlds these women negotiate demand different and often wrenching allegiances. As a result, women of color face significant obstacles to their full participation and contribution to higher education. In their professional roles, women of color are expected to meet performance standards set for the most part by white males. Yet, their personal lives extract a loyalty to their culture that is central to acceptance by family and friends. At the same time, they must struggle with their own identity as women in a society where "thinking like a woman" is still considered a questionable activity. At times, they can experience pressure to choose between their racial identity and their womanhood (Carter, Pearson, & Shavlik, 1988, p. 98).

Black women in the academy differ in their experiences, backgrounds, appearances, educational levels, demographics, occupations, and beliefs. What connects them all is their struggle to be accepted and respected members of society, and their desire to have a voice that can be heard in a world with many views. Carter, Pearson, and Shavlik (1988) note that "historically, black women have been one of the most isolated, underused, and consequently demoralized segments of the academic community" (p. 98). Unlike white women and black men, black women have to deal with a double consciousness of both race and gender. This double consciousness affects how Black women view their ideas, their life decisions, and their place in the world in general.

"Black women have been participants in higher education for more than a century, but they are almost totally absent from the research literature; rarely is the impact of racism and sexism on Black women in academe examined" (Moses, 1989, p. 1). Even though Black women have made significant gains in education, they still struggle for their voice to be heard in the chilly environment of the academy.

This chapter examines the historical participation of Black women in the academy. One cannot discuss issues or experiences pertaining to Black women in the academy without examining how the past continues to inform and influence their experiences in today's academy. Specifically, this chapter explores how education was used as a tool of socialization and liberation in an effort to raise the expectations of Blacks after the Emancipation.

Education as Tool of Socialization

In examining the historical role of Black women in higher education, one must note the historical and traditional role of the academy as a place of intellectual discourse.

> The philosophical and theoretical training of intellectuals is a central and pivotal role of higher education in American society. To see the world differently in patterns and formulations that go beyond the commonplace has been one of the creative and critical burdens of the intellectual. The challenge to institutions of higher learning has been to fine-tune this intellectual quest. Universities and colleges in America have historically and traditionally been citadels of intellectual thought (Coleman-Burns, 1989, p. 147).

Prior to the Civil War, many states developed laws prohibiting the education of Blacks, which made it illegal to teach slaves to read and write. Even though these laws prohibited the education of slaves, some pursued their education and learning in secret. Before institutions of formal learning were established for Blacks, some slaves were taught secretly by someone in the master's house, by religious organizations, by other slaves, or they taught themselves. Noble (1956) notes that "education by imitation—was the main source of learning and, perhaps, the Negroes' first introduction to education. Negro women, many of whom were house servants, had as much opportunity as Negro men did to share in this imitative form of education—and perhaps more" (p. 15).

After the Civil War, it became the mission of religious organizations such as the Methodists, Baptists, Quakers, and Presbyterians to educate the freedmen. Many of these organizations felt it was their Christian mission to help educate and evangelize a mostly illiterate, ignorant, and uneducated group of people who had been ravaged by the institution of slavery. The education of Blacks was, and still is, viewed as both a tool of socialization and liberation.

The early education of Blacks focused on assisting newly emancipated slaves to make them productive members of society. It is estimated that after the Civil War, there were four million Blacks in the United States. Pifer (1973), in *The Higher Education of Blacks in the United States,* stated, "up to the Civil War, as we have seen only 28 Negroes graduate from college; by 1900 this number had increased to about 2,500" (p. 29). Actual enrollment of blacks in that year was apparently about 700 to 800. As noted in Table 1, enrollment increased from 3000 in 1910 to 379,000 by 1970.

Historically, White Protestant missionaries from the North, who established schools for Blacks in the South, were greatly influenced by Puritan morals. "As a consequence they maintained a strict surveillance over the conduct of their Negro students in order to stamp out any tendencies towards frivolous or immoral conduct" (Frazier, 1957, p. 71). Because of this influence, Blacks were required to participate in Bible study, prayer meetings, and attend regular chapel services. "Negro students were supposed to be differentiated in their morals as well as in their manners from the Negro masses. For that reason they were not to indulge in the religious emotionalism of the masses" (Frazier, 1957, p. 77). In an effort to separate Blacks who attended their institutions from other Blacks, they were not allowed to participate in card playing,

Table 1 Enrollment of Blacks in Higher Education from 1900 to 1970

Year	Estimated Enrollment
1900	2,500
1910	4,000
1920	8,000
1930	25,000
1940	50,000
1950	105,000
1960	205,000
1970	370,000

Note: Data adapted from Pifer (1973, p. 29).

dancing, drinking, or smoking. There were also strict regulations placed on male and female relations. All campus visitations were supervised, and female and male students were not allowed to openly socialize with one another.

Frazier (1957) notes that "education was not simply a form of compensation because it set them apart from the Negro masses; it provided a form of compensation as regards their relations with whites. They constantly asserted their educational and 'cultural' superiority to the majority of the Whites whose education was inferior to theirs" (p. 148) As a result of the establishment of historically Black colleges and universities (HBCUs), Blacks developed their own intellectual community.

The Socialization of Black Women in the Academy

"The purpose of education for all women in patriarchal America, as determined by most analyses, has been socialization" (Coleman-Burns, 1989, p. 145). At the end of the nineteenth century, White women founded schools for Black girls to train them to become refined ladies as well as "uplifters" of their race. Religious organizations that established institutions for Black women felt it was their Christian duty to focus on the moral, social, and educational development of young Black women. Because the early education of Black women focused on their social and cultural refinement, some of the institutions established for young Black women were referred to as grooming schools. Ironically, these schools would later facilitate the development of some of the greatest Black women scholars in the world.

White missionaries, who greatly influenced the education of Black women, saw Black women as a key component to uplifting the Black race from its meager circumstances. Therefore, a lot of attention was given to their development. The early education of Black women focused heavily on the idea of "race uplift." Both Blacks and Whites believed ". . . that black women bore the weight of the entire race. If they failed, a whole people failed" (Brazell, 1992, p. 38). Gaines (1996) defines "race uplift" as,

> Popular understanding of uplift, dating from anti-slavery folk religion speaks of a personal or spiritual and potentially social transcendence of worldly oppression and misery. Describing a group struggle for freedom and social advancement, uplift also suggests that African Americans have, with an almost religious fervor, regarded education as key to liberation (p. 1).

White missionaries oversaw every aspect of the Black women's curriculum, dress, and conduct. Bennett College and Spelman College are two of these institutions (often referred to as historically Black women's colleges (HBWCs)). They are the only two remaining Black women's colleges in the United States. The mission of these institutions has always been to educate young Black girls in a nurturing environment. HBWCs have been instrumental in graduating a high percentage of some of the most successful and brightest Black women professionals.

The value system of many of the White women missionaries who played a crucial role in the education of Black women was greatly influenced by the "cult of true womanhood." This "cult of true womanhood" focused on how a woman ". . . was judged by her husband, her neighbors and society could be divided into four cardinal virtues—piety, purity, submissiveness and domesticity" (Welter, 1966, p. 152).

The curriculum taught to Black women tended to focus on moral development, home economics, and training Black women in ladylike behaviors. Noble (1956) states that the reason for this emphasis was:

> Overnight she was to so live that by her ideal behavior the sins of her foremothers might be blotted out. Her education in many instances appears to have been based on a philosophy which implied that she was weak and immoral and that she at best should be made fit to rear her children and keep house for her husband (p. 24).

After the Civil War, many White Southerners wanted Black women to become well-trained domestic servants, as well as help to immortalize the image of the Black mammy (Guy-Sheftall, 1990). To create this image and encourage the development of domestic skills, the curriculum for home economics classes included art, millinery, sewing, cooking, home management, and other activities involved in domestic servitude. The Black mammy image is central to many of the controlling images of Black women. It represents the Black slave woman who cooked, cleaned, and helped to raise the master's children in the slave master's house. For many Whites, the Black mammy image was a very comforting one, which represented a harmless, ignorant woman whose main pleasure was to take care of them. "The mammy image is central to intersecting oppressions of race, gender, sexuality, and class. Regarding racial oppression, controlling images like the mammy aim to influence Black maternal behavior"(Collins, 2000, p. 73).

Education as a Tool of Liberation

> In my mind's eye I see the bronze statue of the college Founder, the cold Father symbol, his hands outstretched in the breathtaking gesture

of lifting that veil that flutters in hard, metallic folds above the face of a kneeling slave; and I am standing puzzled, unable to decide whether the veil is really being lifted, or lowered more firmly in place; whether I am witnessing a revelation or a more efficient blinding (Ellison, 1947, p. 28).

For decades, individuals of African descent were, and many people believe still are, blinded by ignorance that was forced upon them by the institution of slavery. The statue described in this quote is traditionally seen as showing Booker T. Washington, the founder of the institution, lifting the veil of ignorance from the head of a male slave. Ellison, however, is questioning whether or not education was indeed lifting the veil of ignorance from the heads of Black people or just socializing them to fit in the constraints of White society.

Education was seen as the key to unlocking wealth, respectability, and economic development in the Black community after the Civil War and into the twentieth century. The Black community was interested in educating Black women more so than Black men. Coleman-Burns (1989) notes several reasons for this:

> Historically for the black child, it was the mother who determined the status. The education of black women, it was reasoned, would raise the status of the black child. Second, community emphasis was on black woman's education because the type of employment that she could gain beyond being a domestic would more likely be of a higher and more prestigious character than that of the black male. . . . Third, black women, like all women, have been viewed as the carriers of the culture. Schooling was socially a "finishing" process for women, preparing them for society and the transmission of culture to their children. . . . However, the goals and aspirations of black women went far beyond those of whites. An educated woman/mother was viewed by the black community as an asset (p. 153).

The New Breed of Black Woman Intellectuals

> O, ye daughters of Africa, awake! Awake! Arise? No longer sleep nor slumber, but distinguish yourselves. Show forth to the world that ye are endowed with noble and exalted faculties. O, ye daughters of Africa! What have ye done to immortalize your names beyond the grave? What examples have ye set before the rising generation? What foundation have ye laid for generations yet unborn? (Richardson, 1987, p. 30)

This excerpt is taken from an essay by Maria Stewart in 1831 entitled *Religion and the Pure Principles of Morality, The Sure Foundation On Which We Must Build.* Stewart is known as America's first Black woman political writer. The statement is essentially a wake-up call from Stewart to her Black sisters. She asks them to arise and recognize their God given abilities to uplift themselves, as well as future generations.

In 1862, Mary Jane Patterson graduated from Oberlin College, becoming the first Black woman with a bachelor's degree. Oberlin College was one of the first institutions to open its doors to both women and Blacks. A number of the first Black academic women attended Oberlin College. They included such notables as Fanny Jackson Coppin, Anna Julia Cooper, and Mary Church Terrell. These women were responsible for opening schools for black youth and establishing community service organizations, as well as authoring books. They were women who focused on giving back to their communities by developing a dialogue of intellectual discourse among Black intellectuals. At this time, educated Black women saw themselves not only as teachers but as leaders of their race. Their purpose was to enable Black women to become self-reliant and economically self-sufficient.

Anna Julia Cooper's contribution to the academy can still be felt today. Her writings and intellectual discourses are an inspiration to many Black women intellectuals. Cooper's groundbreaking book, *A Voice From the South,* published in 1892, discusses her views on White feminists, the issue of womanhood, and Black men. This book is believed to be one of the first academic writings published by a Black woman in the United States and one of the major contributions to the present Black Feminist paradigm. In her chapter entitled *Womanhood: A Vital Element,* she challenges the fact that Black women have been excluded from leadership positions in the Black community.

By the twentieth century, there had been a shift in the Black academic community: emphasis was no longer simply placed on home economics, teaching, and nursing, but also on liberal arts and the social sciences. Coleman-Burns (1989) notes that at this time

> African American women cultural workers (including scholars, writers, artists, philosophers, authors, artistic performers, and teachers) represent a potentially new genre of American intellectualism. . . . Their potential is limited only by the prejudices and discrimination present in a racist, sexist, and classist society (pp. 146–147).

The twentieth century introduced a new breed of Black woman to the academy who desired to be scholars, leaders of their race, builders of their communities, self-defined and self-sufficient. Coleman-Burns (1989) notes that:

> The black community's priority of education for black women has been unprecedented from any similarly oppressed class. As a result of this commitment to the education of females and the opening up (real or perceived) of white institutions of higher education to larger numbers of blacks in the 1960s, the intellectual imagination of scholarly African American women has been unleashed (p. 146).

Today, the Black community has a strong distrust of Black intellectuals because of the belief that educated Blacks are using the oppressor's language as tools to oppress their own communities. Cornel West (1999) asserts that:

> most intellectuals are in search of recognition, status, power, and often wealth. Yet for black intellectuals this search requires immersing oneself in and addressing oneself to the very culture and society which degrade and devalue the black community from whence one comes. . . . Most black intellectuals tend to fall within two camps created by this predicament: "successful" ones, distant from (and usually condescending toward) the black community, and "unsuccessful" ones, disdainful of the white intellectual world. But both camps remain marginal to the black community—dangling between two worlds with little or no black infrastructual basis. Therefore, the "successful" black intellectual capitulates, often uncritically, in the prevailing paradigms and research programs of the white bourgeois academy, and the "unsuccessful" black intellectual remains encapsulated with the parochial discourses of African-American intellectual life (p. 61).

In keeping with West's belief that Black intellectuals need to develop their own intellectual traditions, Black women in the academy should be conscious of how they use common paradigms to describe Black life.

Over the past couple of decades, Black women in the academy have tried to develop the academic discipline of Black Women's Studies, which is centered on the historical, social, and cultural issues pertaining to Black women's experiences. By developing research that is centered on the experiences of Black women, Black women in today's academy are challenging research that contradicts their experiences.

bell hooks (1981) discusses the use of the words "woman" and "blacks" in literature and how these words are used in a way that excludes Black women:

By verbally denying white women racial identity, that is by simply referring to them as women their status was further reduced to that of non-person . . . From the 19th century to the present day authors will refer to "white men" but use the word "woman" when they really mean "white woman." Concurrently, the term "blacks" is often made synonymous with black men (hooks, 1981, p. 140).

A number of Black women in the academy have begun to discuss some of the inherent depictions of Black women in literature. Fleming (1983) discusses two conflicting images of Black women that can be found in social science literature. These images are the "matriarch" and the "victims." The matriarch is seen as the "strong, competent, self-reliant, even dominant" Black woman, whereas "victims" are "suffering under the double jeopardy of being both black and female in a society that is both racist and sexist" (p. 41). These controlling images undermine Black women's work ethic and discredit the fact that historically they have had to manage both their family life and work. The Black community has always had a high percentage of households led by single Black women. Unlike most cultures, which tend to be patriarchal, the Black community is mostly matriarchal.

Vestiges from the Past

In the academe, Black women have not fared much better. In 1991, according to the U.S. Department of Education, Black women represented 5.8 percent of enrollment in American colleges and universities (and 4.5 percent for Black men). In spite of the high college participation rates, Black women faculty continue to be concentrated among the lower ranks, primarily nontenured, promoted at a slower rate, paid less than their male and white female counterparts, located in traditional disciplines, and primarily employed by two-year colleges (Gregory, 1995, p. 11).

The education of Black women began as a story of empowerment and liberation for the Black community. Since Black woman's entrance into the environment of the academy, she has made considerable gains, but many obstacles still stand in the way of her development within the academy. Currently, some of the issues affecting Black women in the academy include curricular issues, the climate of the environment, the need for a supportive peer culture, mentorship, role models, financial support, retention, and tenure. These issues, along with others, are prompting some Black women to leave the academy for other opportunities outside of the academy.

The academy provides a chilly environment for Black women students, faculty, and administrators. The environment of the academy for the most part, is unreceptive, unsupportive, and lacks in understanding and sensitivity to issues that affect Black women. West (1999) notes that:

> Attitudes of white scholars in the academy are quite different from those in the past. It is much more difficult for black students, especially graduate students, to be taken seriously as potential scholars and intellectuals owing to managerial ethos of our university and college (in which less time is spent with students) and to the vulgar (racist) perceptions fueled by affirmative-action programs which pollute many black student-white professor relations (p. 59).

Presently, there are not enough courses within the academy that give attention to the history of Black women and their experiences. Departments focusing on Women's Studies and Black Studies exist, but between the stories of White women and Black men, the Black woman's story seems to get lost in the equation. In recent decades, there has been a movement to develop a Black Women's Studies Department within the academy. In Atlanta, Georgia, Spelman College has been a forerunner in the development of Women's Research Institutes which focus on courses and research pertaining to the cultural, historical, and social experiences of Black women.

The Black Women's Studies movement has produced a number of publications that focus on developing a framework for research in this area. The book *All the Women Are White, All the Blacks Are Men, But Some of Us Are Brave,* is one of the first to discuss the concept of Black Women's Studies in detail. Hull, Bell-Scott, and Smith's (1982) rationale for the development of Black Women's Studies is that:

> Women's studies courses, . . . focused almost exclusively upon the lives of white women. Black studies, which was much too often male-dominated, also ignored Black women, . . . Because of white women's racism and Black men's sexism, there was no room in either area for a serious consideration of the lives of Black women. And even when they have considered Black women, white women usually have not the capacity to analyze racial politics and Black culture, and Black men have remained blind or resistant to the implications of sexual politics in Black women's lives (pp. xx–xxi).

Hull et al. (1982) also argue for a framework for Black Women's Studies that includes a focus on "pro-Black feminist" and "anti-racist" perspectives.

Another obstacle affecting Black women is the lack of a supportive peer culture, role models, and mentorship in the academy. Retention rates for Black students at predominantly White institutions are very low, due in part to Black students' lack of support, mentorship, and role models (Allen, 1996). M. Elizabeth Tidball (1974) notes that women teachers as role models for women students are a critical ingredient in a college environment that turns out talented women. Research on women's colleges offers insight into the contributions of special focus institutions and the development of successful and talented women. Research has shown that the environment in women's colleges offers personal support, a critical mass of women, role models, a supportive peer culture, inclusion in the curriculum, and a strong institutional mission of excellence. Research also confirms that historically Black women's colleges have been the most productive institutions in the development of successful Black women (Wolf-Wendel, 1998).

> It has taken a long time to recognize that the educational climate must be improved not only for women students but also for women professionally in the educational process. As more is understood of human development, it will become increasingly apparent that the two are related, that the nutritive environment for women undergraduates is closely related to the environment that prevails for women faculty and administrators, and that one cannot expect a high return on the investment in women students if institutions are uncommitted or hostile to women academic professionals (Tidball, 1973, p. 131).

Conclusion

Black women in the academy differ in their experiences, backgrounds, appearances, educational levels, demographics, occupations, and beliefs. What connects them all is their struggle to be accepted and respected members of society and their desire to have a voice that can be heard in a world with many views. The road to gaining access to higher education for Black women has not been an easy one. It has been one of struggle, perseverance, and enlightenment. In analyzing the education of Black women, one must take into consideration that the educational system was not developed for Black women, but for wealthy White males. Education was offered to Black women as a tool of socialization and as a compromise to assist Blacks after the Civil War.

Through education, Black women have been able to define themselves, educate their Black youth, and express themselves. At the same time, they are an inspiration to their communities and their families. Many of the issues that affect Black women in the academy cannot be solved overnight because they are deeply entrenched in practices that are centuries old. The key to success for Black women is in the development of their own intellectual tradition separate from alliances with other minority groups whose frameworks are not always in agreement. Only when Black women organize like their foremothers did can they take their rightful place in the walls of the academy.

Bibliography and Suggested Readings

Allen, W. R. (1996). Improving Black student access and achievement in higher education. In C. Turner, M. Garcia, A. Nora, and L. I. Rendon (Eds.), *Racial and ethnic diversity in higher education* (pp. 179–188). Needham Heights: Simon and Schuster.

Brazell, J. C. (1992). Brick without straw: Missionary-sponsored black higher education in the post-emancipation. *Black Higher Education 63*(1), 27–46.

Carter, D., Pearson, C. & Shavlik, D. (1988). Double jeopardy: Women of color in higher education. *Educational Record,* Vol. 68/69 *Fall/Winter,* 98–103.

Coleman-Burns, P. (1989). African American women—Education for what? *Sex Roles, 21½,* 145–160.

Collins, P. H. (1990). *Black feminist thought.* New York: Routledge.

Collins, P. H. (2000). *Black feminist thought: Knowledge, consciousness, and the politics of empowerment.* (2nd ed.). New York: Routledge.

Cooper, A. J. (1892). *A voice from the South.* Xenia, Ohio: The Aldine Printing House.

Ellison, R. (1947). *Invisible man.* New York: Random House.

Fleming, J. (1983). Black women in black and white college environments: The making of a matriarch. *Journal of Social Issues, 39*(3), 41–54.

Frazier, E. F. (1957). *Black bourgeoisie: The rise of a new middle class.* New York: The Free Press.

Gaines, K. K. (1996). *Uplifting the race.* Chapel Hill, NC: The University of North Carolina Press.

Gregory, S. T. (1995). *Black women in the academy.* Lanham, MD: University Press of America.

Guy-Sheftall, B. (1990). *Daughters of sorrow: Attitudes toward black women, 1880–1920.* New York: Carlson.

Guy-Sheftall, B. & Bell-Scott, P. (1989). Finding a way: Black women students and the academy. In Carol S. Pearson, Donna L. Shavlik & Judith G. Touchton (Eds.), *Educating the majority: Women challenge tradition in higher education* (pp. 47–56). New York: Macmillan Publishers.

hooks, bell (1981). *Ain't I a woman: Black women and feminism.* Boston, MA: South End Press.

Hull, G. T., Bell-Scott, P. & Smith, B. (Eds.). (1982). *All the women are white, all the blacks are men, but some of us are brave.* Old Westbury, NY: The Feminist Press.

Moses, Y. (1989). *Black women in academe: Issues and Strategies.* Project on the status of education of women. Washington, D.C.: Association of American Colleges.

Noble, J. (1956). *The Negro woman's college education.* New York: Garland.

Perkins, L. M. (1988). The education of black women in the nineteenth century. In John M. Faragher and Florence Howe (Eds.), *Women and higher education in American history* (pp. 64–86). New York: W.W. Norton.

Pifer, A. (1973). *The higher education of blacks in the United States.* New York.

Richardson, M. (Ed.). (1987). *Maria W. Stewart, America's first black woman political writer.* Bloomington, Indiana: Indiana University Press.

Tidball, M. E. (1973). Perspective on academic women and affirmative action. *Educational Record, 54*(1), 130–135.

Tidball, M. E. (1974). The search for talented women. *Change, 6,* 51–52, 64.

Welter, B. (1966). The cult of true womanhood: 1820–1860. *American Quarterly 18,* 151–174.

West, C. (1999). The dilemma of the black intellectual. In C. West, *The Cornel West Reader* (pp. 302–315). New York: Basic Books.

Wolf-Wendel, L. E. (1998). Models of excellence: The baccalaureate origins of successful European American women, African American women, and Latinas. *The Journal of Higher Education, 69*(2), 141–183.

Dr. Jennifer E. Obidah

Dr. Jennifer E. Obidah is an assistant professor in the Graduate School of Education and Information Studies at the University of California, Los Angeles. She completed her undergraduate degree in sociology at Hunter College in 1989; a masters degree in African American studies at Yale University in 1991; and her doctorate in education at the University of California, Berkeley in 1995. Her areas of research in education are the social and cultural contexts of urban schooling, focusing specifically on issues of school violence, multicultural education, racial and cultural differences between teachers and students, teachers as critical pedagogists, and teacher preparation.

Dr. Obidah has presented papers at the annual meetings of the American Educational Research Association, the Youth-At-Risk Conference, Ethnography in Education Forum, the National Association of Multicultural Education, the Association for Moral Education, the International Conference on Educational Change at the University of South Africa, Pretoria, and the International Association of Teacher Educators in Namibia. Her publications include *Because of the Kids: Facing Racial and Cultural Differences in Schools* (Teachers College Press, 2000) with Karen Teel; "On Living (and Dying) with Violence: Entering Young Voices into the Discourse," a book chapter in Stephanie Spina (Ed.) *Smoke and Mirrors: The Hidden Context of Violence in Schools and Society* (Rowman & Littlefield, 2000); "Born to Roll: Graduate School from the Margins," a book chapter in Carl Grant (Ed.) *Multicultural Research: A Reflective Engagement,* (Falmer Press, 1999); "Life after Death: Critical Pedagogy in an Urban Classroom" in *Harvard Educational Review* (1995); and "Mediating the Boundaries of Race, Class, and Professorial Authority" in *Teachers College Record* (2000).

3

IN SEARCH OF A
THEORETICAL FRAMEWORK

Jennifer E. Obidah

What separates academic writing and other types of writing is the theoretical framework, that is, a review of published empirical studies that provide written evidence and counter evidence with which the researcher synthesizes and "frames" her own study. Few of us would deny that a theoretical framework is integral to graduate instruction and requirements (course papers, theses, dissertations, and so forth), is demanded in grant proposals, conference papers, and journal articles, and is still a fundamental requisite for what merits as good academic scholarship. In short, it is virtually impossible to enter and succeed in academe without such knowledge.

In this chapter, I discuss why African American scholars, and perhaps other minority scholars, may have difficulty in developing a theoretical framework. One reason may be the canonization of deficit theories purported to explain the social, emotional, and intellectual development of African Americans. Rather than an analysis of such theories, my discussion in this chapter focuses more on the *making* of the theories: why they were written, and why they continue to influence educational research. More specifically, I examine how constructs of race in American society influence the development and maintenance of deficit theories. This chapter concludes with an analysis of the usefulness of postmodern theoretical concepts in offering alternative explanations to those posited by deficit theories of African American underachievement, and provides avenues by which African American and other scholars can enter and redefine elements of the theoretical discourse.

Canonizing Deficit Theories of African American Underachievement

In postsecondary institutions across America, scholars-in-training will read or hear about sociopolitical theories of cultural deprivation (Coleman, 1966; Moynihan, 1965), underclassness (Auletta, 1983; Wilson, 1987), and psychological theories of limited intelligence (Jensen, 1969; Herrnstein & Murray, 1994) as some of the explanations for African American students' underachievement in schools. These theories are preserved in the canon of educational discourse. Though disputed, even at the time they were initially published, deficit theories have maintained a lasting quality in educational thought; hence, their canonized status. At best, in the process of disputing these theoretical explanations, scholars are forced to reiterate and thereby accord them some validity. At worst, other scholars have revisited and re-presented these theories as legitimate, objective, scientific research (see the work of Herrnstein and Murray (1994), which attempted to reassert the validity of Arthur Jensen's (1968) claim of African Americans' limited intelligence, a claim made twenty-six years earlier). To better understand how these theories, though debated and often proven false, continue to influence current educational thought and teaching practices, it becomes important to attend to the making of these theories—that is, who wrote them and why.

Beyond a view of theories as philosophical explanations of the world, theories also have implications for the lived experiences of people in society. For example, there were implications for a young scholar named Arthur Jensen when his research titled "Social Class, Race and Genetic Implications for Education" was published. Jensen's study first gained attention as an invited address at the annual meeting of the American Educational Research Association in New York City on February 17, 1967. This address then accessed a wider audience through its publication in the *American Educational Research Journal* (AERJ) in January 1968. A year later, in 1969, an issue of the *Harvard Educational Review* (HER) was comprised only of an elaborated version of Jensen's paper. For the life of a junior scholar, to have his work showcased in such reputable journals as AERJ and HER assured him tenure and promotion at an esteemed university, a national reputation for his contribution to the field, and overall success in his academic career. Interestingly, Jones-Wilson (1990) points out that Jensen's study revived the genetic deficit theory that had prevailed in the United States at the turn of the century. Meanwhile, as Jensen's life was being positively affected by the attention he received for his research, the lives of African Americans were simultaneously adversely affected.

Jensen's study was published only four years after Moynihan's (1965) policy analysis of the state of the Black family and what he perceived as the debilitating effect of their matriarchal family structure. Thus, the prevalent view posited in educational research and policy during this decade was that of the uneducability of African American students resulting from either their genetic or cultural deficiencies: African Americans failed in both the nature and nurture domains of human development.

Ironically, these deficit theories and political reports were also published during a time when African Americans were challenging their unequal citizenship and White Americans were facing the demise of a status quo that had been in place since slavery. Additionally, many of the studies on which these theories were based were conducted in the wake of the 1954 Supreme Court decision to make school segregation illegal. Charles Payne (1984) in his study of the continued academic underachievement of African Americans in schools discussed ways in which educational theory maintained victim-blaming perspectives of these students' failure. Payne asks us to "consider the sheer range and variety of questions which social scientists have traditionally ended up explaining stigma with stigma" (p. 9). He gives as examples, among others, the following questions and subsequent answers:

> Why are some people poor? Because their essentially matriarchal backgrounds failed to give them the achievement orientation so necessary in our competitive society. Why can't some children learn to read? Because their home backgrounds do not offer the intellectual nourishment conducive to learning (Payne, 1984, p. 9).

Payne concludes that "the underlying similarity between much sociological thinking and the thinking of lay persons results from the fact that the two are molded by a common culture" (p. 12). He further contends that this created a major problem of "rediscovering as theory, verities of the culture learned at mother's knee" (p. 15). It is these ideas posited and affirmed in scientific inquiry that helped to mold negative socially constructed identities with which Black people struggled. In a conceptual analysis of researchers' work and scholarship in society, Banks (1998) makes a similar point. Banks asserts that claims of neutrality merely enable a researcher to support the status quo without publicly acknowledging that support. In short, given the race biased society that is America, it is inconceivable that theories, which legitimized racial stigma, resulted from objective scientific research. This web of interactions between negative public opinions of African Americans, supported by White researchers positing those same opinions as objective research, in the midst of African Americans fighting against their unequal treatment and status in society, demonstrates the complexity of life during that period; a complexity that needed to be explored by future generations of social scientists in order to make better sense of the inequities that continue in our educational systems. One area of the complexity that has been explored in the last decades is the influence of racism on social scientists' development of theoretical frameworks.

The Influence of Race Constructs

Postmodern scholars have successfully unveiled the masquerade of ethnocentrism previously cloaked in the legitimacy of academic disciplines. Giroux (1992) points out that "modernist discourse in various forms rarely engages how white authority is inscribed and implicated in the creation and reproduction of a society in which the voices of the center appear either invisible or unimplicated in the historical and social construction of racism as an integral part of their own collective identity" (p. 116). Giroux argues that normalized whiteness operated in the work of scholars in such a way as to render their authoritative voices neutral and their identities unimplicated and invisible.

Scholars consigned the struggle of subordinate groups to master narratives suggesting that the oppressed needed to be remade in the image of a dominant white culture in order to be integrated into mainstream society. Giroux (1992) recommends a broader examination of the constructed boundaries of ethnicity, race, and power that would "make visible how whiteness functions as a historical and social construction" (p. 117). Thus, most social scientists were unaware of, or did not take into account, the extent to which their racialized identities influenced their perspectives and the "results" of their research. Moreover, in reference to earlier discussed deficit theories, it is unsurprising then that the makers of these theories—unconsciously influenced by constructs of the "other" engrained in their culture—could publish theoretical positions loaded with such potentially destructive implications for the lives of African American students. Additionally, and most unfortunately for the education of African American children, educators who were ineffective with this student population could place the responsibility for their own and the school's failure outside of the school (Erikson, 1996) and could justify their decision with scientific research.

What I've discussed in the last pages are not unique insights—the theories or the arguments substantiating their impact on the educational experiences of African American students. These arguments have been asserted over and over again since the making of deficit theories and their continued influence on the educational practices of some teachers of African American students. What is rarely discussed however, is the emotional response felt by African American scholars-in-training when they first encounter these theories in graduate school.

After defying many odds—economic, academic, discriminatory, and prejudicial—to attain higher education, it is unsurprising that African American graduate students would experience an emotional response to the legitimization of such theories by virtue of their continued existence and influence on educational praxis. The emotional response is often captured in thoughts such as "they're saying this about us!" Such a response felt by African American graduate students may temporarily block the learning of a framework with such theories at the center. Moreover, the graduate student may engage in what McLaren (1989) refers to as a "cultural politics of resistance." Students' cultural politics of resistance fundamentally challenges the established power and authority in teaching and learning situations, such that "what may look like idiosyncrasy, passivity and indifference among students really marks the point where [a teacher's] political project runs into the [perceived] subaltern's fundamental otherness" (McLaren, 1989, p. 189). In short, students who are opposed to learning what they perceive as false information will utilize some mode of protest to demonstrate their opposition. These students may present a real problem to a professor unaccustomed to being challenged. Unfortunately, these challenges to the established authority may result in sanctions against the students, such as alienation by the professor and fellow students, and a lack of the mentorship that is crucial to a successful academic career. In short, there are risks involved in confronting normalized constructions of "otherness" that are codified in academic knowledge. Thus, not only are these students going through the usual rigors of graduate school, they are also battling psychological and other degradations promoted through educational theory. Fortunately, more theoretical shifts have occurred in educational research.

Theoretical Shifts in Educational Research

Continuing a tradition built on the momentum of the civil rights movement, many scholars attempt to move beyond the traditional paradigmatic boundaries of educational theory to provide a more cogent analysis of African American experiences. In the last twenty years, important shifts have occurred in educational research. More researchers now wrestle with the roles of structure, culture, and agency in the reproduction of social inequality, and are less inclined to isolate one factor of human development or experience as the primary factor of the problem being studied. Scholars now attempt to determine how factors of human existence—grounded in the objective and subjective dimensions of race and class—mitigate or magnify the effects of each other. For example, postmodernism has entered theories of social and cultural reproduction (Bourdieu, 1977; Bowles & Gintis, 1986), cultural production and resistance (McLaren, 1989; Willis, 1977), and critical pedagogy (Freire, 1967; Giroux, 1992; Shor, 1996) into educational discourse. Additionally, theories of multiculturalism have emerged from empirical studies that examined the effects of racism and prejudice in educational and teaching practices (Banks, 1995; Delpit, 1995; Gay, 1992; Ladson-Billings, 1994). Even though these theories may have their own flaws, nonetheless they widen educational discourse to include other explanations of the complexities of urban life and schooling.

For example, social and cultural reproduction theorists attempt to explicate the relationships between schools and the capitalist structure of American society—specifically, the role of schools in maintaining and perpetuating the social inequality that naturally results from capitalism. An important contribution to this line of inquiry is Bourdieu's (1977) concept of "cultural capital" which has made a significant contribution to reproduction theory. Cultural capital—the general cultural background, knowledge, dispositions, and skills that are passed from one generation to the next, where some people's cultures are more valued than others within the context of schooling—uncovers mechanisms utilized in educational systems by which some students' cultural expressions are perceived as advantageous or debilitating to their potential for academic excellence. This approach to studying the relationship between culture, schooling, and unequal outcomes for students critiques the view that some students have a culture and other students are culturally deprived. I elaborate with the example of African Americans' fight to obtain an education.

African American Education Post-Slavery

Today, African American students disproportionately are experiencing many problems in schools, primarily as a result of the ways in which the educational system is currently structured. These problems include significantly lower performance on standardized tests, more reported discipline problems, poor attendance, and higher rates of school drop-outs (Fine, 1991; Ogbu, 1990; MacLeod, 1987). Nonetheless, during the early years of the twentieth century—and some would argue even before—African Americans held education in high regard (Banks, 1995; DuBois, 1953). In *The Souls of Black Folk*, W.E.B. DuBois (1953) analyzes the identity struggle among African Americans that resulted from a history of slavery and a persistent denial of access to literacy. African Americans saw literacy as integral to freedom. DuBois recounts that after the Voting Rights Act of 1870, African Americans began to see a new vision of liberty:

> Slowly but steadily, in the following years, a new vision began. It was the ideal of "book-learning." Here at last, Black Americans seemed to have discovered the mountain path to Canaan, the biblical land of freedom (DuBois, 1953, p. 19).

As DuBois states, African Americans saw literacy as a goal—both realistically and symbolically—that led to freedom from slavery and toward the attainment of full citizenship in America. However, all the while believing in and striving for the American educational ideal, African Americans were simultaneously operating from an acute awareness of mainstream America's institutionalized rejection of them as equal participants in this society: their cultural capital then was treated as nonexistent in American society and today it continues to be undervalued. Cummins (1993) asserts three ways in which school practices can affect racial minorities: 1) the classroom interactions between teachers and students; 2) the relationship between school and minority communities; and 3) the intergroup power relations in society as a whole. In each of these areas, he writes that all racial minorities can be "disabled and disempowered"(Cummins, 1993, p. 106) by differential treatment. In this way, social scientists who study African American student underachievement today can use Bourdieu's notion of cultural capital, along with an American historical context, to help explain this phenomena.

Nonetheless, African American families and schools are increasingly perceived as oppositional rather than mutually interdependent institutions that educate the same children. Scholars posit other reasons why African American students today tend to reject education as a vehicle for social mobility (Fordham, 1988; Ogbu, 1990). John Ogbu's tri-classification system is one of the most commonly cited theories. Ogbu notes three types of minorities in American society: autonomous minorities (such as the Mormons), voluntary minorities (for example, immigrants who choose to live in America), and involuntary or castelike minorities (that is, people brought to America against their will) which are, historically, a group to which African Americans belong.

Ogbu (1990) argues that involuntary minorities reject school because they consider schools as institutions that help to maintain their second-class status in society. He writes that castelike minorities possess "a negative dual-status, limited-mobility frame of reference that does not encourage striving for school success" (p. 53). He further contends that "while their [African Americans'] folk theories stress the importance of education, an emphasis on the appropriate or necessary effort does not accompany their verbal endorsement" (p. 53). He continues:

> This [lack of effort] is probably because historically (in terms of jobs, wages and social recognition) involuntary minorities have not been adequately rewarded for their educational achievement. Therefore they have come to view the inadequate and unequal reward of education as a part of the institutioned discriminating structure which getting an education cannot eliminate (Ogbu, 1990, p. 53).

In Ogbu's argument, the fault of African American students' educational underachievement lies neither with their intelligence nor with the absence of "quasi-academic training" that middle-class children are purported to experience at home. In this way, his arguments move us beyond those theories of the past. Additionally, he establishes the impact of historical traditions on present-day dilemmas in education. However, Ogbu's description of involuntary minorities presents a highly deterministic depiction of native-born minority groups in America. His research does not permit exceptions of minorities who do not behave in ways that are consistent with the criteria and the descriptions that are implied by the labels: autonomous, voluntary, and involuntary. For example, studies have been completed which suggest that the characteristics attributed to involuntary and castelike minorities are also found among members of non-minority cultural groups such as working class White males (MacLeod, 1987; Weiner, 1985; Willis, 1977). Moreover, Ogbu's thesis does not fully address the role of discriminating practices and discrepancies that transpire within the confines of a school. To elaborate, even if students come to school predisposed to rejecting an education because of preconceived notions that such an education continues their oppressed positions in the society, the oppressive acts that actually manifest within the schools—through teacher-student interactions (Obidah & Teel, 2000; Ladson-Billings, 1994; Erikson, 1996), unfair disciplinary practices (Brown, 1970; McCadden, 1998), and other forms of negative evaluation—confirm those beliefs that students already hold and intensify their predispositions. In other words, these students aren't only rejecting school because of historical frames of reference, their rejection also results from the realities of their lived experiences in schools. The insights of Samona Joe, an African American urban school teacher, are worth quoting at length here:

> Those of us born outside the group whose language, values and norms of behavior are the basis upon which schools operate, are less likely to be reared according to those same norms. Partly as a function of

how we, as African Americans view the world, and partly as a func-
tion of how we must live daily life in this world, we raise ourselves
and our children with different values, languages, and behavioral
expectations. These differences are not negative in and of themselves;
but it is via these differences that the likelihood of understanding, surviving, and thriving in a white middle-class normal school setting is
greatly reduced. This reduced likelihood is further exacerbated by the
fact that we as African Americans disproportionately end up in the
lower-ability groups, slower academic tracks, and generally weaker
echelons of school settings which reinforce the negative outcomes of
these differences (Joe, 1993, p. 6).

I posit that it is more than a rejection of schooling, as Ogbu argues. What
is occurring today is a resistance by students to the "go with the flow" nature
of the status quo. Moreover, they are demanding respect from a society they
perceive does not afford them any. In some cases, this respect is demanded
even at the cost of the promise of upward mobility; a promise that often goes
unrealized in even the best circumstances. Students are engaging in what Paul
Willis conceives of as "cultural production." Willis (1977) defines culture
production as "the active, collective use and explorations of received symbolic,
ideological and cultural resources to explain, make sense of and positively
respond to 'inherited' structural and material conditions" (p. 123). Willis provides an important perspective on notions of culture. From the perspective of
culture production, all cultures, including the working class and minority cultures, are viewed as cultures in and of themselves, not simply as cultures that
arise in opposition to domination. This analysis is important because it provides a theoretical space for examining the legitimate cultural resources of
racially and socioeconomically oppressed people.
Oftentimes the cultures of dominated groups are perceived by mainstream
cultures merely as responses to these groups' oppressed status. Recall the limitations of Ogbu's arguments discussed earlier. Culture production challenges
this perception. It affirms agency as the primary existence lived by African
Americans and other minority groups, as opposed to the reactionary existence
often ascribed to them. In addition, culture production also affirms their development of cultural resources that are separate from the received symbolic,
ideological, and cultural forces that maintain these groups' dominated status.
In short, what is apparent today is that African American students on all levels (K-12 through graduate school) resist openly the abandonment of those
cultural resources emerging from their culture production. A growing number
of these students command a repertoire of overt and covert mechanisms to
combat debilitating frames through which their identities are referenced. In

order to survive and succeed such experiences, African American and other scholars develop theoretical frameworks from the margins.

These frameworks utilize a range of theories including postmodern, multicultural, feminist, and those of grassroots social activism. Additionally, these theoretical frameworks interrogate taken-for-granted aspects of educational inquiry and areas of research. These theoretical frameworks serve as the backdrop for studies that explore the multiple meanings embedded in topics such as "teacher-student reactions," "curriculum and instruction," and "excellence in academic achievement." These scholars do not assume that these topics carry the same values and belief systems in every context and with every group of people in a society. Lastly, and most importantly, these scholars assert the power of human agency to change the world at any given moment.

Conclusion

I conclude this chapter by noting the importance of theoretical frameworks to academic writing. I also noted that such frameworks are expected to be taught and learned in graduate schools of education, and the skills involved in framing educational thought in this way should be demonstrated by scholars who expect to succeed in academic careers. I have not argued for or against the use of theoretical frameworks in this chapter. Rather, as the title of this chapter alludes to, I've discussed some of the challenges I believe that African American and other minority scholars may face in their development of a theoretical framework.

The primary purpose of the perspectives put forth here is to demonstrate that 1) educational theories have implications for the lives of both the researcher and the researched, 2) that developing educational theories are not neutral endeavors, 3) that they evolve from particular social, historical and political contexts, and that 4) with recent paradigmatic shifts in educational theory, traditional notions about the purpose of theoretical frameworks must shift to also include scholars' political projects. For scholars today who still combat the legacy of past deficit theories of academic achievement, developing a theoretical framework cannot be divorced from a political project. The lives of children are at stake.

Bibliography and Suggested Readings

Auletta, K. (1983). *The underclass.* New York: Vintage Books.
Banks, J. A. (1998). The lives and values of researchers: Implications for educating citizens in a multicultural society. *Educational Researcher, 27,* 4–17.

Banks, J. A. (1995). Multicultural education, historical developments, and practice. In J. A. Banks & C. A. M. Banks (Eds.), *Multicultural education: Issues and perspectives* (2nd ed.). Boston: Allyn & Bacon.

Bourdieu, P. (1977). *The outline of a theory of practice.* (Richard Nice, Trans.). Cambridge: Cambridge University Press.

Bowles, S. & Gintis, H. (1986). *Schooling in capitalist America.* New York: Basic Books.

Brown, J. (1970). The Black athelete. In M. Libarle & T. Seligson (Eds.), *The high school revolutionaries* (pp. 42–57). New York: Vintage Books.

Coleman, J. S. (1966). *Equality of educational opportunity.* U.S. Department of Health, Education, and Welfare.

Cummins, J. (1993). Empowering minority students: A framework for intervention. In L. Weis & M. Fine (Eds.), *Beyond silenced voices: Class, race, and gender in United States schools* (pp. 101–118). New York: State University of New York.

Delpit, L. (1995). *Other people's children: Cultural conflict in the classroom.* New York: The Free Press.

DuBois, W. E. B. (1953). *The souls of black folk.* Greenwich, CT: Fawcett Publications.

Erikson, F. (1996). Transformation and school success: The politics and culture of educational achievement. In E. Jacob & C. Jordan (Eds.), *Minority education: Anthropological perspectives* (pp. 27–51). Norwood, NJ: Ablex Publishing.

Fine, M. (1991). *Framing dropouts: Notes on the politics of an urban public high school.* Albany: State University of New York Press.

Fordham, S. (1988). Racelessness as a factor in black students' school success: Pragmatic strategy or pyrrhic victory? *Harvard Educational Review, 58,* 54–85.

Freire, P. (1967). *Pedagogy of the oppressed.* New York: Continuum.

Gay, G. (1992). The state of multicultural education in the United States. In K. Adam-Moodley (Ed.), *Education in plural societies: International perspectives* (pp. 47–66). Calgary: Detselit.

Giroux, H. A. (1983). Theories of reproduction and resistance in the new sociology of education. *Harvard Educational Review, 52,* 257–293.

Giroux, H. A. (1992). *Border crossings: Cultural workers and the politics of education.* New York: Routledge

Herrnstein, R. J. & Murray, C. (1994). *The bell curve.* New York: The Free Press.

Hilliard, A. (1995). *The maroon within us.* Baltimore: Black Classic Press.

Jensen, A. (1968). Social class, race, and genetics: Implications for education. *American Educational Research Journal, 5*(1) 1–43.

Jensen, A. (1969). How much can we boost I.Q. and scholastic achievement? *Harvard Educational Review, 39,* 1–123.

Joe, S. (1993). *Classroom color lines.* Paper presented at a symposium entitled Race and Racism in Teaching and Learning. Annual Meeting of the American Educational Research Association. Atlanta, GA.

Jones-Wilson, F. C. (1990). Race, realities and American education: Two sides of the coin. *Journal of Negro Education, 59*(1), 119–128.

Ladson-Billings, G. (1994). *The dreamkeepers: Successful teachers of African American children.* San Francisco, CA: Jossey-Bass.

MacLeod, J. (1987). *Ain't no makin' it: Leveled aspirations in a low-income neighborhood.* Boulder, CO: Westview Press.

McCadden, B. M. (1998). Why is Michael always getting timed out? Race, class and the disciplining of other people's children. In R. E. Butchart & B. McEwan (Eds.), *Classroom discipline in American schools: Problems and possibilities for democratic education* (pp. 109–134). Albany: State University of New York Press.

McLaren, P. (1989). On ideology and education: Critical pedagogy and the cultural politics of resistance. In H. A. Giroux & P. McLaren (Eds.), *Critical pedagogy, the state and cultural struggle.* Albany: State University of New York Press.

Moynihan, D. P. (1965). *The Negro family: The case for national action.* Washington, DC. U.S. Government Printing Office.

Nieto, S. (1992). *Affirming diversity: the sociopolitical context of multicultural education.* New York: Longman.

Obidah, J. E. & Teel, K. (2000). *Because of the kids: Facing racial and cultural differences in schools.* New York: Teachers College Press.

Ogbu, J. (1990). Minority education in a comparative perspective. *Journal of Negro Education, 59*(1), 45–56.

Payne, C. M. (1984). *Getting what we asked for: The ambiguity of success and failure in urban education.* Westport: Greenwood Press.

Shor, I. (1996). *When students have power: Negotiating authority in a critical pedagogy.* Chicago: The University of Chicago Press.

Weiner, L. (1985). *Between two worlds: Black students in an urban community college.* Boston: Routledge & Kegan Paul.

Willis, P. (1977). *Learning to labor: How working class kids get working class jobs.* New York: Columbia University Press.

Wilson, W. J. (1987). *The truly disadvantaged.* Chicago: University of Chicago Press.

Dr. Mary V. Alfred

Dr. Mary V. Alfred immigrated to the United States from the British Caribbean Island of St. Lucia. She completed a bachelor's degree in occupational education with a specialization in office and business administration and a master's degree in counseling psychology, both from the University of Central Texas. She completed her doctorate degree at the University of Texas at Austin, where she majored in adult education and human resource development leadership. Her dissertation, *Outsiders Within: The Professional Development History of Tenured African American Women in the White Research Academy,* was nominated as dissertation of the year in 1995.

From 1981 to 1999, Mary served as faculty, and later program coordinator, in the division of Vocational and Workforce Education, Department of Office Administration at Central Texas College. She provided vision and leadership for a program with the primary focus of preparing adults to reenter or advance in the work world.

Dr. Alfred is currently Assistant Professor at the University of Wisconsin–Milwaukee in the Department of Administrative Leadership, Division of Adult and Continuing Education. Her pedagogy includes leadership development, diversity, and human resource development. Her research interests include career development of minority professionals in majority organizations, diversity in education and the workplace, and learning and development among people of color.

Dr. Alfred belongs to various professional organizations and has contributed to the leadership and development of many nonprofit organizations. She is currently serving as a steering committee member of the Adult Education Research Conference, the governing body of the U.S. Association of Adult Educators. In 1999 she received the *Cyril O. Houle Fellowship* in Adult and Continuing Education. This fellowship program recognizes nine emergent scholars (five from the United States) in Adult and Continuing Education who show promise of making significant contributions to the field. Mary's Houle program research is entitled, "The Sociocultural Contexts of Knowing: Epistemology, Learning, and Self-Development among Immigrant Women of Color in the United States."

4

SUCCESSS IN THE IVORY TOWER

LESSONS FROM BLACK TENURED FEMALE FACULTY AT A MAJOR RESEARCH UNIVERSITY

Mary V. Alfred

True, I am a woman, and I am Black. I ask you to take a painful journey with me. The waters are high and the treasures are buried deep. What are these precious treasures that I long to find and labor for in the walls of the ivory institutions? They are the forgotten achievements of Black women. When I find them, where will I place them; back in stacks of forgotten records, or will they be placed on a shelf where explorers such as I can easily capture the beauty of the Black woman's experience in higher education? (Payton, 1981, p. 223)

Life in the ivory tower is very attractive. It provides faculty with freedom to pursue their own research interests, autonomy and control over their work, and opportunities for creative and intellectual development. However, several writers alert us to the negative experiences of Black female faculty as they struggle to gain access, inclusion, and a piece of the good life in predominantly White institutions of higher education (Granger, 1993; Lopez, 1991; McKay, 1997; Smith, 1992). The problems of access, inclusion, and promotion are even more acute in predominantly White research universities where Black female faculty make up only 1.2 percent of the total faculty (National Center for Education Statistics, 1994). Despite the adversities, some women have achieved tenure and promotion, earning their place in the halls of White academia. This chapter results from research that examined the professional development history of five Black tenured female faculty at a predominantly White research university in the Southwest. The participants included Jean, the first Black dean in the history of her major research institution; Myra, professor and director of African and African American Studies; Sara, professor of social work and director of a research institute; Elizabeth, associate professor of journalism; and Kendra, associate professor of engineering.

The research on which this chapter is based examined the professional development experiences of these women, particularly those that contributed to their success in the White male-dominated academic institution. More specifically, the study qualitatively explored the influence of the Black culture and the White dominant culture on the professional development experiences of the participants, their experiences with the White institutional culture, and the strategies they employed to navigate the White academic culture. The study found that meeting and overcoming challenges were central themes in the participants' professional development journeys. These women navigate the White academy through the power of self-definition, knowledge, voice and visibility, and a fluid life structure. Together these forces of power form an interconnecting framework for understanding the participants' success in the White research academy.

Naming Ourselves: The Power of Self-Definition

One of the most illuminating findings of the research is the role of positive self-definition in the participants' management of White-dominated cultures. The defining of self, or self-definition, is the manner or ways in which a woman rejects externally defined controlling images of her Black womanhood (Ward, 1995). These self-definitions enabled the women to use African-derived conceptions of self and community to resist negative evaluations of Black womanhood advanced by dominant groups (Collins, 1991).

Because of the strong interconnection of the Black family and the community during their early developmental experiences, these women grew up with a distinct sense of themselves as Black people. This unique sense of difference created an awareness of expectations in the White culture. They knew that they were different, and therefore, knew that they would be treated differently. They had learned that in order to preserve their inner selves as Black women during their interactions with the White male-dominated culture, they would have to use creative strategies to manage the culture and still emerge with a distinct sense of self. For these women, positive self-definition was manifested through (1) the rejection of negative marginality, (2) finding a safe space, and (3) the rejection of external definitions.

Redefining Our Marginality:
Rejection of Negative Marginality

Park (1928) is credited with the marginal man concept, which typifies the double consciousness that Blacks experience in the White dominant culture. Park defines the marginal man as

> A cultural hybrid, a man living and sharing intimately in the cultural life and traditions of two distinct peoples; never quite willing to break, even if he were permitted to do so, with his past and traditions, and not quite accepted because of racial prejudice, in the new society in which he has sought to find a place. He is a man on the margin of two cultures and two societies which never completely interpenetrated and fused (p. 892).

Although Park did not develop his marginal theory with Blacks in mind, for the most part, his concept seems to fit the status and experiences of Blacks in White American society. His statement, "He is a man [woman] on the margin of two cultures and two societies" (p. 892) does not reflect the experiences of the women studied. The participants did not see themselves on the margin of their two cultures but as active participants in both cultures. Although their token status places them outside their collegial group within the institution, their involvement in their academic community as well as their participation in their Black cultural community make them central players in both lifeworlds.

Park also suggests that marginality leads to psychological conflict, a divided self, and a disjointed person. His statement denotes that marginality is something to be avoided because of the problems that result from such experiences. Contrary to his suggestion, participants in the study define their marginality as a positive attribute. To them, it's a privilege to be marginal. Myra uses the term "creative marginality" to describe her outsider-within stance in the dominant culture. She explained that her marginality allows her to move freely in her various lifeworlds because of her competence in them all. Myra used a discussion she had with another Black woman to explain her concept of creative marginality. As she recounted,

> I talked to a woman at the ski summit and we were talking about being in the box or being outside the box. She said her image of herself is standing on the edge of a cube. It's like the box is at an angle and she is standing on the edge as opposed to being in the box; she is dancing on the edge. . . . That's exactly how I like being marginal.

Audre Lorde (1984) notes that in order to survive, those of us for whom oppression is as American as apple pie have always had to be watchers.

Watching generates a dual consciousness in African American women, one in which Black women become familiar with the language and manners of the oppressor. Being on the edge of the box provides Black women with a special angle of vision from which to watch and learn the behavior of the oppressor and plan their survival strategies.

Standing on the edge of the box, as opposed to being in the box, affords bicultural individuals the freedom to navigate their various cultural worlds without the constraints of any particular world. Collins (1991) suggests that our outsider-within position in the dominant culture places us in a unique position that affords us a distinctive view of the contradictions between the dominant group's actions and their espoused ideologies. As one participant noted, "We know everything about them, and they know nothing about us. We are in a very special position." Because of the privilege of knowing, watching, seeing, and learning that our marginality affords us, we should use that privilege to produce new knowledge about the Black experience.

The findings of the study refute the notion that marginality is problematic and causes psychological conflict. They also challenge the popular belief that Black women, because of their underrepresented status in the White academy, are a marginal group. Marginality is a state of mind and can only become problematic if one lacks a strong sense of cultural identity. If one is rooted in her culture and has a definite sense of herself and her place in that culture, then I argue that she will perceive her marginality as a positive attribute rather than as a handicap. Myra, for example, attributes her Black cultural identity to positive interactions within her family and the Black community lifeworlds during her early developmental period. She said,

> I was always aware of Black people and White people. I don't think I ever had any identity crisis about who I wanted to be, and I think it's because when I first started growing up, all Black folks talked to each other. White people were not people to look up to; they just lived there. They were the other people of society. I always had a sense of difference. I never thought I was the same as them, ever.

Articulating a similar sentiment, Sara said, "I think I absolutely grew up with that very knowledge that I was Black."

The women grew up in nurturing Black environments where Black cultural pride was part of their ancestral and community legacies. They knew that as Black people, they were different from White people. They had a unique sense of difference. They did not see themselves as subordinate to White people, but as different from White people, and none felt that the difference made them subordinate. They use their marginality to enhance their position in the academy. By seeing their marginality as an asset instead of an obstacle, these women use their marginal positions to watch, observe, and learn the behaviors of the dominant group while preserving their own cultural identity and self-definition. When I asked Jean, an executive officer, about the myth that women in leadership positions emulate the behaviors of White men in order to be competitive with that group, she remarked,

> I couldn't behave like anything other than who I am. That wouldn't be real, and I have a hard time carrying on unreal stuff. That makes me very uncomfortable. I think I can be who I am and what I am, but it does not hurt to know how some people might play the game. I think awareness is important, but I don't think I have to emulate anybody's behavior.

By watching, observing, and becoming aware of the way the dominant group plays the game, Jean develops her own strategy, based on her self-defined standpoint, for playing and winning the game. By being aware of how others play the game, these women develop the competence necessary to successfully perform roles in the dominant culture—a major contributor to their success. The perspective from which these women view their marginality was found to be a central element in Black women's definitions of themselves as survivors, survivors with the ability to float in and out of different class and ethnic cultures while still emerging with a strong sense of who they are. Instead of accepting their marginality as disabling, they reconstructed their own definition to reflect positive rather than negative images of their marginal status in White-dominated cultures.

Having a Place of Refuge: Finding a Safe Space

Having a safe space is a method by which the women preserve their constructed definition of the self when the environment becomes disconcerting. According to Ward (1995), "the safe space serves as a prime location for the Black woman to resist objectification as the Other" (p. 153). The findings from this study indicate that participants were able to identify and access places or people in the Black community where their objectification as the Other was minimized. bell hooks (1989) refers to these safe spaces as "homeplace." She describes homeplace as

> a safe place where Black people could affirm one another, and by so doing, heal many of the wounds inflicted by racist domination. . . . We can make homeplace that space where we return for renewal and self-recovery, where we can heal our wounds and become whole. (p. 42)

Elizabeth, for example, resists institutional marginalization by retreating to the safe place she has created in her home. As she explained,

> I won't allow myself to feel marginal at this university. I guess if this meant more to me, if it were my whole life, then perhaps I may have a different view of it; but it's only part of my life. . . . I love my work, but this is not my main life. . . . I am very happy with my family. I have my husband and my daughter, and we are very happy; we have lots of fun together. We have a beautiful home to come to. This is not my only reality. When this becomes too much, I can go home and forget it, at least for a while.

Elizabeth sees marginality as something you allow to happen. Refusal to be marginal suggests a power within to control the definition of one's self. Elizabeth's home and family provide a refuge where she can escape external definitions of her marginality.

Sara's safe space, on the other hand, consists of her childhood community—an all-Black academic community. Going back to her community gives her a sense of wholeness and reminds her of the support, the love, and the safety she received from the family and community. This is particularly important to Sara because she works in an environment where she sometimes feels like an outsider. As she explained,

> I think the times I feel like an outsider are really when I go to meetings in which I don't know anybody else, like some of the committees that I serve on. Sometimes I go, and I get the feeling that when I walk in, there is a surprise that I am there. I hear some of the interactions that suggest that some of the other faculty know one another. Those are the times I feel like an outsider because I know nothing about them, and they know nothing about me. . . . When we go home, there is such a feeling of well being. It feels good to be there. We still know the people, and they know me because of my father. The neighborhood is still predominantly Black. I try to go back at least once a year.

Sara's childhood community provides a safe space where she can recreate and solidify her definition of self, a definition that is sometimes challenged by experiences in the White academic life world.

Retreating to a safe space is a method of resistance that Black women embrace to escape forces of oppression prevalent in the dominant society. The immediate and extended family, churches, African American community organizations, and even the individual psyche are important locations where African Americans retreat to safety. This safe place becomes a house of refuge where Black women can resist objectification as the Other. In this safe place, the Black woman can reconstruct any image of herself that has been threatened as a result of her interactions within White-dominated institutions.

Refusing the Labels of Others: Rejection of External Definitions

> Called Matriarch, Emasculator and Hot Momma. Sometimes Sister, Pretty Babe, Auntie, Mammy, and Girl. Called Unwed Mother, Welfare Recipient, and Inner City Consumer. The Black American Woman has had to admit that while nobody knew the troubles she saw, everybody, his brother and his dog, felt qualified to explain her, even to herself (Collins, 1991, p. 67).

Race, class, and gender oppression continue because of the powerful ideologies that have been constructed to justify their existence. The stereotypical images ascribed to Black women help to perpetuate the dominant group's ideology of Black women's inferiority. By their refusal to accept others' definition of their Blackness and their femaleness, the women in this study are breaking down the negative images that thwart their successful existence in the dominant culture. They define themselves as survivors, and their survival depends on their definition of their own identity and on their rejection of stereotypical images of themselves as Black women. Myra, for example noted, "There is oppression, but my attitude is not victim of oppression but somebody who is privileged to be part of the most dynamic culture on the planet."

Jean, for example, in her vehement refusal to be marginal said, "No I won't allow them to make me feel marginal if that is what they are trying to do. If I ever feel that it is too much, I know how to brush off my vitae and move on." Her refusal to allow others' perception of her place within her collegial group to influence her self-definition is a classic example of these women's refusal to be objectified as subordinate Others. On another occasion, Jean said,

> You deal with different levels of that stuff [discrimination], and I think this university has a long way to go. . . . This notion of being a token, I don't buy that; that doesn't mean people don't see me that way, probably my colleagues, especially here at this university. I have felt they are very lucky to have me, and that's because no one has given me anything. I have paid my dues, and I feel pretty secure about what I do.

Jean's positive definition of herself and her confidence in her abilities to perform her job make it possible for her to refuse others' definition of who she is
as a Black female academician in a White research university. Elizabeth also
noted, "Some people try to put me in a box, but it does not affect what I try
to build on." Sara, on the other hand noted,

> Oh, I just refuse to be what people want me to be. No, I won't do that.
> I know a lot of times, I don't feel necessarily that I fit in. You almost
> have to force yourself to stop being self-conscious about that and view
> it really as their problem. I do not allow myself to be marginalized by
> this other group because it's their problem, not mine.

By refusing to take ownership of the dominant group's definition of them
as subordinate Others, these women are dismantling the negative images that
surround them and are creating and maintaining positive definitions of themselves—definitions that portray the uniqueness of their combined categories,
female and Black. By creating their own self-definitions, they reject the majority group's domination of the minority group. bell hooks (1989) asserts that as
subjects, people have the right to define their own reality, establish their own
identities, name their history. . . . As objects, one's reality is defined by others, one's identity created by others, one's history named only in ways that
define one's relationship to those who are subject (p. 42).

The tendency for the dominant group to objectify Black women and Black
women's refusal to be objectified is one of the major challenges the participants face in the academic culture.

Getting to Know: The Power of Knowledge

Along with self-definition, the power of knowledge is very significant to Black
women's survival in an academic culture that professes the pursuit, creation,
and disbursement of knowledge. Knowledge of the academic culture and role
expectations contribute to the abilities of Black women to meet cultural expectations and thus contribute to their own success in the White academy.

Learning Our Way: Knowledge of Academic Culture

The culture of the academy is based on the concepts and symbols of academic
freedom, the community of scholars, collegial governance, individual autonomy, and service to society through the production of knowledge, the trans-
mission of culture, and the education of the young (Clark, 1972). In this study,
participants placed great emphasis on the importance of cultural knowledge in

successfully managing the academic culture. Knowledge of the culture was first enhanced through their role performance as teaching and/or research assistants, and this early participation in the culture broadened their understanding of the assumptions, values, and ideologies of members of the White academy.

By watching, observing, and learning the practices of others, these women developed a frame of reference from which to pattern their own actions and behavior. Elizabeth, for example, said that her mentor from graduate school was grooming her for an academic career by giving her a visual image of academic culture. As she explained,

> [My mentor] was bringing me along, even though at the time, I didn't know that's what he was doing. He gave me a picture that exemplified an ideal of wouldn't this be great, working with ideas, working with graduate students? Wouldn't this be great not to have a full-time job?

By working with her mentor, she had a picture of life in academy. Elizabeth further suggested, "during the Ph.D. program, you need to get a teaching assistantship or a research assistantship, a job that will connect you with other professors if that is possible. Those of us who had jobs within the university were the insiders; we knew the faculty, and we knew the culture." By interacting with significant members of the culture, the women learned its rules and expectations and such knowledge made them a member of the culture. Myra, in referring to her present institution noted, "I don't feel like an outsider in the university because I understand the way things run here." Her knowledge of the way things are run represents a source of power that strengthens her ability to meet the expectations of the academy.

From their experience as tenured faculty, participants suggested that one way to learn the culture was to interact with its members. By interacting with the culture, the Black woman enhances her visibility within her academic community. For example, Myra said, "Interact but don't spend a lot of time socializing. While you are interacting, find a few that you can work with and make those productive relationships. Know the politics, and let your work speak for itself." Myra also noted that interacting with members of the culture not only facilitates knowledge of the culture, but it opens the way for developing meaningful relationships with those who share similar interests. To new faculty, she suggested, "try to make friends; do have coffee with those folks if you can, and do find out what interests them. Talk to them; make them know you. Do the social stuff, but also do the academic stuff."

Kendra noted that academic culture also varies with discipline and suggested that a faculty member become knowledgeable about the culture of her specific discipline. "Find out from the people who are on the faculty you want to be associated with what is required. It varies from department to department." Kendra's statement substantiates the findings of Bowen and Shuster's (1986) study of American professors in which they found that faculty members in different disciplines exhibit different attitudes, values, and personal characteristics. Because academic culture varies with each discipline, there is no unified academic culture, only many disciplinary cultures. Clark (1972) suggests that the development of competence in a disciplinary culture begins in graduate school when the individual begins to develop some form of cultural identity and begins to understands the symbolic meanings of professional activities.

For the five study participants, socialization processes were facilitated through their participation as graduate students and through their insider positions as assistants and proteges of influential members within the culture. In addition, early interactions with significant members of the culture gave them a competitive advantage for developing the competency necessary to successfully manage the culture.

Serving Competently: Knowledge of Role Expectations

Research studies on the process of tenure in research universities often reveal the lack of knowledge that participants have about the process. In a study of junior faculty's perceptions of the tenure process in research universities, Verrier (1992) found that many of the participants were unclear about the process, had a preoccupation with knowing where they stood in the process, and craved specific indices or clearly defined road maps. Contrary to Verrier's findings, the results of this study suggest that these women clearly understood the cultural expectations with regards to the tenure process. Knowing the culture facilitates knowing the culture's expectations.

Participants, through their affiliation with the culture as research and teaching assistants, as well as through their relationships with significant mentors during graduate school, had some knowledge of the culture's expectations before they joined the ranks of the professorate. They knew the political workings of the culture. Meeting cultural expectations was further enhanced by the departmental support they received during the tenure process. Kendra's school, for example, has a committee in place with the express purpose of ensuring that junior faculty members become aware of tenure expectations. According to Kendra, the committee meets with you individually twice a year. It's a very nice thing. They look at your resume and see where you are in terms of publications, research, etc. . . . They will let you know what you need to do. . . . They really spell it out in terms of what you need to do. I mean you are aware of where you are deficient.

Such awareness enhances participants' knowledge of the culture and increases their opportunities for successful participation.

Each woman articulated the significance of research and publication in the right journals, the importance of networking with colleagues to gain their support and establish visibility (a critical element in the tenure review), the significance of teaching, and the importance of service to the academic community. As Sara said, "I think in terms of the tenure process, the expectation is to publish in the mainstream kind of journal in your field, to get some recognition, and most importantly, to have a research agenda and to follow that to get some research funding." Kendra also noted, "You need to be clear on what they are looking for [during tenure evaluation]. They ask for your research and publications, your community service, your teaching, and the committees that you have served on. . . . You are given about five years to pull this together."

These women came into the academy aware of its cultural rules. Although they found some of the rules inappropriate, they chose to follow the rules to ensure their success in the culture. When Jean and I were discussing the issue of cultural expectations, she said, "I always said, even before I went up for tenure, I know the rules of this game that I have chosen to enter, like them or not, these are the rules. If I want to succeed in this system, then I have to abide by the rules. . . . Know the rules and play the game by the rules."

Knowledge of the rules enhanced Jean's ability to meet the expectations that guided the tenure process. Myra also articulated the importance of playing the game by the rules. She said, "There are rules, follow the rules." To Myra, knowing the culture and its expectations means knowing not only the explicit but also the implicit expectations that the culture has of Black women. She noted, "You really have to do what you are supposed to do, and you have to do a lot of it because being an African American, people are gunning for you. Practically everybody is gunning at you." Myra is suggesting that, in order to avoid the guns of others in the academy, the Black woman should exceed cultural expectations. The message, in order to be equal, you have to be better, is part of her ancestral legacy, and it is a constant life script after which the Black woman patterns her life.

While these participants are aware of the cultural expectations of the research academy, they are also aware of cultural practices that create obstacles for Black women at tenure review time. They noted that in some instances, academic disciplines impose barriers when evaluating Black women's scholarship because it does not fit the discipline's narrowly-defined Eurocentric and masculinist criteria. The White-male-dominant culture, with its narrowly defined criteria and expectations, sometimes has difficulty understanding Black women's scholarship and experiences that do not neatly fit into those criteria. As Jean described,

> I have seen it happen with a lot of Black faculty across the country, many of whom I have written letters in support of when they are going up for tenure. I have to try to translate that person's work and service in a manner that they can understand and is meaningful to the academy.

The issues surrounding Myra's tenure battle clearly demonstrates Jean's argument. As an anthropologist, she studied human development and education in Africa. To the school of education, her research agenda was not focused enough on education and she was, therefore, initially denied tenure. This lack of understanding of Black faculty members' scholarship and experience contributes to the low tenure rates of Black female faculty in predominantly White research universities.

Speaking Out, Standing Tall: The Power of Voice and Visibility

Listening to the voices of others while using their own voices to define themselves as Black women and to articulate their competence have been powerful forces in the participants' successful management of the White academy. By listening first to the voices of family and members of the Black community during their early development the participants learned ancestral legacies which later guided their participation in majority cultures. From the message, "do the best you can, be the best you can be, don't conform to stereotypes of what Whites think about Blacks," Sara learned to be the best. Most importantly, so that she would not conform to stereotypical images of Black womanhood, she learned that she had to first define herself. Sara also said, "I had been told by many of the teachers that they [Whites] would think that they were better than we were, and we needed to prove ourselves. We had to be better." The need to be better in order to be seen as an equal is part the driving force behind Black women's professional success in predominantly White institutions.

By listening to the voices of family and community members, participants in the study developed a strong cultural identity, determination, confidence, and the strength to resist being objectified as subordinate Others. They learned the value of hard work, of staying focused in their professional development endeavors, of being resourceful, self-reliant, and persistent. Most importantly, by listening to the voices of others, they learned the cultural values and expectations of their White and Black cultural lifeworlds. Such knowledge prepared them to successfully participate in both the Black and the White cultures of their lives.

By listening to the voices of others, the women in this study developed their own voice and used that voice to demonstrate their competence, to resist oppression, and to articulate their constructed knowledge of themselves. For the Black woman, a voice is the identification, access, and vehicle through which the knowledge she has constructed of herself and of her various lifeworlds may emerge. These women's voices are manifested in their research and publications, in their contributions to university and academic affairs, and in their contributions to their academic community through professional organizations and conference presentations.

Getting White academic professionals to listen to the voices of Black women is a particular challenge. Because their Blackness and femaleness render them invisible in White institutions, their voices are often silenced (Collins, 1991; Ward, 1995). Even when Black women speak, Whites do not always hear what they say because White professionals have their own preconceived ideas of what Black women should be talking about. Sara said that when she makes presentations about her research, people are always surprised to find that she is not "talking Black." She noted, "There is a lot to overcome in the sense that some of the research that I do is not on a racial issue. For example, whenever I go out to speak on a particular topic that has nothing to do with race, people are kind of surprised that I am there to speak about it." The challenge of getting others to see beyond her Blackness and her femaleness and to listen to her voice is one that confronts Black academic women.

Using their voices to resist oppression and exclusion, and to articulate their positions is evident in the participants' stories. When Elizabeth's dean tried to oust her from an important committee for which she was nominated, she did not walk away gracefully. She spoke out against the exclusionary practices of her department and maintained her position on the committee. As she recounted,

> I told her I was going to stay on the committee. I told her that I was
> appointed and that she could not get me off. I felt that it was very

important for me to be on it. I felt that I could contribute more than most of the other people on the faculty. A lot of people do have problems with standing up, speaking out, and I don't have a problem with that.

Myra, too, did not walk away gracefully when she was denied tenure at a major White research university. She used her voice and her constructed knowledge of herself to fight the system and she won. She was told that her African Americanist research was too popular in orientation. While she wrote for two popular publications, she submitted none of that work for her tenure review. She explained,

> So I wrote lots of stuff for [two popular publications] but I didn't submit any of that. I submitted academic stuff from the *Journal of Modern African Studies,* the *Journal of Religion in Africa* and the kinds of refereed academic journals I was supposed to write for. They also said that my work wasn't focused enough on education, and I said, well you are defining education in a very narrow way. I did research on human development and education in Africa. I believe that's education. They hadn't specified that I had to study the United States. I told them, more or less subtly, I was sorry that my worldview was not narrow enough for them, and that I was also surprised that a major institution would want me to have such a narrow worldview. They said my African Americanist writings were popular and were rather nonscholarly, and I said, I'm sorry, I don't know what you are talking about. The only African Americanist publication that you could have read is my master's paper now published as a book in Europe. I submitted two reviews of it from European journals that said it was a major contribution to knowledge in the area. So I don't know what is too popular about that. They said it was a major scholarly piece, and I'm sure you read those reviews, although they were written in French.

The battle continued and every time they wrote, Myra wrote a stinging rebuttal. She understood the root of her problem. As an anthropologist who worked in the school of education, she did not engage in the stereotypical research that is normally carried out in the school of education. She continued,

> I was supposed to study why Black kids can't read. They said I didn't do that type of stuff, and I told them that it wasn't in the job contract. You can never expect me to study why Black folks can't learn because that's blaming the victim. You can expect me to study why the United States can't teach Black kids to read but Cuba can. How come the United States can't teach a Black kid to read unless his parents make

over $35,000. That's what you can expect from me. So I understood their problem with me, but I just said, at least critique me well. You all critique me poorly, I'm going to critique your critique.

Myra felt she needed bigger guns and she elicited the help of a major African American state politician. She held a press conference to publicize her dilemma and used other strategies to place pressure on the system. After a three-year battle, she won her fight and was promoted to associate professor.

The participants agree that, as Black women, we should use our voices to challenge the system, but it should be done in a professional manner. As Jean said,

> I think there are ways to challenge, and I don't think a loud voice or accusations are the way to do it. You need to be more subdued. It does not mean that you have acquiesced everything. . . . You won't find me screaming, talking about the White man did this and the White man did that, but I think I can stand up for the principles I believe in.

Elizabeth also said, "Be willing to speak up and challenge things in a professional manner." Emphasis on the proper use of voice is crucial to getting the dominant group to listen to the voices of Black women. The Black female faculty member who can get the dominant group to listen to her voice will increase her visibility among that group—a significant element in the academic success model.

This study found that voice and visibility go hand in hand in the demonstration of competence. Although Black women are rendered invisible by virtue of their femaleness and their Blackness, successful Black academic women are rendered highly visible by their academic institutions. As one participant said, "The University has my face plastered all over campus." In the academy, the development of visibility started during graduate school, was promoted through mentoring relationships, and enhanced by the employing institution and the women's participation in regional, national, and international organizations. The effects of such visibility are the opportunities they provide for career development and enhancement. These participants were recruited for faculty positions because of their visibility, either through national organizations, through their established scholarly record, or as a result of mentoring relationships during their doctoral program (in the case of their first faculty position where they were nominated by their mentor).

Kendra noted that one's visibility within her academic community becomes crucial at review time. She said, "You need to be visible in the community that you say you are an expert in. You need to be visible at your national conferences and in your publications. They ask other people who are experts in the field, 'What do you know about this person?' " Elizabeth also emphasized the importance of remaining visible within the academic community. As she said, "You need to be active and visible in the national organization. I was visible in the national organization, and I think that is important."

Findings suggest that for a Black woman to become powerful in the academy, she has to be known, and in order to be known, she must be visible within her academic community. For Black female faculty to become successful, they must be visible among the community of scholars who judge their activities and their performance.

Bridging the Cultural Divide: Fluid Life Structure and Bicultural Competence

An individual's mode of participation within her various sociocultural life worlds depends upon the fluidity or rigidity of the life structure. "The life structure is the design of a person's life at any given time. . . . It is the individual's pattern of involvement in relationships, roles, activities, and physical settings" (Wolfe, O'Connor, & Crary, 1990, p. 958). The life structure is the individual's mode of participation within her sociocultural worlds. This study found that the participants' success in the academy is partly due to their fluid life structure, which enables them to float in and out of their various sociocultural groups. By having a fluid life structure, participants were able to navigate their bicultural worlds with little of the strain and stress Bell (1987) found to be associated with biculturalism. They saw their bicultural lives as interconnected rather than separated. For example, when I asked Kendra about the duality of her life, she said, "No, I don't have a dual life. I cannot distinctly separate my lives. This is all my life. What I am finding is that we may have some cultural uniqueness, but what has brought us together is our work. My professional and personal life is just a continuum."

Jean, on the other hand, agreed that she had a Black life and a White life, but she did not see any distinct separation between the two. As she remarked, "I guess there is a Black life and a White life. Work is White and everything else is Black, meaning social contacts and all that, but that is all my life; I cannot distinctly separate the two. I cannot tell where one ends and the other one starts. They are all parts of my life." Sara also indicated her inability to distinctly separate her life into a Black world bounded by a White world. She noted,

When I go home, it is really totally apart from the university world. What I am in my private life at home, I am still connected to the university in a sense that I am writing and doing things related to my work. I am just not connected on a social basis. . . . I think I am a part of both worlds. It is hard to separate the two. It is all my world.

Seelye (1994) suggests that a truly bicultural person acknowledges that she is not merely "50 percent X and 50 percent Y, but unique blends of X and Y with a variety of successful behaviors to choose from when dealing with X's and Y's" (p. 29). He notes that the bicultural person does not deny the influence of one or another culture on her character but sees her life as a composite of all experiences originating from her various life worlds.

The participants' inability to see the distinct separateness of their lives is evidence of their bicultural life structure. The power of Black women to pattern their mode of interactions to fit their Black and White life worlds is what La Fromboise, Coleman, and Gerton (1993) term bicultural competence. They note that to be biculturally competent, one must possess a substantial degree of personal integration and individuation to avoid the negative consequences of a bicultural living situation. Elaborating on the importance of a bicultural living condition, Rashid (1984) suggests that biculturalism is an attribute that all Americans should possess because it creates a sense of efficacy within the institutional structure of society along with a sense of pride and identification with one's ethnic roots. For African Americans, he notes, it is a vital prerequisite for coping with the racism and classism that permeate this society. These women were found to have high self-esteem and Black cultural identity, elements that Seelye (1994) finds necessary for becoming biculturally competent.

Sister to Sister: Listening to the Voices of Our Tenured Sisters

In this study, the women did not define themselves as victims but as survivors. They creatively manage White academic culture by employing a variety of strategies that enable them to survive and acquire tenure, thus securing their places in the academy. Because these women have survived, they have chosen to bequeath to academic aspirants their gift of survival. To end this chapter, I have allowed each participant to deliver her message in her own voice. Each participant offers her own mode of survival and offers additional advice to make our journey to tenure more manageable.

Sara's Message

- I think in terms of the tenure process, the expectation is to publish in the mainstream kind of journals in your field, to get some recognition, and most importantly, to have a research agenda and to follow that to get some research funding.

- Do what you need to do to get tenure. After you get tenure, you still have demands because the next step is full professor, and you still want to achieve that. You must not lose that focus.

- Do what is expected of you. You need to start working with other people to get joint co-authorship of publications, thus maximizing the number of your writings. Begin to become more visible. Become a good departmental citizen, in a sense of being able to work well with others, so you can have the support of your peers when you go up for tenure. Don't be an isolated person.

- Interact but don't spend a lot of time socializing. While you are interacting, find a few that you can work with and make those productive relationships. Know the politics, and most of all, let your work speak for itself. Do the work so when you turn in your materials, you don't have to say, well if they only look at this or if they only look at that. Your work must speak for itself.

- You really have to stay focused the whole time, just like you did for your dissertation and for your doctoral work. You have to be focused continually, and it is easy to lose focus. It is easy to get your attention diverted, especially if you have worked on a doctoral program and a lot of times, you are burned out and you don't want to focus, but you really need to.

- I think the most important thing is to be at a school where you think you can work with the faculty, and especially to have someone who will support you because if you go to a major research university like this, your publications are going to be the most important thing.

- Preparation for an academic career really begins in the doctoral program. A lot of things go on during the doctoral program, in a sense that you are making connections with all sorts of classmates who you might eventually publish with. You almost have to map it out so that almost any relationship that you have is in some way going to be interconnected to future relationships. You need to really nurture those and to use them to make things happen.

- In many ways, you have to be OK with yourself. You have to build networks. You will have to reach out and do those kinds of things, or it's not going to happen. If you are a Black female at a university like this, you are not going to come across many more Black males. They are not here; the ones that are here are probably married. So you might as well forget it and build a network outside the university.

- If you can't be comfortable in the college or school environment where you are and you don't feel comfortable within the community, you can be a very unhappy person.

- A lot of times you may feel that you do not necessarily fit in. I think you almost have to force yourself to stop being self-conscious about that and view it really as their problem and not allow yourself to be marginalized by this other group.

Elizabeth's Message

- You need to identify an organization or a person who is going to support you, whom you have a good rapport with and you can work with and someone with whom you have similar interests. Sometimes you have to initiate that and sometimes others will initiate it, but more than likely, you would have to initiate it.

- You need to be active and visible in the national organization. I was visible in the national organization, and I think that is important. You need to be as professional as you can be and also be willing to speak up and to challenge things in a professional way.

- The preparation [for a faculty career] starts during the Ph.D. graduate school program. After that, I think you are kind of on your own. You need to develop it there; you need to develop the confidence because once you get out there, unless you have somebody to support you, you are on your own.

- I think you really have to have somebody to work with, somebody who has that area of expertise, and then you may be the second author for a while, but still you are doing publication.

- During your Ph.D. program, you need to get a teaching assistantship or a research assistantship, or a job that will connect you with other professors if that is possible. Those of us who had jobs in the university were the insiders; we knew the faculty and we knew the culture.

- You need to create your own opportunities for your career development. Don't expect the university to have something in place for developing you.

- The race baggage that we carry, don't let it affect your professional life; don't let it affect your relationships with other members of the culture.

Jean's Message

- Know the rules of the game that you have chosen to enter and play the game by the rules. If you want to succeed in this system, you have to abide by the rules whether you agree with them or not. Don't enter the game and then try to change the rules, unless there is enough support behind you to do so. Know the rules and play the game by the rules. That's the way the system is, rightly or wrongly.

- Know yourself and be comfortable with yourself as a Black woman. You must feel secure about yourself and your work in order to survive in this environment.

- When it comes time to challenge the system, you have to know your stuff; you just have to be rational. You have to know exactly what you want; you have to give them help on how they can get there, but don't just protest on foolish stuff. I think there are ways to challenge, and I don't think a loud voice or accusations are the way to do it.

- I don't think you have to emulate anyone to perform your role successfully. But it doesn't hurt, however, to know how other people might play the game. I think awareness is important, but you don't have to emulate anybody's behavior.

Myra's Message

- As a new assistant faculty member, try to make friends; do have coffee with those folks to be accepted if you can, and do find out what interests them. Talk to them; make them know you. Do the social stuff, but also do the academic stuff. Write the articles, get the articles published, turn them out so that if they criticize you, you can ask, about what. You cannot half step your way and then say well, they are just racist. That will not work.

- There are rules, follow the rules. Even if you write critical pieces, publish them in the right journals. Make sure it is refereed. Try to find friendly publications. Try to know somebody who is doing something, and try to get your stuff in through the back door if you can. That's the real system; that's the old boys' network; so we need an old girls' network.

- Try to find somebody who will help you. They may not look like you expect them to look. It may not be the sister; it may not be the brother; it may be a White person; it may be a White man.

- You really have to do what you are supposed to do, and you have to do a lot of it, because being an African American woman, people are gunning for you. Practically everybody is gunning at you. African American men, although they are saying they are on your side, may resent you, especially if you have power over them.

- Try to have a parallel life. Do not make the university your only life. It should not be your only reality. You must develop social relationships outside of the university.

Kendra's Message

- You need to be visible in the community that you say you are an expert in. You need to be visible at your national conferences and in your publications. They ask other people who are experts in the field, "What do you know about this person?"

- Find out from the people who are on the faculty in your school or department what is required. It varies from department to department. You need to be clear on what they are looking for. What are the criteria that are going to be used to make a judgement about you, whenever that judgement is made?

- You want to look good to the people who are evaluating your work. They ask you for your research and publications, your community service, your teaching, and committees that you have served on. They check everything, so your facts had better be straight.

- You are given about five years to pull this together, and coming in from the life of a graduate student, this is very different. You must remain focused at all times.

Conclusion

The five women featured in this chapter have found success (measured by tenure and promotion) in the academy through their successful management of the academic culture as well as their personal lives. They continue on their journey through the ivory tower armed with their powers of self-definition, knowledge, voice and visibility, and a fluid life structure. Their power of self-definition allows them to create positive images of themselves and reject stereotypical images that characterize them as subordinate Others. Their knowledge of the culture and its expectations continues to play significantly in their ability to competently perform roles necessary for continued growth and development. Visibility within the academic community increases opportunities for career development, career advancement, and career mobility. The dimension of voice to demonstrate competence, to articulate constructed knowledge of the self, and to resist oppression was found to be an important strategy that contributes to academic success. Having a fluid life structure makes it possible for members to gain the competence necessary to float in and out of their various sociocultural worlds and to capitalize on the opportunities of both worlds. These five dimensions form an interconnecting framework for promoting Black women's professional development in the White academy.

Bibliography and Selected Readings

Alfred, M. V. (1995). *Outsiders-Within: The professional development history of black tenured female faculty in the white research academy.* Unpublished Doctoral Dissertation. University of Texas at Austin.

Bell, E. L. (1987). The power within: Bicultural life structures and stress among black women. *Dissertation Abstracts International, 4340.* (University Microfilms No. 87-22-233).

Bowen, H. R. & Schuster, J. H. (1986). *American professors: A national resource imperiled.* (ERIC Document Reproduction Service No. ED 272 086).

Clark, B. R. (1972). The organizational saga in higher education. *Administrative Science Quarterly 17,* 178–184.

Collins, P. H. (1991). *Black feminist thought: Knowledge, consciousness, and the politics of empowerment.* New York: Routledge.

Granger, M. W. (1993). A review of the literature on the status of women and minorities in the professorate in higher education. *Journal of School Leadership, 3,* 121–135.

hooks, b. (1989). *Talking back: Thinking feminist, thinking black.* Boston: South End Press.

LaFromboise, T., Coleman, H., & Gerton, J. (1993). Psychological impact of biculturalism: Evidence and theory. *Psychological Bulletin, 14(3),* 395–412.

Lopez, T. R. (1991). *Some African American and Hispanic voices from the University of Toledo.* (ERIC Document Reproduction Service No. ED 328 153).

Lorde, A. (1984). *Sister outsider.* Trumansberg: The Crossing Press.

McKay, N. Y. (1997). Black women in the halls of the white academy. In L. Benjamin (Ed.), *Black women in the academy: Promises and Perils* (pp. 11–22). Gainsville FL: University Press of Florida.

National Center for Education Statistics. (1994). *Digest of education statistics: National study of post-secondary faculty.* Washington, DC: U.S. Government Printing Office.

Park, R. E. (1928). Human migration and the marginal man. *The American Journal of Sociology 33*(6), 881–893.

Payton, L. R. (1981). Black women in higher education: Power, commitment, and leadership. In G. L. Mims (Ed.), *The minority administrator in higher education.* Cambridge: Schenkman Publishing Co.

Rashid, H. M. (1984). Promoting biculturalism in young African American children. *Young Children, 39*(2), 13–24.

Seelye, N. (1984). *Teaching culture.* Lincolnwood: National Textbooks.

Smith, E. (1992). *A comparative study of occupational stress in African American and white university faculty.* New York: Edwin Mellen Press, Ltd.

Verrier, D. A. (1992). *On becoming tenured: Acquiring academic tenure at a research university.* ASHE Annual Meeting Paper. (ERIC Document Reproduction Service No. ED 352 908)

Ward, W. G. (1995). *Successful African-American doctoral students at predominantly white post-secondary institutions: A cross-case analysis from an outsider-within perspective.* Unpublished Doctoral Dissertation. University of Texas at Austin.

Wolfe, D., O'Connor, D., & Crary, M. (1990). Transformation of life structure and personal paradigm during the midlife transitions. *Human Relations, 43*(10), 957–973.

Dr. Gloria D. Thomas

For **Dr. Gloria D. Thomas,** the youngest of eight children, growing up in the blue collar town of Chester, Pennsylvania, did not provide the financial resources to place education as the family's top priority. As a result, Dr. Thomas learned creative ways of seeking intellectual stimulation wherever she could find it. She gained much from her older siblings, asked questions of everyone she met, and sought out educational opportunities in schools and the community that would enhance her academic growth.

With much assistance and motivation from the Swarthmore College Upward Bound program, of which she was a participant throughout high school, Dr. Thomas enrolled in Swarthmore College as an undergraduate. In 1985, she was the first in her family to receive a four-year college degree. Having enjoyed the intellectually stimulating atmosphere of this small liberal arts college, Dr. Thomas subsequently spent seven years there working in the admissions office. Although she treasured the work and the environment, after spending a total of fifteen years on Swarthmore College's campus (as an Upward Bounder, an undergraduate, and an admissions officer), she yearned to pursue new challenges. Faculty, staff, and alumni of the college had become like her own family and were very supportive of her pursuit of doctoral studies.

In 1993, Dr. Thomas moved to Ann Arbor to pursue a doctorate degree at the Center for the Study of Higher and Postsecondary Education at the University of Michigan. She received various University of Michigan fellowships to support her educational endeavors. To enhance her graduate experience, she taught a number of undergraduate courses at the Center for Afro-American and African Studies and worked on a variety of research projects examining the work lives of women faculty. She coordinated a support network for women of color faculty at the Center for the Education of Women. Having recently completed her doctoral studies, she is thankful to close friends and family who provided the support that carried her through the doctoral journey.

5

THE DUAL ROLE OF SCHOLAR AND SOCIAL CHANGE AGENT

REFLECTIONS FROM TENURED AFRICAN AMERICAN AND LATINA FACULTY

Gloria D. Thomas

Introduction

Research has shown that faculty of color—African Americans, Asian Americans, Hispanic/Latino Americans, and Native Americans—experience less satisfying careers in academe, often due to hostile, unsupportive environments (Astin, Antonio, Cress, & Astin, 1997; Carter & O'Brien, 1993; Carter & Wilson, 1996). They are also less likely than their white counterparts to experience supportive or mentoring relationships with senior colleagues (Blackburn, Hollenshead, Coen, Thomas, Waltman, & Wenzel, 1999; Turner & Myers, 2000). Women of color in academe report experiencing double jeopardy since they frequently bear the brunt of both race and gender biases (Turner & Myers, 2000). In other cases, class, age, and sexual orientation are additional personal characteristics frequently used to keep women in subordinate roles (Lorde, 1995).

Research on Black women, in particular, has found that they are concentrated in the lowest academic ranks, are primarily non-tenured, are promoted at slower rates, and are paid less than their male and White female counterparts (Gregory, 1995). In spite of the inequities faculty of color experience in their academic careers, many successful scholars say they stay in academe because they love teaching; they have some supportive administrative colleagues or mentors; they experience a sense of accomplishment in their careers; and they enjoy the interaction with other faculty of color (Turner & Myers,

2000). My ongoing research on the career experiences of women academics at a research university corroborates many of the above findings for women of color, especially for African American women and Latina scholars. In addition, this research suggests that many African American women and Latina scholars see a personal mission of *social change* as a fundamental part of their professional responsibilities. This finding warrants more emphasis and attention as an aspect of career success for women of color in academe. Previous studies merely hint at this phenomenon. For example, Astin et al. (1997) report in their work that one of the biggest differences between faculty of color and their White colleagues is that faculty of color embrace a personal goal of promoting racial understanding. Turner and Myers (2000) cite John Hope Franklin's 1968 statement that "a black scholar has a clear responsibility to join in improving the society in which he lives" (p. 56). Turner and Myers also note the intentional decision of bell hooks to write for a wider public audience as opposed to a narrow academic audience—a strategy she employs to combat the prevailing hegemonic expectation that women of color scholars assimilate and adopt the normative behaviors inculcated during the socialization process for academics. Although these studies suggest that social change is important, the significance of social change among women of color scholars has not been examined in depth. In this chapter, I share excerpts from interviews with tenured African American and Latina scholars, to illuminate their experiences as agents of social change in predominantly White universities.

The Interview Data

Between 1997 and 1998, I conducted semi-structured, in-depth interviews with twenty-four women of color scholars[1] from various disciplines and ranks at the University of Michigan for two separate projects. For both projects, I used a similar interview protocol. The first set of interviews, with mostly tenured women of color scholars, documented their career experiences for a 1999 video documentary entitled, *Through My Lens*.[2] The second set of inter-

---

1. Of the total twenty-four women of color interview respondents from both projects, eight of the women were African American tenured scholars and six were non-tenured; five of the women were Latina tenured scholars; the rest were Asian and Native American tenured and non-tenured scholars.

2. *Through My Lens* is a 27-minute video documentary produced by the Women of Color in the Academy Project at the University of Michigan. The production is based on interviews with women of color faculty in various ranks and across disciplines, and with key academic administrators. For more information about obtaining a copy, contact the Center for the Education of Women at the University of Michigan.

views, with a mixed race group of women, was part of my dissertation research, entitled *Academic Career Success for Women at a Research University: How They Define It and What Factors Contribute to Their Achieving It*. In this chapter I focus solely on tenured African American and Latina female faculty, a subset of the women interviewed for the larger research project. We focused primarily on tenured women for the purpose of making the video because the women would have to share their stories publicly and reveal their identities. Those of us involved in the project did not want to jeopardize opportunities for tenure for junior faculty. Further, I draw only from the quotes of African American and Latina scholars because they were the ones who cited their commitment to social change.

Commitment to Social Change

Broadly defined, the term *social change* means an alteration of social structures or culture over time. From the interviews that I have conducted with women faculty, the findings suggest that many African American women and Latina faculty see their functions as agents of social change as fundamental to their roles as scholars and as crucial among factors of career success. In fact, African American women and Latina faculty respondents consistently reported that they define academic career success partially on the basis of their achievements related to social change, and that they persist in their careers, in spite of experiences of hostile and unsupportive environments, because they have accepted the obligation to promote social change in and out of the academy.

In focusing on this particular issue of social change, I am not claiming that all African American women and Latina scholars accept the pursuit of social reform in and out of the academy as their professional obligation. In fact, I am cautioned from drawing such an oversimplification by a reply bell hooks (1994) gave in an interview on this very topic. In response to the question, "Do you feel that you as a Black woman are changing things in the academy?" hooks replied . . .

> Black women change the process only to the degree that we are in revolt against the prevailing process. However, the vast majority of Black women in *academe* are *not* in revolt—they seem to be as conservative as other conservatizing forces there! Why? Because marginalized groups in institutions feel so vulnerable. I've been . . . thinking a lot about how often I feel more policed by other Black women who say to me: "How can you be out there on the edge? How can you do certain things, like be wild, be inappropriate? You're making it harder for the rest of us (who are trying to show that we can be 'up to snuff') to be 'in' with the mainstream" (1994, p. 233).

bell hooks's observation may have some truth to it—perhaps many Black women academics are conservative and not in revolt. However, it is important to note that in interviews I conducted with upwards of sixty women of color and White women, African American women and Latina faculty frequently cited social change as central to their career purposes and objectives. The only other one to make such a reply was a White woman, full professor in the social sciences. My data demonstrate that this phenomenon of social change is one that is especially significant to African American women and Latina faculty. In the following pages, I use excerpts from their interviews to show how their commitment to social change is both a part of 1) how these women define academic career success for themselves, and 2) what keeps them in academe.

Defining Academic Career Success as Social Change

African American women and Latina faculty responded to the broadly stated question, "How do you define career success?" For many of these scholars, career success means achieving the accomplishments that are traditionally rewarded in the academy, particularly at a research university—publishing, gaining respect and recognition as a national or influential scholar in one's field; getting grants/funding to do research; and having an impact on the intellectual development of students. Some African American and Latina respondents also noted that success for them means doing the kinds of professional work they enjoy and having meaningful personal and/or family lives outside of academia.

In addition, African American women and Latina scholars frequently cited one nontraditional component of career success—being involved in social change through various means and processes in order to reform individuals or communities.

For example, Freda,[3] a Latina in the Humanities, talked about making such changes through her students, her teaching, and her research. She stated,

> The definition of success that I have is my own internal one. And it has to do more with the kinds of change that I see in my students . . .
> I'm not as concerned with having students cover all the theories and read all the major authors that they're supposed to read . . . because that is, I think, one front to a kind of capitalist education . . . I'm interested less in that kind of accumulation of knowledge as I am in how knowledge can change people and can change forms of life and

---

3. Pseudonyms have been given to all interview respondents to protect their identities.

can change communities. So, for me, success has to do more with my own teaching and with the kinds of impact and changes that I can see happening in my students and through my teaching. And also, through my work, through my research. If an article can make a difference in terms of how people think about culture, how people think about Latinos, then I am being successful . . . as a tool for social change. And so that's sort of more my idea of success, whether the academy validates that or not.

Susan, an African American scholar in the social sciences, also believes she should teach for social change. But she extends her commitment beyond the classroom into her own lifestyle. Striving for social and environmental justice is both a personal and professional mission for her.

I can't separate career success from personal success. In fact . . . one of the struggles for me here is being able to walk my talk. The most important thing to me is having a certain integrity between what I'm trying to accomplish with my students and my classes . . . and who I am as a person. That has to do with making a difference, with working . . . struggling to make a more just world, a more socially and environmentally just society . . . I'm involved a lot with the sustainability movement of looking at who has access to what resources and the fact that, as a country with only four percent of the population, we're using up half the world's resources . . . [I'm] trying to engage students in becoming part of the debate against that kind of use of resources. But in my personal life, I do the same thing. [My] house is actually partially a solar home. I have a south-facing house. I heat my house with a wood-burning stove. I get up half an hour early to build a fire. I grow my vegetables. I can them . . . I try to walk my talk, and that talk has to do with social and environmental justice.

Pamela, an African American scholar in the biological health sciences, discussed her views of social change as community-based, outside the realm of academia. For her, social change means maintaining a certain connectedness to her community roots and using her education to make a difference in that community as opposed to no longer fitting in that community. With such a community focus, she defined her academic career success this way:

Making a difference; embracing a concept of the community; being a change agent; working for change; fundamental change, not surface, not window dressing . . . but fundamental change; being connected to real people; never being so educated that I couldn't go home. By choice, most of the organizations . . . that I'm involved in outside of academia are working class, grassroots organizations. Some of them are women's organizations. But real people; for me that was what I needed to do to stay grounded.

While these definitions of academic career success uniquely incorporate components of social change, they all demonstrate how significant it is to these women to alter social structures or cultures in which they live and work. Freda works for social change through her students and through her research. She suggests that her pedagogical objectives, contrary to those traditionally carried out in academe, are to help students find ways to use knowledge to inform themselves and change communities.

Susan's commitment to social change extends beyond the classroom and her research and into her way of living. Her commitment to social and environmental justice issues has the potential to influence her students in the classroom, as well as global environmental policies.

Pamela cites her commitment to social change through her community connections. Twice, she makes reference to people in her community as "real people" whom she strives to stay connected to, thus suggesting that there is something about the people in academe that is not genuine, not "real." Moreover, her comments about the dissonance between "being so educated" and not being able to "go home," and about "real people" keeping her "grounded" further imply that the inauthenticity of the academic world involves academics' lack of attention to issues and concerns of the people at home, or the community. She makes it clear that although she is a part of academe, she is not inattentive to her own personal roots and those she has departed from in order to join the academic world.

Staying in Academe to Make a Difference

It is not unusual for people of color to take nontraditional paths into careers in academe. Among the women of color I interviewed, some worked as nurses, trade book publishers, secretaries, social workers, medical technologists, and a host of other jobs and professions prior to starting their academic careers. Needless to say, this group of women had a magnitude of career options available to them. However, for reasons as varied as their prior professions, all of the African American women and Latina faculty represented here eventually ended up in academic careers, and all of them subsequently achieved the rank of tenured associate or full professors at a major research university.

In all of my interviews with women from various ethnic/racial backgrounds and from across the disciplines, I asked, "What keeps you in academe?" The most frequently cited factors that White women mentioned included the flexibility of the profession, which provided more time for family; the intellectual challenge; the funding to do their research; or simply the fact that they were happy in the profession. While some African American women and Latinas cited these same factors, they also cited issues of social change that were not mentioned by White women.

In one example, Louise, an African American woman in the social sciences, stated that one of the reasons she stays is to support new junior faculty she helped to recruit. As she told me,

> [There's another] reason I stay . . . I was part of recruiting two women faculty several years ago . . . I said, "Ok, I'll be part of the recruitment process." Then I realized that that was a commitment, at least on my part. You don't recruit them and say "goodbye." . . . I needed to be there if there were things that needed to be done. Well, we are now in the midst of the second one's promotion to tenure . . . But those two that I personally said I will be there for, I've been there . . . [O]ne was a big, ugly fight, but a successful one. The other one is in process [of being reviewed for tenure] and I think will be OK.

Linda, a Latina in the social sciences, discussed how her commitment to academe stems from the impact her work has had on changing the way social work and psychology are practiced. As a result of her efforts, as well as those of many other like-minded scholars, these disciplines, she says, have begun to "empower" the so-called "pathological" people they study.

> Social work . . . and psychology [have] traditionally played a role of being oppressive to people of color and women and gays and lesbians and people with disabilities . . . We look at eugenics and all the things that social workers have done . . . So my feeling, as a feminist and a progressive-type person, was that I [wanted] to be in social work trying to [make] change so we were not always having that role; so that we can figure out ways in which we [could] be progressive and liberating and work with people around social justice issues.

Similarly, Susan, an African American scholar, talked about the changes she's been able to make in her discipline as one way that she gives back to people who helped her along the way. She cites this as one of the primary reasons she has persisted in the academy. She tells this story:

> I think that I'm making a real difference in my field in architecture. I think that I have opportunities to try to turn things around. Right

now, I'm involved in something that is enormously exciting. I have become . . . the president-elect of the accrediting board in architecture. Now that's amazing. And one of the issues on the table is whether there should only be one degree in architecture. Apparently, all of the mainstream people got together about five years ago and voted that this should happen. And I went to a conference in May and questioned that, in a multicultural world where we're trying to think of diversity, that we would think that there should only be one way to be an architect. Sure enough, as soon as I said that, all these other people came out of the walls and said, "You know, I wanted to say that too." . . . I'm the troublemaker who gives other people the courage to say what they were really thinking . . . that things are just not right. I don't mind taking the flack. So, I'm out there to try to change things for other people. I had people who did that for me . . . I think I do make a difference.

Freda, a Latina scholar, told me the story of how she has influenced the development of Latino Studies, a discipline that emerged out of political protests. She makes it clear that the field of study is, itself, one of social change.

When you talk about issues of language and the relationship of language to economic access or to economic well being, when you're talking about language and education, you cannot say that this is not political. And it's very risky and it's very challenging too. But Latino Studies is a political field. It's also a political field, not only because of the way that it studies people [but] because it also addresses the history and the conditions of a particular group of people—which are pretty much working-class and pretty much marginalized from the mainstream economy and a people that have been historically colonized. So these things are political facts, and we cannot erase those. And so I think many of the scholars who work in this area are very aware and very conscious about why we are here and we're not here just because we had good grades or because . . . our scholarship is excellent and so on. It's also because many people sacrificed their lives and sacrificed their energy and sacrificed their freedom to allow for these spaces to be created.

Freda went on to explain how her academic career has been dedicated to shaping a field of study that is a part of her very own culture as well as that of numerous Latino students in colleges and universities—a culture that previously had been ignored by the academy:

When I finished my Ph.D., I finished it in Latin American Literature, which is a pretty mainstream, traditional area of study. I liked what I had done with my Ph.D. thesis and all of that, but I knew that inside me I felt like I needed a change. I really was not totally convinced that this is what I wanted to do for the rest of my life. And when I moved, my first job was in California, after my Ph.D., and I discovered that there was this whole world of Latino students in California; that there were professors who were teaching Chicano History, Chicano Literature, Puerto Rican Literature. And I came to a point in my life when I decided that, if I was going to stay in academia, I had to do something that I was really invested in. I felt that now I had the skills to do critical thinking, to do critical writing, and I really wanted to do something that was much more connected to who I was, to my culture, to what it meant being a Puerto Rican woman in the United States. I felt that if I didn't do that and that [if there wasn't] some kind of urgency and immediate need for me to continue in academia, then I might as well have gone into something else.

Finally, Freda noted that her roles in this burgeoning field of Latino Studies were to serve as a role model for the students and to be a part of history in the making.

I realized that there was a historical need and an important need to have Latino professors in this country because of the students that I was starting to see in my classes. [T]here was a need for role models. And that also there was a need to change the curriculum. And to present and address this whole other field of study which became Latino studies or which was already becoming Latino studies then. And for me, [it] was very exciting to have been part of that history, in my own way. So that's another part of the career. You know, that it's not just a career, but it was also a social motivation behind staying in academia.

In the responses that address why these women stay in academe, these African American women and Latina scholars talk about changes they are actually making in their disciplines, in their academic units or departments, or in their students and colleagues' lives. Invariably, they all conclude that a major part of what keeps them in the academy is their ability and wherewithal to be influential in their own respective ways. Taken together, these examples provide evidence for the commitment to social change in and out of the academy that these African American and Latina scholars have made as a fundamental part of their personal and professional duties.

Conclusion

These quotes from African American women and Latina scholars from a major research university bespeak their commitment to changing social structures in and out of the academy. Though few, if any, referred to themselves as feminists, their struggles for social change relate to what Aída Hurtado (1996) calls "women of color's 'no-name feminism.'" In such struggles against the patriarchal status quo, most women of color, like those represented here, do not have the luxury of separating gender oppression from their own racial/ethnic oppression, so their battles are fought on behalf of women as well as those of their racial/ethnic groups.

Since these women have not only survived the often-oppressive forces of the academy, but have also thrived in them, one might conclude that their work toward social change has helped to make them the industrious and successful individuals that they are. Their works, individually and collectively, have translated into changes that embrace alternative views and perspectives beyond what is traditionally upheld in their particular academic units or departments, throughout the university, and in some cases throughout their entire disciplines. According to Audre Lorde (1995) people choose to respond to systematized oppression in one of three ways: "Ignore it, and if that is not possible, copy it if we think it is dominant, or [challenge] it if we think it is subordinate" (p. 267). The examples provided in this essay show that these women obviously see many problems in the current structure and culture of the academy. Accordingly, they have chosen to challenge these problems as a means of reform in order to seek more inclusive alternatives.

I refer to one final comment that Freda made about why she feels so committed to social change in the academy. Freda stated,

> So I think we constantly live being defined by others, and we're constantly being reminded that somehow we don't belong here. It just feels very wrong. It feels very wrong to have people make comments like that and have these attitudes when I think that, in many ways, they could have been doing a lot more for the same issues that we're struggling for. Their luxury, though, is that they don't have to. They have a choice and we don't.

In closing, my response to her remark is that I wish more academics—men and women as well as those of all racial and ethnic backgrounds—accepted social change as part of their personal and professional responsibilities.

Bibliography and Suggested Readings

Astin, H. S., Antonio, A. L., Cress, C. M., & Astin, A. W. (1997, April). *Race and ethnicity in the American professoriate, 1995–96.* Los Angeles: Higher Education Research Institute, Graduate School of Education and Information Studies, University of California.

Blackburn, R. T., Hollenshead, C., Coen, P., Thomas, G., Waltman, J., & Wenzel, S. (1999, November). *University of Michigan faculty work-life study.* Ann Arbor: Center for the Study of Higher and Postsecondary Education and the Center for the Education of Women, University of Michigan.

Carter, D. J. & O'Brien, E. M. (1993). *Employment and hiring patterns for faculty of color.* (American Council on Education Research Briefs 4(6)). Washington DC: American Council on Education Research, Division of Policy Analysis and Research.

Carter, D. J. & Wilson, R. (1996). *Minorities in higher education: Fourteenth annual status report.* Washington, DC: American Council on Education, Office of Minorities in Higher Education.

Gregory, S. (1995). *Black women in the academy: The secrets to success and achievement.* New York: University Press of America.

hooks, b. (1994). *Outlaw culture.* New York: Routledge.

Hurtado, A. (1996). *The color of privilege: Three blasphemies of race and feminism.* Ann Arbor: University of Michigan Press.

Lorde, A. (1995). Age, race, class, and sex: Women redefining difference. In A. Kesselman, L. D. McNair, & N. Schniedewind (Eds.), *Women: Images and reality: A multicultural anthology* (pp. 267–272). Mountain View: Mayfield Publishing Co.

Turner, C. S. V. & Myers, S. L. (2000). *Faculty of color in academe: Bittersweet success.* Boston: Allyn and Bacon.

Dr. Lisa D. Williams

Dr. Lisa D. Williams recently completed her doctorate in social justice education at the University of Massachusetts, Amherst. She also received a graduate certificate in advanced feminist theory through the Women's Studies Department. She holds a bachelor of arts in economics and sociology from Rutgers University and an M.B.A. from Cleveland State University. While a full-time faculty member in the UMASS Women's Studies Department, Dr. Williams taught Introduction to Women's Studies, Critical Perspectives in Women's Studies, Black Women and Activism, and Women of Color and the Legal System. She also taught courses on Social Diversity in Schools (K-12), Intergroup Dialogues, and led a seminar on Faculty Teaching for African American, Latino, Asian, and Native American graduate students.

Dr. Williams is a native of Teaneck, New Jersey, with ancestral roots in Charleston, South Carolina, and St. Croix, Virgin Islands. She has close family ties with her extended family and with her parents, Vernon and Hortense; her brothers, Vernon, Jr., and Derek; and her twin sister, Lori. She currently lives with her fourteen-year-old daughter, Laci.

Dr. Williams is very active on campus and in the community working with teenagers, students, parents, community groups, and women's groups. She consults with schools, colleges, businesses, and nonprofit agencies on issues of diversity, multicultural organizational development, and prison and healthcare issues. Dr. Williams has been the recipient of many awards including a Teaching Excellence Award. She was recently selected to the International Who's Who of Business and Professional Women. Through her research and activism, Dr. Williams is committed to creating a space and a voice for African American Women and other groups who have been consistently marginalized by mainstream society. Her compassion and commitment to helping others is driven by her strong faith and belief in God.

6

COMING TO TERMS WITH
BEING A YOUNG, BLACK
FEMALE ACADEMIC IN U.S.
HIGHER EDUCATION

Lisa D. Williams

Introduction

The experiences of young Black women and their increasing presence in academe mandate understanding their cultural perspectives, respecting their differences, and acknowledging the many contributions they bring to the academy. There needs to be a deeper understanding and analysis of Black women in the academy and not a simplified one that masks the multiple layers of their different identities. Thus, the purpose of this chapter is not to just identify the "problems" of young Black women in higher education. Rather, I illuminate and highlight some of the major issues which seem to impact young Black women in higher education by centering on my own experiences as a doctoral student, faculty member, and researcher.

Some of the research on faculty of color in academe suggests that they experience severe marginalization (Johnsrud, 1993). While some researchers attribute the marginalization of faculty of color to poor institutional fit, cross cultural and social differences, and lack of support (Smith, Wolf, & Busenberg, 1996), others suggest feelings of isolation, experiences with prejudice and discrimination, lower salaries, low professional ranks, and lack of tenured status (Tack & Patitu, 1992).

Caught between Race and Gender

Historically, women of color and particularly Black women, have been jeop-ardized by being both Black and woman. Guy-Sheftall (1995) writes "that black women have struggled against racism and sexism and many other 'isms' during our involuntary sojourn in this country and that these courageous efforts have been ignored, misinterpreted, or maligned" (p. 25). Living in the backdrop of New York City, just a stone throw away—six minutes outside of the Big Apple—I sometimes wondered where I would end up professionally. I never imagined that I would be teaching Women's Studies or Social Justice Education at a major research university in a small New England college town where there are few Black women students or faculty.

The relative absence of Black women scholars on campus, however, can lead to the erroneous belief that Black women are not qualified to be scholars, professors, administrators, or even doctoral students. One negative conse-quence resulting from this dilemma is that many Black women faculty report that their qualifications are constantly challenged (Gregory, 1995).

According to Collins (1991), Black women's lives are inextricably linked to a history of racist and sexist oppression that institutionalizes the devalua-tion of African American women as it idealizes their White counterparts. For Black women, issues of gender are always connected to race because the two are inseparable. This itself is a paradoxical situation. While their race and gen-der make them so visible on the outside, when they are devalued, ignored and disrespected, they are sometimes left feeling invisible inside.

For many Black women, higher education requires self-discipline and awareness not only of their academic environment but of their social environ-ment. Many of my students and colleagues have confided in me that despite their persistence to achieve on campus, they feel that they are considered unqualified to be in higher education. They have been confronted with the stereotypes, overtly and covertly, which suggest that most young Black females are poor, academically unprepared, and not qualified to be in higher educa-tion. They have also been targeted as being simply *affirmative action cases* with little regard for the skills and intellect that they bring to campus.

Thus, several personal incidents motivated me to write this chapter on the topic of being a young Black female in higher education. One incident in par-ticular involved a situation that occurred in my Women of Color and the Legal System course, which I taught last semester. As I prepared the outline and syl-labus for this gender and legal course, I could never have imagined the learn-ing that would come out of this teaching experience.

The first day, I walked into a class filled with the excited faces of students of different races and cultures—some who were pleading to get into this new class, which was already oversubscribed. They explained that they were excited to discuss issues pertaining to women of color and the legal system. Moreover, they welcomed the opportunity to read the research about women of color and the issues surrounding their interaction with the legal system. In addition, they knew they would be expected to simultaneously tease out the reality of these women's daily lives and their ongoing battles of gender and race issues.

For this course, one assignment required the students to find a courthouse, observe what they saw and how it impacted women of color, and then to report back to the entire class. Hesitant, but eager to complete their assignment, they headed off to their local courthouse to observe legal trials and proceedings. Midway through the course, when the students returned to share their experiences, one woman of color described how the judge in the courtroom she visited asked her to approach the bench so that "her" case could be heard. In response, the student explained to the presiding judge that she was in court to complete a class assignment. Ironically, but not suprisingly, the judge responded to this young student that the reason he called her to approach "his" bench was simply because the majority of defendants that approach him in "his" courtroom are Black and Hispanic. Thus, this young woman of color fit the description of a typical defendant, based on the judge's own historical and statistical analysis of who he sees in his courtroom on a daily basis.

On the surface level, this may seem like a simple case of mistaken identity. On a much deeper level, this incident reinforces the notion that all people of color can easily be mistaken for each other and, more importantly, can be readily mistaken for suspected criminals. Statistically, research does show that Black women comprise the fastest growing imprisoned population (Davis, 1998). However, this teachable moment highlighted the deeper injustices within the legal system. The judge clearly focused on race as a determining factor in deciding who needed to approach his bench. Based on this scenario, it is questionable if this judge would have targeted a White individual to approach his bench.

Nevertheless, Angela Davis (1998), who has made a commitment to highlighting the biases in the criminal justice system, challenges academics not to forget the responsibility we have to the larger community. In her article she states,

> Finally, if the presence of increasing numbers of black women within the academy is to have a transformative impact both on the academy and on communities beyond the academy, we have to think seriously about linkages between research and activism, about cross-racial and

transnational coalition strategies, and about the importance of linking our work to radical social agendas (p. 30).

In other words, Black women in the academy have a responsibility not to forget their sisters who are involved with the criminal justice system. Needless to say, the above student's revelation of her experiences provoked a "heartwrenching" discussion of "race dynamics" in America, particularly as it pertains to woman of color and the legal system.

Furthermore, the judge's actions and comments in this example substantiate the need for addressing the experiences of being a young woman of color. Specifically, his comments raise a number of issues pertaining to why it's important to come to terms with being a young Black female in higher education. While this is only one small example of the underlying dynamics of race and gender, I'm sure it will resonate with many Black women who read this book and have recollections of being accused of doing something wrong because of their combined race and gender.

Shifting the Center

As a full-time faculty member in the Women's Studies Department, I had the opportunity to teach Introduction to Women's Studies. The goal of this course was to place women's experiences at the center of interpretation. This course was designed to introduce the basic concepts and perspectives in Women's Studies. It also focused on women's lives with a particular emphasis on the ways in which gender interacts with race, class, sexual orientation, and ethnicity. The central aim of this course however, was to foster critical reading and thinking about women's lives, including the ways in which the interlocking system of colonialism, racism, sexism, ethnocentrism, and heterosexism shape women's lives.

On one occasion while teaching this course, a White female student commented that she appreciated hearing and learning about heroines such as Fannie Lou Hammer and Sojourner Truth, but that she would rather focus on Women's issues rather than Black issues. In other words, in her eyes, Black women such as Hammer and Truth, were not considered to be "real" women, just "Black" women. Unfortunately, this sentiment is echoed by many young White middle-class students who don't realize the inconsistency of this statement. Yet, this was a clear example of how one group can attempt to shift the center toward their own liking and comfort zones. Through this experience, I had to come to terms with the fact that many White students had never had a Black professor prior to stepping into my classroom. In other words, I wasn't just teaching the subject, I became the subject—a young, Black female who was shifting the experiences of Black women from the margins to the center.

Recently, race feminists have articulated how the dominant group attempts to shift the center. "When people who are not regarded as entitled to the center move into it, however, briefly, they are viewed as usurpers" (Grillo & Wildman, 1997, p. 47). As a young Black woman in the academy teaching in a predominantly White campus, I know that because of my race and gender, I am not considered the center by many in the dominant group. I also know from experience that issues pertaining to Black women's lives and their historical accomplishments are not a high priority for some groups. Arguably, to be in the center would mean that those in power would have to shift out of the center. Grillo and Wildman state that "Another tactic used by the dominant group is to steal back the center using guerilla tactics where necessary" (p. 47). Thus, anytime Black women's issues make a move to the center, there seems to be some type of overt or covert repercussion. Consequently, it became clear to me that I was not solely a professor teaching a subject; at times, I became indistinguishable from the subject of Black woman.

For many, Black women are still marginalized from mainstream academe. In her essay, Russell (1997), a law professor, describes how an unidentified person placed a magazine cover of a gorilla in her mailbox at her law school. The picture of this gorilla was an attack on both her intellect and her human dignity. Once again, this example represents how Black women are continuously assaulted on many different levels despite their academic and intellectual accomplishments. The fact that the individual(s) who perpetuated this act did not have to reveal him/herself, lends credence to the silent protection they obviously felt they had in the academy. The gorilla was allowed to "gaze" at Russell and as a result, caused her to seek refuge in the "comfort" of her own office, if there is such a place in the academy. In retrospect, Russell notes, "the reality is that black woman can expect to have only dysfunctional relationships in the academy" (p. 111). If dysfunctionality is an expectation in the academy, as Russell suggests, then one might question why we, as Black women, seek to enter such a place. There are probably as many answers to this question as there are Black women. The main point however, is that while the academy may be a place of higher learning and positive experiences for Black women, it can also be a place where Black women need to constantly be on guard.

"For Crying Out Loud"

As a faculty and staff member, I have worked with many young women of color who were silently screaming to get more information about themselves and about women who looked liked them, acted like them, talked like them, and dreamed some of the same dreams they did when they were their age. Many were crying out for someone to hear what they had to say and what issues they wanted to discuss. They were determined to hear the whole story about their foremothers, such as Ida B. Wells and Zora Neale Hurstson. They wanted to grapple with issues afflicting Black women: poverty, reproductive rights, AIDS, violence against women, and welfare—issues which, to some extent, eat away at the foundation of Black communities.

Sista to Sista: Connecting Theory to Practice

To address the real issues of Black women, I made a concerted effort to bring real Black women into the classroom. Bringing real live Black women into the classroom was just as much a teaching experience as it was a learning experience. Guests in my Black Women and Activism course included prison workers, community activists, a medical doctor/law student, a professor/activist, an assistant pastor, a licensed social worker, and an engineer. The students listened, sometimes in tears, as these down-to-earth, intelligent Black women reiterated horrid examples of the racism and sexism they experienced before, during, and after obtaining their degrees in medicine, law, theology, education, counseling psychology, social work, sociology, business, and engineering. The experiences of these powerful Black women helped shatter the myths some of my students held prior to coming into these classes. Typically, the discussions following these presentations were deeper and more honest because "history" in the books came into contact with "herstory" in a real life setting. Placing these Black women scholars/activists front and center facilitated an environment where students couldn't take a break from what they were reading and come back to it later. Most were intellectually and emotionally forced to come to grips with some of their thoughts right on the spot and had to face the reality of the inequities of the socially unjust system in which we all live. The issues of racism, classism, sexism, were embedded throughout all of these discussions.

Having a Say: The Role of Mentoring, the Role of Voice

It is common knowledge that W.E.B. DuBois rightfully predicted that the problem of the color line would be the problem of the twentieth century. Unfortunately, unless there are some revolutionary changes in the very near future, his prediction will also clearly guide us into the twenty-first century and beyond. Attacks on affirmative action continue to have damaging effects for Black students and faculty alike. If there are no Black students in the pipeline, there can be no new Black faculty emerging from the pipeline. Furthermore, if there are no emerging young Black females in the faculty pipeline, then who will serve as mentors for future generations of young Black women? If an individual has not been mentored, how can that individual effectively mentor someone else? Can only a few Black woman scholars focus on new forms of Black feminist theory?

These questions lead me to reflect on why Black women's voices need to be heard in the academy. Specifically, my research on Black math and science faculty, who are few and far between, highlights the necessity for us (Black women) to do our own work. As a doctoral student, faculty member, scholar, and mentor, I have had to feel my way through the academy by negotiating many obstacles and challenges.

Young women of color have sought me out as a mentor because they are also trying to negotiate their way through the higher education process. Not surprisingly, researchers have identified mentoring as a vital ingredient in the most successful faculty careers (Johnsrud, 1993). Blackwell (1988) discussed networking and mentoring of Blacks in graduate and professional education and helped bring attention to the need for mentoring of Black students.

> If Black students are excluded from social and educational networks and if they are not included in the network spawned by mentor-protégé relationships, their movement 'through and up' in the world of professional ranks may be impeded and perhaps, unnecessarily traumatic (p. 4).

Blackwell found that women were less likely to participate in mentoring relationships, and Black women were less likely than White women and Black or White men to participate in mentoring relationships. Blackwell further suggested that more research be conducted on mentoring and the impact it has on graduate success. Such research would be useful when one considers the growing body of literature revealing that many scholars of color experience severe marginalization on predominantly White college and university campuses (Aguirre, Hernandez & Martinez, 1994; Boice, 1993; Nakanishi, 1993; Olivas, 1988).

In addition to mentoring, there has been much discussion in the literature about the need for Black women to serve as role models. Allen (1997) critiques the role model argument on the grounds that it degrades Black women's true contributions to the academe. In her essay, *On Becoming a Role Model,* Allen states,

> In the final analysis, it is plain that we should applaud black female role models, but reject the journalist's version of the role model argument—that the principal reason for adding black women to a faculty that may already include white women and black men is that they are role models (Allen, 1997, p. 86).

Allen points out serious limitations of the role model argument and stresses that some colleges try to hide behind the fact that Black women think, research, and write as well as Whites. In other words, their sole purpose is not just to be a role model.

When being mentored, I am constantly reminded by one of my mentors about the connectedness in my work. She always says, "Lisa, as you move forward in life you will realize that everything you do is all connected somehow and in some way, even though you may not see the connections at the moment." This constant reminder, coupled with the following quote by Patricia Hill Collins (1998), forces me to remember the purpose of why we, as Black women, need to have a "voice and a say" in higher education.

After so many years of being silenced, individual voices like mine can provide comfort, if not inspiration to individuals from many groups who, like African American women, have been similarly silenced. I also know that, lacking a collective voice, individual voices like mine will become fainter until, one day, many may forget that we ever spoke at all (p. 76).

Conclusion: In the Shadow of My Sisters

Who am I teaching? What am I teaching? How am I teaching? Why am I teaching? These are just a few of the questions I grappled with on a daily basis. I ask similar questions in regards to my research and service commitments. There are no easy answers to these questions, but I do know that the road I've taken to receive my doctorate is not the end all, but rather a small step in a life-long journey. The academic awards and honors that I've received over the years can certainly be regarded as accomplishments, but more importantly, they are reminders of the tasks that lie ahead. It is easy to achieve something and then rest on one's laurels, but while many are resting, life goes on. History has taught us this lesson time and time again. While many rested with some of the accomplishments from the Civil Rights Movement, others were already strategizing to strip the civil rights of certain groups, including Blacks and other groups of color. Over the years, I have learned that if you are trying to make changes for the better, there is always work to be done.

In brief, I can honestly state that I feel fortunate and proud to be existing in the shadows of intelligent and courageous Black women who put their lives on the line to make a way for young Black women trailblazing behind them. Fannie Lou Hammer, Audre Lorde, June Jordan, Anna Julia Cooper, Ida B. Wells-Barnett, Sojourner Truth, Harriet Jacobs, Mary McLeod Bethune, and a host of others, including the oftentimes lesser known women in my family and in my community. These woman have individually and collectively helped to shape the way I think, act, and speak.

Reflecting back, I truly believe that I have made a difference in the lives of the individuals I have taught and worked with in the academy. Yet, I also know that these same students and colleagues have made a difference in my life as well. Through my experiences in higher education, I have learned the importance of survival by bridging alliances with others across race, class, gender, religion, abilities, sexuality, and age. As with any research about higher education, however, there remains much more to discover about Black women. Specifically, there is a continuing need to tease out the dynamics that contribute to the multifaceted experiences of young Black women and to place much needed attention on the role they play as scholars, researchers, faculty, and students. Finally, we must continue to create a critical space in which to transform and challenge misconceptions about young Black women in higher education.

Bibliography and Suggested Readings

Aguirre, A., Jr., Hernandez, A., & Martinez, R.O. (1994). Perceptions of the workplace: Focus on minority women faculty. *Initiatives, 56*(3), 41–50.

Allen, A. (1997). On Being a role model. In A. Wing (Ed.), *Critical race feminism: A reader.* New York: University Press.

Blackwell, J. E. (1988). Faculty issues: Impact on minorities. *The Review of Higher Education, 11*(4), 417–434.

Boice, R. (1993). The early turning points in professional careers of women and minorities. *New Directions for Teaching and Learning, 53,* 71–93.

Collins, P. H. (1991). *Black feminist thought: Knowledge, consciousness, and the politics of empowerment.* New York: Routledge.

Collins, P. H. (1998). *Fighting words: Black women and the search for justice.* Minneapolis: University of Minnesota Press.

Davis, A. (1998). Black women and the academy. In J. James (Ed.), *The Angela Y. Davis reader.* Cambridge: Blackwell Publishers.

Gregory, S. (1995). *Black women in the academy: The secrets to success and achievement.* Washington DC: University Press of America.

Grillo, T. & Wildman, S. (1997). Obscuring the importance of race: The implication of making comparisons between racism and sexism (or other isms). In A. Wing (Ed.), *Critical race feminism*. New York: New York University Press.

Guy-Sheftall, B. (Ed.). (1995). *Words of fire: An anthology of African American feminist thought*. New York: The New Press.

Johnsrud, L. K. (1993). Women and minority faculty experiences: Defining and responding to diverse realities. In J. Gainen & R. Boice (Eds.), *Building a diverse faculty, New directions for teaching and learning* (pp. 3–16). San Francisco: Jossey-Bass.

Nakanishi, D. T. (1993). Asian Pacific Americans in higher education: Faculty and administrative representation and tenure. *New Directions for Teaching and Learning, 53*, 51–59.

Olivas, M. A. (1988). Latino Faculty at the border: Increasing numbers key to more Hispanic access. *Change, 20*(3), 6–9.

Russell, J. (1997). On being a gorilla in your midst, or The life of one black woman in the legal academy. In A. Wing (Ed.), *Critical race feminism* (pp. 110–112). New York: University Press.

Smith, D., Wolf, L. E., & Busenberg, B. E. (1996). *Achieving faculty diversity: Debunking the myths*. Washington, DC: Association of American Colleges and Universities. ERIC Document Reproduction Service No. ED 348 785.

Tack, M. W. & Patitu, C. L. (1992). Faculty job satisfaction: Women and minorities in peril. *ERIC Digest, 4*, 92–96.

Ms. Rochelle L. Woods

Ms. Rochelle L. Woods attended the University of Illinois at Urbana–Champaign, where she majored in sociology and minored in Afro-American studies. She worked for three years as a work-study student in the Afro-American Studies and Research Program where she was nurtured and mentored by the faculty and staff, in particular Professor Dianne Pinderhughes, Valinda Littlefield, and Amita Althaus. In 1992 and 1993, Ms. Woods participated in the CIC Summer Research Opportunity Program, completing research projects with mentors Professor William Trent and Dr. Ife Williams. She received a bachelor of arts degree in sociology with departmental distinction from the University of Illinois in 1994.

In the summer of 1994 she began doctoral studies in the Department of Sociology at the University of Michigan at Ann Arbor. After receiving a master's degree in 1995 and achieving doctoral candidacy in 1996, Ms. Woods received a grant from the Minority International Research Training Program sponsored by the Foggarty International Center of National Institute of Health. This funding allowed her to conduct dissertation research in Johannesburg, South Africa. For significant periods of time between 1996 and 1998, she lived in Johannesburg, conducting research and collecting data on post-Apartheid education in South Africa. She is currently writing her dissertation: *Intruders in the Ivory Tower: Everyday Racism at a Historically White University in South Africa.*

In addition to her academic work, Ms. Woods has vigorously pursued opportunities to serve the community. She is a member of Alpha Kappa Alpha Sorority, Inc., and is active in several student organizations on the University of Michigan campus. In addition, since 1995 she has served as a volunteer at the Domestic Violence Project in Ann Arbor, working as a non-residential counselor and on the speaker's bureau to assist survivors of domestic violence and to educate the community about domestic violence. In 1998, Ms. Woods and a colleague (Robyn Kent) established the College Planning Program. This program is designed to encourage and assist Black, Latino/a and Native American high school students in the Ann Arbor/ Ypsilanti area in gaining admission to four-year colleges and universities.

7

INVISIBLE WOMEN

THE EXPERIENCES OF BLACK FEMALE DOCTORAL STUDENTS AT THE UNIVERSITY OF MICHIGAN

Rochelle L. Woods

If anyone should ask a Black woman in America what has been her greatest achievement, her honest answer would be, "I survived." (Pauli Murray as quoted in Jewell, 1993).

In the last few decades, there has been a substantial increase in the proportion of Black women pursuing doctoral degrees and faculty positions at prestigious colleges and universities across the nation. However, despite affirmative action and diversity rhetoric, Black women's presence in academia remains scarce. The University of Michigan is one of the nation's top universities in terms of awarding doctorates to Black females (Top 100 degree producers, 2000). Unlike most predominately White universities, the University of Michigan has a critical mass of students of color, particularly Black women doctoral students. In most social science departments, Black women and other women of color comprise a significant group within the overall student population. The University of Michigan offers doctoral students of color[1] an attractive, multi-year funding package, but the environment within departments is often far from welcoming. After Black women are admitted, they must struggle

---

1. "Students of color" denotes Blacks, Latino/as, and Native Americans.

to establish mentoring relationships and to attain prized research and teaching positions. Their chosen research areas, which often focus on communities of color, are devalued and marginalized by faculty. This chapter examines the experiences of Black women doctoral students in the social sciences at the University of Michigan. The chapter highlights the struggles and obstacles these students face in their pursuit of doctoral degrees.

Black women in the academy often find themselves marginalized and excluded from meaningful participation in their universities and academic departments. In her groundbreaking work, *Black Feminist Thought,* Patricia Hill Collins argues:

> While Black women historians, writers and social scientists have long existed, until recently these women have not held positions of power in universities, professional associations, publishing concerns, broadcast media, and other social institutions of knowledge validation. Black women's exclusion from positions of power within mainstream institutions has led to the elevation of white male ideas and interests and the corresponding suppression of Black women's ideas and interests in traditional scholarship (Collins, 1991, p. 7).

The fact that the presence of Black women in academe is currently more evident than in previous decades, obscures the fact that educated Black women have not obtained equality with Whites, male or female. Collins (1998) points out the irony of this notion:

> Relying on the *visibility* of African-American women to generate the *invisibility* of exclusionary practices of racial segregation, this new politics produces remarkably consistent Black female disadvantage while claiming to do the opposite (p. 14).

Studies of Black women have documented the everyday racism and discrimination that these women face in their daily lives. In her 1990 book, *Everyday Racism,* Essed examined the experiences of African American women in the United States and Surinamese women in the Netherlands. She found that in universities, the workplace, and public places, Black women consistently faced poor treatment from Whites. Such treatment included 1) having their intelligence, qualifications, and authority constantly called into question; 2) being excluded from important activities; and 3) having Whites judge them according to negative stereotypes (for example, all Blacks are lazy). A similar study conducted by St. Jean and Feagin (1998), which involved interviews with over 200 college-educated Black women, had similar findings. They argue that

Black women experience a "gendered discrimination" which involves "negative White reactions, individual and institutionalized, to Black female characteristics" (p. 16). They further argue that "gendered racism . . . assaults Black women by misrecognizing or ignoring, among other attributes, their humanity and spirituality" (p. 18).

At predominately White universities, Black women academics are not exempt from the issues of racism that plague other Black women. They often have difficulty gaining tenure and promotion, receive less pay, and are forced to carry out research and teaching activities in hostile environments (Gregory, 1995; Moses, 1997; Turner & Myers, 2000).

A study of women of color in sociology doctoral programs revealed that they faced a "hidden curriculum" in graduate departments in which they were treated as intellectually inferior and often considered "affirmative action cases" (Margolis & Romero, 1998),

> Intense competition for admissions, assistantships, grants and fellowships ignites a hostile environment for students of color when they compete for scarce resources with white students. When universities implement affirmative action programs and policies in a racially hostile environment, student of color constantly find their qualifications called into question (p. 8).

The authors also found that women of color in sociology graduate departments were excluded from prized research and teaching positions, denied mentoring by faculty, discouraged from conducting scholarly work on communities of color and the devaluation of ethnic, racial and gender studies.

This chapter highlights the struggles of Black female graduate students who attempt to succeed in doctoral programs despite being denied participation in important aspects of graduate training, such as mentoring. The findings discussed in this chapter are based on based on interviews, focus groups, and informal conversations with twelve Black women who are advanced doctoral students and seven recent doctoral recipients in the social sciences[2] at the University of Michigan. I specifically included women with the following characteristics:

- These women, because of their status and experiences as advanced doctoral students and doctoral degree recipients, have obtained substantial knowledge about academia and its processes.

---

2. The "social sciences" represented in this paper are psychology, sociology, social work, and education.

- These women have all been successful in navigating their respective doctoral programs. Among the doctoral students discussed herein, all have achieved candidacy for doctoral degrees and several were also ABD.[3]

- These women are highly qualified: Many have multiple master's degrees and/or bachelor's degrees from prestigious universities, were heavily recruited by their respective graduate departments, and have received prestigious fellowships and awards.

- All of the women are *survivors*[4] of the University of Michigan, who have either recently (within the past twelve months) completed doctorate degrees or are well on the way to completing their dissertations.

The Black women in this study face difficulties on a variety of levels: 1) they have difficulty establishing and maintaining mentoring relationships, which is exacerbated by the lack of faculty of color; 2) their scholarly work was marginalized and/or demeaned because it focused on issues related to communities of color or women; and 3) they are viewed as less intelligent than other students, which merely compounds the problems they have in other facets of their lives as doctoral students.

When and Why I Entered: Black Women's Expectations of Doctoral Programs

Several factors caused the women in this study to pursue graduate school. The most common factors were the desire to broaden their knowledge and skills, to advance occupationally, and to build solid careers with the highest credentials. Given the wide variety of universities nationwide that offer doctoral programs, I sought to understand what brought these women to Michigan. One woman provided the following reason:

> Throughout my undergraduate and my master's program, I heard phenomenal things about these people, so I came here because I thought that this program would be a good break for me. It would be

3. ABD is an acronym meaning "All But Dissertation." A student has this status when they have completed all preliminary exams and formally defended a dissertation proposal.

4. I chose not to include less experienced doctoral students or what I term "casualties" of academe (that is, those who began doctoral programs but did not finish) because although they have valuable insights, they did not navigate the process successfully.

an opportunity for me to really expand and to be an integral part of a program at a very prominent school.

Several women also cited the combination of a good funding package and the school's reputation:

> I came for the money and the reputation, because Michigan offered me the wonderful Rackham Fellowship. They basically offer you four years of funding. I thought to myself, getting paid to go to school, whoo-hoo! Michigan was ranked in the top five. As a Black woman, I knew that would help, coming from a top five school that was recommended by my undergrad. Plus, there was someone from my undergrad who came here before me. I knew if they could get in, that meant I could get in. There were also a lot of people of color here that were like really, really thrilled and they told me, come on, it's a nice place.

While funding and reputation were major factors for many of the women in their selection of Michigan, equally important was the strong presence of other students of color.

> When I first came here for a visit, I was picked up at the train station by a Black woman who was a graduate student here several years ago. I stayed with another Black woman graduate student that the department had arranged. At first I thought, "these must be the only two here." But once I actually went to the department and there were all these Black students and Latinos, I was really shocked. And they were all so friendly and welcoming.

While these women came to Michigan with high expectations for both themselves and their respective academic departments, they quickly began to encounter a variety of problems. The following discussion examines the nature of the problems encountered by Black women and their struggles to complete their doctoral programs.

Mentoring . . . What's That?

One of the major challenges faced by almost all of the women in this study was establishing mentoring relationships with faculty members. Given that many Blacks are first generation college students, they generally lack knowledge of the doctoral process. Mentoring is the best way to fill that gap, yet many Black women struggle to find faculty members who are willing to work with them. The following statement captures one woman's reflections about her problems in finding a good mentor:

> Well, I knew that we would have advisors who I thought their job was to help you. But my advisor wouldn't even talk to me. I tracked her down in the hallway and I said, hello, how are you? She looked at me like, who are you? She wouldn't even talk to me . . .

I probed further to get an understanding of why this advisor would not want to talk. She explained,

> Well, I just, I don't know, it was just not important, it was not important, I was just not important. I felt that the other professors were the same way, none of them here would speak to you in the hallway if they see you. Even if you just saw them in class, when they see you in the hallway it's like they don't know who you are. You are just not important to them.

In this situation, this student was rebuffed by her advisor even though she attempted to develop a relationship with her. Through this experience, and through interacting with other faculty members, she and other Black women came to understand that they were unimportant to faculty. Despite many setbacks, some Black women are able to establish relationships with faculty members. These relationships, however, are often short-lived and never develop into real mentoring.

> I expected that I would work with someone and have my interests meet with theirs. My experience was not that at all. One person told me, this is my line of research, you come on board, and I did go on board. But there was never any kind of bringing any of *my* ideas into the discussion. So, I eventually left the project. So that was a big letdown for me.

Another doctoral candidate shared her experience,

> When I came here, I just knew I was going to work with [professor HJ] and [professor AB] and become a phenomenal academician with this background like nobody had ever had before. It didn't happen, didn't happen. [Professor HJ] was always busy, [professor AB] always said well you come see me, come see me. These were just not like you're welcome. I took my prelim, I passed my prelim, passed it, still never heard anything. I kept appealing to people, can I work on this project, can I work on that project, can I work on this project. Ultimately I ended up over at ISR with [professor FR], and she and I had to battle.

As the two statements illustrate, Black women have consistent struggles maintaining relationships with faculty. In both cases the Black women found it difficult to work with faculty because their opinions and ideas were either devalued or ignored altogether.

There are few, if any, Black women or other women of color faculty members in social science departments. Those who exist tend to be non-tenured. This affects the extent to which Black women are able to establish mentoring relationships and the quality of mentoring they receive. A student interviewed by Margolis and Romero (1998) highlights this problem:

> It would be one thing if there were no women of color on the faculty and women of color could still get a mentor, that's one sort of problem. But neither of those things are happening. One, there's no one who is going to mentor us and two, there are no women of color on the faculty. So the two sort of compound one another (p. 12).

It is clear that for many Black women, the absence of women of color on the faculty seriously hinders their ability to find mentoring because they often receive poor treatment from White professors and are neglected by Black male professors. In terms of mentoring, the following statements highlight the unique situation for Black women at Michigan.

> We don't even need to discuss White men, and even White women. For the most part they end up in their networks because they have that mentorship dynamic going on. So women of color are stuck here, we can't relate to the brothers because they just don't feel it. Most of them work with the Black men professors. And we're stuck in this corner. And the White women don't get it, you know, they think, "oh we're all women." No, we're, we are all women biologically but we do not have the same set of issues, be it department-wide, your family background, whatever. So we're stuck in this corner. There's a group of us, especially in the social sciences, with no faculty that's like us. So we're in this special corner. There's only been one Black female sociology professor since I've been here.

While Black women's experiences are influenced by race, Black women also recognize the salience of gender in their relationships with White and Black faculty. Because of their position at the intersection of race and gender, these Black women have come to understand how they are "singled out."

> I'm in this research group run by [professor CY] and it's all Black folks. I'm one of two Black women in the group. When we have meetings we

just sit there while they laugh and talk and discuss the work and they barely even talk to us. And when I dare to ask a question, they talk down to me, so I stopped asking questions. These are all Black men, too. When I think about the race and gender, I think of a 4 by 4 box of colored men, colored women, White men, and White women. We're so different because we know in sociology, if you're male and you're colored you end up in ISR within the first two weeks. And you get that opportunity because other men of color say come on, we've got you.

In contrast to the poor experiences Black women have with White faculty and Black male faculty, many have found support with women of color faculty, often from outside their academic department. One woman described positive experiences with a Black woman faculty member who was helpful to her in the job search:

I went to [professor GL] and I felt so comfortable. This is another sister. I felt comfortable just telling her, you know, read my letter, these are my weaknesses, and tell me what I'm doing wrong. She was very helpful. It's not like I didn't want to hear it because I can take criticism, but she gave me so much feedback. If it had been a White man, I probably wouldn't have been able to do it.

Another woman concurred:

Even [professor GL], I don't know her well, I've met her four times maybe. But every time that I've met her she always says, "come talk to me, if you need some information about this, come talk to me." I've never gotten that from the White people here. If I did, when I did go talk to them, it was like the dead end, you know. That's the end of it, you know, if you go talk to them, they look at you like, who are you and what do you want. I had a friend who said they look at you like you're just visiting from the dead. You walk in and it's like, where did you come from; or, oh my God, here she comes again.

While these women report positive relationships with Black women and other women of color faculty, these relationships are hard to form because of the scarcity of women of color faculty at predominately White universities like Michigan.

Marginalization of Research

Another major problem faced by Black women is the marginalization of their research areas. Black women often choose research topics with relevance to their backgrounds. Such research may center on issues salient to communities of color, or on other issues of race/ethnicity, class, and gender. Often, when people of color pursue research topics that relate to their personal experiences and background, they are accused of not having objectivity or of being too close to the topic to conduct quality research, yet Whites are not privy to the same criticisms when their research focuses on Whites (Margolis & Romero, 1998). Women in this study reported similar problems: Their research topics were demeaned by faculty.

> I think that translates to our research interests as well. A lot of us find issues related to women of color et cetera to be important topics of study. But I'm not sure those same research interests are given the kind of weight as other sort of "non-racialized" topic areas. Unless it's a White man doing it, then it's scholarly. Now, when we do it, it's interesting reading. I was in one class and the professor wanted me to change my topic. You know what they told me, they said, you just write about such sad, depressing things. And I was dealing with child welfare issues! They [White faculty] think that you're supposed to do it like this, because that is the Eurocentric approach to writing and to research.

While Black women often faced criticism from White professors concerning their choice of research topics, they also were cautioned by other people of color, who encouraged them to de-emphasize the racial and or gendered aspects of their research.

> Because of my research interests, in my job applications I've talked about my work with women of color and work that I did with students of color. [A faculty member of color] had to tell me, she said, "this is good, but you are promoting yourself too much as a diversity person." I thought, well these are the things I'm proud of, these are the things I want. She said, "no you can't do this because they'll think you can't relate to the White man. You're not enough of a true scholar." She continued, "you can't talk, you can't put the emphasis on diversity. You have to talk about other aspects of the whole study." So it's interesting how, these are your commitments, but you can't say too much about them.

Although Black women felt that the advice given was well-meant, it still sent a message to up-and-coming scholars to steer away from topics related to race, class, and gender. The previous statements indicate that they are aware that such work is devalued in the academy and as a result, their opportunities will be limited. The women in this study expressed a strong commitment to doing research that was relevant to the "real world."

They Think We're Dumb!

Perhaps the most salient issue that the participants in this study raised was the concern about being viewed as unintelligent. This has long been an issue for Blacks in the United States. Beginning with slavery, Blacks were depicted as a race with an inability to learn who were inferior to Whites (Davis, 1977; hooks, 1981; Collins, 1991). In the academy, women of color, despite their advanced education, are still the subject of this racist ideology used to subordinate Blacks and other people of color. The women in this study asserted that White faculty viewed them as unintelligent. The following statements from several women underscore this point:

> They think we're dumb.
>
> They think we're not as smart as Whites.
>
> They do not think we are as smart, at every stage. If I hear the words, "oh you're so articulate" one more time. If I hear, "oh you really write well." At every stage, you get the sense, like it's a surprise that we actually can put two words together, that we've read and understand Marx, Weber, Durkheim. I actually think that that is a BIG issue. They don't think we're smart.

The problem of being seen as intellectually inferior affects many interactions Blacks women have with White faculty. In the following case, a woman knows she cannot go to her professor with questions about statistics because he will view her poorly:

> But then later on, you realize you can't go to professors with those kinds of problems. If you have a problem with stats when it's, you just don't feel comfortable taking every problem to a professor. They're going to think less of you.

Another woman pointed out the predicament many Black women face:

> If you don't know what multiple regression is or what a slope or an intercept is, they may think you don't belong here. You know what I mean? They may treat you that way from then on.

Conclusion

Emerging from the preceding discussion is evidence that Black women in pursuit of doctoral degrees at historically White universities face a plethora of obstacles. First, they must operate in a system which is largely unsupportive. The Black women in this study have reported having difficulty establishing and maintaining good mentoring relationships, which are important in providing guidance and feedback on writing and research, and in establishing professional networks. Second, they face the problem of having their chosen research areas marginalized and demeaned. Often the research done by Black women and other women of color is rooted in a strong commitment to researching topics of relevance for communities of color and issues of gender, yet these women have found White faculty to be unreceptive to their work, or they are accused of lacking objectivity. Even faculty of color can be complicit and "caution" women of color against focusing too heavily on issues of race, class, and/or gender. Finally, despite the educational advancements made by these doctoral students, their intelligence is often called into question by Whites. This leads to a hostile and alienating environment where Black women's development as doctoral students is hindered.

Despite all the obstacles Black women face, they have survived. They have already received doctorate degrees or are well on their way. These women are success stories. But what about the Black women and women of color who were not able to overcome these obstacles? Clearly there is much work to be done to ensure that doctoral programs are places where all students have a supportive environment in which to be trained as scholars and academics.

Bibliography and Suggested Readings

Collins, P. H. (1991). *Black feminist thought: Knowledge, consciousness, and the politics of empowerment.* New York: Routledge.

Collins, P. H. (1998). *Fighting words: Black women and the search for justice.* Minneapolis: University of Minnesota.

Essed, P. (1990). *Everyday racism.* Alameda, CA: Hunter House.

Gregory, S. (1995). *Black women in the academy: The secrets to success and achievement.* New York: University Press of America.

hooks, b. (1981). *Ain't I a woman: Black women and feminism.* Boston: South End Press.

Jewell T. L. (1993). *Black woman's gumbo ya-ya: Quotations by Black women.* Freedom: Crossing Press.

Margolis, E. & Romero, M. (1998). "The department is very male, very white, very old and very conservative": The functioning of the hidden curriculum in graduate sociology departments. *Harvard Educational Review, 68*(1), 1–32.

Moses, Y. T. (1997). Black women in academe: Issues and strategies. In L. Benjamin (Ed.), *Black women in the academy.* Gainesville: University Press of Florida.

St. Jean, Y. & Feagin, J. R. (1998). *Double burden: Black women and everyday racism.* Armonk: M.E. Sharp.

Top 100 degree producers. (2000, July 7). *Black Issues in Higher Education,* 7(10), 48–89.

Turner, C. S. & Myers, S. L. (2000). *Faculty of color in academe: Bittersweet success.* Needham Heights, MA: Allyn and Bacon.

Dr. Dionne A. Blue

Dr. Dionne A. Blue received her doctorate in integrated teaching and teaming in 2000 from The Ohio State University. Blue is an alumna of Spelman College, where she received a bachelor of arts degree in English. She is also a graduate of the master of arts program in literacy education at Washington State University. After working one year as interim coordinator for the African American Student Center at Washington State University, Blue returned to graduate studies with the desire to contribute to the academic and social development of African American students. Her research interests examine the ways in which students of color at the postsecondary level construct and negotiate race/ ethnicity and identity within the context of academia. Her cognate areas are multicultural education, language, literacy and culture, and social foundations of education.

A member of Delta Sigma Theta Sorority, Inc., Dr. Blue has received both public service and graduate associate research awards during her tenure as a graduate student. She has presented several research papers and other scholarly endeavors at universities and conferences across the country. She is currently a guest lecturer at The Ohio State University, Lima campus. Her professional goals include being a college professor and developing support systems for students of color. Blue is a native of Newark, New Jersey, and her hobbies include reading, music, travel, and outdoor recreation.

8

BREAKING THE SILENCE

RACIAL IDENTITY DEVELOPMENT OF POST-BACCALAUREATE AFRICAN AMERICAN WOMEN

Dionne A. Blue

Prologue

You know what, little girl, your mouth is going to get you into trouble one of these days. That was an oft-repeated threat, and sometimes promise, from my mother throughout childhood. I always had a lot to say, and thought that there was no reason that I should not be able to say whatever it was, and clearly no reason that I should not be heard. I received straight A's in school, but always with the criticism "talks too much in class." I asserted myself as someone searching for the voice that I could clearly call my own: one with opinions different from my parents, yet representing a will separate from that of my friends. I sided with bell hooks (1989), in that "I made speech my birthright—and the right to voice, to authorship, a privilege I would not be denied" (p. 6).

In college, nestled within a community of young African American scholars, I was always smart enough, and usually informed enough to follow along with, if not actually fully participate in, any conversation. Topics on anything Black, and/or female, would alert my senses, and anything I did not know about, I was willing to either ask someone I trusted, or read vigorously until I could easily speak just as intelligently as my peers could.

But one day I stopped talking. I was a graduate student at a large, predominantly White University, and no longer felt knowledgeable enough, secure enough, competent enough, or even compelled enough, to speak—on any topic. We talked about things that I did not know about—or at least not in the ways they talked about them. I thought that because I did not say things in the ways my White classmates did, I must certainly not be as smart as they were. Yet, I resisted the scholarly language they often used. I felt like a fraud when I tried to use academic language—I felt it betrayed me. It made me sound like someone else: someone I did not recognize, someone without ownership of the words being spoken. I was immobilized between having neither the "right" things to say nor the "right" ways to say them. I likened my paralysis of speech to the inability to play a musical instrument. The power of language and speech is like an elegant grand piano holding within it the passion and beauty of symphonies; however, despite a desire to play, the inability to do so renders the instrument useless. It becomes a secret that you cannot decode: a beautiful locked box for which you have no key. I wanted to learn to play beautiful music, but I wanted the music to be a part of who I was already, rather than converting me into someone else.

I found my indoctrination into academic language and identity alienating. I wondered, as Marlon Riggs (1992) queries, whether my tongue was "at times, in effect, not [my] tongue, if [my] tongue had really become their tongues, and if, in fact, it was their tongues that were in [my] mouth, pressing against, crowding out [my] own" (p. 103). The thought of speaking with the tongue of the intellectual mainstream was not acceptable to me as a Black woman who was already not included in the conversation. So rather than speak with a tongue that was not my own, I moved into subversive silence. Although I used silence as an act of resistance, it was silence nevertheless, and as Gilmore (1997) states, there is usually little to nothing achieved as a result of silence. Specifically, "silence does not cause the fear to disappear. Silence does not make me feel more secure. Silence does not dispel ignorance" (p. 53). By being silent, I only hurt myself, yet I knew no other recourse.

The more I listened to my colleagues and classmates, the more I realized that they were not necessarily more knowledgeable than I, but they knew how to communicate in a way that was validated in academia. I found the generalizations my professors used to describe "us" as Americans in various contexts did not take into account my unique position as a Black female with middle-class values and poverty-level economic status. As a young Black woman in graduate school I felt "oppressed and violated by the rhetoric of dominant ideology, a rhetoric disguised as good 'scholarship' by teachers who are unaware of its race, class and gender 'black spots' " (Anzaldúa, 1990, p. xxiii). Fortunately, I soon discovered scholarship by Black women and other women/people of color who validated a different way to know and be known—one that saw people of color as the center of their own experiences rather than as the margin of someone else's experiences. Women such as Audre Lorde, Gloria Anzaldúa, bell hooks, and Alice Walker taught me that I did not have to betray who I was as a person, specifically a Black woman, in order to speak or write in a way deemed scholarly or intellectual.

No longer having an excuse not to speak given the new tools with which I was armed, did I value these alternative ways of being and knowing? Did I even trust what I had to say? Years of western, hegemonic education had caused a certain amount of self-hatred to grow within me. I did not have faith in the voice that told me "this is who you are, this is the way you should see yourself—validated and empowered. This is your voice." I was still afraid.

Because I remained one of the few people of color in my classes, and if for no other reason than that, I was obligated to overcome my fear. I had a responsibility to myself as someone relegated to the margins of race and gender, to confront both my fear of academic language and my fear of my own intelligence as "greater than or equal to" anyone else's. As bell hooks (1989) asserts, "for us [women of color], true speaking is not solely an expression of creative power; it is an act of resistance, a political gesture that challenges politics of domination that would render us nameless and voiceless" (p. 8). As a matter of resistance and survival, I utilize the work of critical and feminist scholars as an alternative to more hegemonic voices, and am now prepared to speak. The opinionated, defiant little girl in me, the one who knew no fear, would not allow me to retreat into invisibility. That little girl still has plenty to say, and she will not let me keep quiet.

Introduction

Throughout history, Black women have had a precarious relationship to the rest of society. As both the "second sex" and the "last race" (duCille, 1996), we have been constructed and portrayed in the most negative light from all possible perspectives, which has served not only to silence Black women in many ways, but in some cases has erased Black women altogether. Conceptions of Black female identity and Black feminist consciousness emanate from this struggle to regain voice: out of an obligation to both explain and defend their/our existence, both in the world and in the academy. As the group to be

found at the negative end of Black/White and male/female "self/other" bina-
ries, the ways in which Black women are socially constructed and defined
directly influences how those with power and/or privilege can construct and
define themselves. Working within these frames, while at the same time striving to change them, has forced Black women to create alternative spaces that
are self-defined and to some degree self-regulated.

Much like the autobiographical scenario previously described, many Black
women and girls encounter a host of obstacles, particularly in academic settings, based on gender and racial inequalities both inside and outside of Black
communities. This chapter examines some of those difficulties in the context
of the racial identity and schooling experiences of four African American
women participating in a larger study of identity development among students
of color. By looking at the stories of four collegiate African American women
in the context of my own story as a African American woman scholar/
researcher, I hope to "provide insight into both our particular realities and the
broader requirements of social living, complete with the conflicts and struggles
that define our individual interpretations of lived experiences" (Dillard, 1996,
p. 3). Among those conflicts and struggles are negotiating racial incidents both
in and out of school, and the effects of marginalization on self-perception and
academic achievement. In order that these interpretations may be put into context, there are certain identities that must be routinely reflected upon because
they so routinely affect our lives. Among them are racial and gendered identities, because struggles against the "isms" associated with these identities can
greatly affect all of those who genuinely labor for a more inclusive reality.

Racial and Gender Identity: Positioning Them/Ourselves

In order to discuss the unique positioning of Black women in the United States,
one must begin by looking at the complex ways in which race, class, gender,
and sexuality are constructed. In addition, the "isms" enacted upon and manifested within Black women's lives must also be examined, as well as the position Black women are then placed in within the hierarchies produced by these
constructions. For example, Lorde (1984) critiques the attitudes and perceptions Black communities have had regarding Black women's sexuality, and the
ways in which Black women's bodies have been appropriated within both Black
and White communities. Her analysis of these issues helps to provide a framework for Black women who seek not just to understand and explain, but to
redefine and reinvent our lives in our own terms using our own definitions.

These are women who reject and defy stereotyped images of mammies, maids, sexual deviants, exotic others, single mothers, welfare abusers, and super women. These images, which have permeated the American mind for centuries, have made Black women's bodies a site of domination and Black women's minds a breeding ground for internalized oppression and self hate (duCille, 1996; hooks, 1992; Yamato, 1990). The re-inventions and re-constructions Black women have come to use include attention to personal experience and "testifying" as ways of establishing truth and creating knowledge. Leaning on nontraditional, or in other words, non-White, non-male ways of making meaning, Black women have begun to avert these negative images while giving validation to images that are more authentic and appropriate.

Many scholars of color recognize the need to examine the intricate relationship between race, class, gender, and sexuality, rather than compartmentalizing or dissecting one issue from another. In other words, they recognize that one's view of the world cannot be "de-raced"; for that matter, neither can it be un-gendered, un-classed or de-sexualized. These are the filters that we use to see our experiences and none of these filters can be separated from another, nor can we be fully understood as any particular one without the others. Given that, examining these intersections is the only way to bring about liberation for all women and all people (Anzaldúa, 1990; Collins, 1991; Guy-Sheftall, 1995; hooks, 1992; Lorde, 1984). That is to say, a one-dimensional examination of the effects/roles of race or gender, without also critiquing the ways that race is engendered and that gender is racialized, will never bring about true liberation on either the personal or societal levels. For example, historically White feminism has failed in many cases to also effectively critique White privilege rather than solely male patriarchy, while at the same time, Afrocentric paradigms have often failed to effectively critique the role of gender oppression and male privilege, particularly within Black communities. Black women, who are oppressed on all sides of those equations, are left without the luxury to ignore any one aspect of race, class, gender, or sexuality in favor of another.

The Crossroads of Racial Identity and Pedagogy

Because oppressive values and assumptions are so intertwined in our society, they often are no longer questioned, but have instead become the norm (Maher & Tetreault, 1997; Sleeter, 1995; Tatum, 1992). Until those assumptions can be challenged and changed, education will continue to reinforce privilege on one side and prejudice on the other. Fortunately, scholars of color have begun to provide both frameworks and models for education that do not reinforce oppression but that are critical, multicultural, and that lend themselves to the transformation of society and the development of positive cultural identities for people of color (Delpit, 1995; Freire, 1994; hooks, 1994; Ladson-Billings, 1994).

For example, Tatum (1997) relates the discussion of identity formation specifically to the schooling experiences of people of color, using the revised Cross (1995) model of racial identity development and Black Feminist theory (Collins, 1991) as part of her theoretical framework. Using the sitting patterns of students in the high school cafeteria as a metaphor, Tatum (1997) reveals the complexities students of color face in schools as they attempt to negotiate their perceptions and acceptance of themselves as racial beings in opposition to, and sometimes in conflict with, how they are perceived by their White counterparts. She states that in racially mixed settings, students are more prone to align themselves according to racial or ethnic background in response to the/a real or perceived threat of racism. Moreover, "joining with one's peers for support in the face of stress is a positive coping strategy" that students of color may employ in those situations under the often times stressful tensions around race (Tatum, 1997, p. 62). Tatum comments that educators are at times uncomfortable with the idea of prioritizing those situations where students can have experiences that are identity-affirming, rather than stressful, or that provide information on students' histories and the contributions of their specific cultures, because teachers have not traditionally received that information as part of their own educational experiences.

Fordham (1988) examines the relationship between academic success and cultural affiliation, which also has implications for identity development and self-perception. She asserts that African American students who wish to succeed academically must sometimes adopt a persona of "racelessness," which in turn disassociates them from the fictive kinship found within Black communities. In other words, the students in her study who were successful constructed their social identity in ways very different from those who were not considered academically successful. Fordham's work seems to be presented in the type of "either/or" fashion that encourages the limited view that culture must be negated in order for Black students to achieve success. This dichotomy may not necessarily allow for alternative ways to negotiate the real or perceived gap between home and school cultures for African American students. In other words, although the students in the study disassociated with their ethnic identity in order to gain perceived success in school, there is little to no mention of other ways or examples that would allow students to maintain affiliation and identity within their culture, yet still be what is labeled a "high achiever," enabling them to take on identities of success, as has been put forth by other scholars (Ladson-Billings, 1994). Fordham concludes that the choice to adopt racelessness in order to succeed is too high a price to pay and that the "option is unacceptable" for Black students, yet the entire basis of her argument is that it is not only necessary to adopt such a persona to succeed, but that it is maybe even impossible *not* to do so. Fordham's research is very important because it brings to light issues faced by youth in the Black community as they attempt to overcome barriers academically, socially, and politically; however, there seems to be a need to negotiate the "master the possibilities" approach of some identity theories (Markus & Nurius, 1986) with the realities of cultural sacrifices described by Fordham.

Conceptualizing Race

Discussions pertaining to race, race-based theories, and racial identity have become as volatile and ambivalent as the category of race itself, yet race has remained a primary category for constructing difference. Omi and Winant (1993) have suggested that race can be considered neither solely a biological category nor solely a social category. They suggest instead that race must be considered a socially constructed category that has physical manifestations and repercussions. As McCarthy and Crichlow (1993) maintain, "racial difference is the product of human interests, needs, desires, strategies, capacities, forms of organization, and forms of mobilization." They state further that these variables are manifested in the form of "grounded social constructs" such as identity, and are "subject to change, contradiction, variability, and revision within historically specific and determinate contexts" (p. xv). Race is differentiated as the primary foundation for conceptualizing this text because, as McCarthy and Crichlow state, "the race question brings into the foreground omissions and blind spots. It exposes callouses [*sic*] and bottlenecks in even the most radical and ameliorative of approaches to social themes of 'exploitation,' 'domination,' 'resistance,' and 'human emancipation'" (p. xviii). In other words, looking at issues of access and equity in various contexts, and in this specific case the racial identity development of African American women in higher education, the lens of race illuminates those places where schooling at all educational levels, particularly postsecondary education, has fallen short of the promise of providing a democratic education for all people. Although I address the roles of pedagogy and programming given the particular effects of race and institutional racism, in no way is that an attempt to compartmentalize race-related issues within what Ladson-Billings (1996) would call a "constellation of subjectivities." On the contrary, as Yamato (1990) argues, racism, classism, sexism, and all of the other "isms" need one another to survive. She states that "all these ism's are systemic, that is, not only are these parasites feeding off our lives, they are also dependent on one another for foundation" (p. 22). Therefore, given the complexity and interconnectedness of identity delineators such as race, class, gender, and sexuality, race is discussed as merely a springboard for conceptualizing the various issues around identity development among African American women in higher education contexts.

Composing Our Lives: Identity Construction among African American Women

The following portion of the text revolves around the lives of four African American women: Raquel, Janet, Consuela, and Tonya. Each grew up in mostly middle-class, predominantly White communities, a dynamic that was reflected in their K-12 and undergraduate schooling experiences. While each have had a variety of experiences in these contexts, there were many aspects of these experiences that were common among them. While their schooling experiences have been diverse demographically, their stories reflect similar themes around issues of race and identity, including the effects of those experiences on their perceptions of themselves throughout their development into Black women.

Negotiating Racial Encounters

Each of these four women has had various experiences marking significant stages in their racial identity development. According to the Cross revised model of Nigrescence (1995), these events are characterized as the "encounter" stage, in which a significant experience causes an individual to reassess his/her racial identity. Consistent with Cross's theory, the race-related encounters these women have had included both positive and negative events, and taught them how to negotiate being people of color, particularly Black women, in what they perceived to be a "White" world. While only two specific cases are described here, each woman was asked to reveal the most significant racial event that had happened in their lives, and the effects of those event(s) on their racial identity development and/or on the ways in which they constructed race. None could name just one event; they felt for the most part that there had been several critical moments in which they were explicitly made cognizant of their humanity as racialized individuals.

Generally, they relayed experiences with individuals of diverse racial, social, political, and economic backgrounds; however, they note their most significant experiences in opposition to White mainstream culture, rather than to another racially marginalized ethnic group. That is not to say that none of these women have had negative experiences with members of their own or other non-White ethnic groups, but for the purpose of describing the "most significant racial experience" they had ever had, they chose incidents involving Whites. Some of the experiences described with regards to racial events involved people they knew well and/or someone with whom there was some level of trust, while others had significant racial experiences with strangers. Finally, each of these women, in addition to whatever other experiences they may have had, explicitly mention the significance of being Black students attending predominantly White institutions.

Student #1: Raquel

Because Raquel has lived in diverse environments, she has had a variety of interactions with a variety of people throughout her life. While such a background may have kept her from some of the more blatant racial incidents described by other women in the text, she has nevertheless had quite a few experiences with the implicit forms of racism that many face each day just by nature of their ethnic background. Raquel describes incidents from high school and college, respectively, which were critical in helping her understand both the complexities and subtleties of race for women of color.

Event #1

> Much to my surprise, I was nominated for the homecoming court. I had never even dreamed that that would happen to me, and ended up winning homecoming queen. I was totally shocked and surprised—and happy! I was cool enough to be voted for homecoming queen. But then the dance rolls around and nobody will take me. There was one brother there who I was like "come on, let's go. Since I'm homecoming queen, we get in for free; our pictures are free. I'm gonna borrow this dress from my friend, you just put something on. I got a coupon for dinner, we can have a $10 dinner." And the deal sounded good enough to him that we were able to go. My dad literally was even trying to figure out who could take me to the dance. Now I'm cool enough to be voted homecoming queen, but you cannot take me to the dance.

She goes on to offer the following analysis of the experience:

> It was the whole, "folks didn't know what to say to their parents about going out with a Black person." They were intimidated. That just kind of shows that it's okay to associate with Black people to an extent, but when you get to a certain point there's a line you can't cross. It's not that I ever was hoping to go out with any of those guys, not that I was interested in them hooking up with me or taking me home. But it's just the whole thought. Because of that it probably was more significant, because it's like "I'm not even trying to date you; I'm just trying to go fulfill my obligation as homecoming queen, dance my one dance, and cut out. You can't even do that with me? You'd rather sit at home than do that?"

Raquel's experiences may not be unlike other African Americans', particularly African American women, who may have felt accepted among their White peers until the awkward stage of puberty, when the decisions adolescents make around dating become more clearly racialized (Twine, 1996). Her reaction to winning as prestigious a title as prom queen among her White peers, yet being unable to get one of them to accompany her to the dance, was one of anger and hurt. At the same time, it allowed her to see, as she later stated, that there was a line that she "could not cross" with them, an occurrence that continued to manifest itself in various ways throughout her schooling experiences.

Event #2

> When I got there [college], I was adjusting pretty quickly to what the environment was like socially, but things definitely took a turn and changed for me within that first year. I don't know if I can really identify what the turning point was—what turned it around. I first identified or hung most closely with the people from my dorm you know, proximity thing, here's who I live with. I had a roommate who was from my high school, she was White, everybody else on the floor was White, and they were in the White Greek system. "Oh, here's where we're going, to this party tonight. We're going to this party, everybody come." I'm on the floor, you know, I'm part of the group; I'm going too. And it was definitely a different social scene, but it wasn't radically different from what my high school friends—not my tight "homies"—but my high school friends, were like. But somewhere there within my freshman year I did get hooked up with [African American student organizations], and all of the "sister" [Black women] groups, to the Black fraternities.

I think what happened was that I was always open to doing things with my [White] friends that they wanted to do. But once or twice, you know maybe there was a party, and you know for Black folks it was special occasion stuff, not every weekend was a party. And I remember one Halloween party, where I was inviting my folks: "okay you guys, let's go to my Halloween party, let's all dress up." One person came with me, out of everybody on the floor, and she wanted to leave after like fifteen minutes, because she felt uncomfortable. And it's like "you know, you guys expect me to always change and adapt to yours, but you can't even try mine, and that's getting old." I don't know that that was *the* thing that did it, but somewhere along the line, I just felt like this is a lot easier to do if I'm with my Black peers. I don't need this to also have to deal with. "I don't necessarily feel like this party is all that fun, all y'all doing is up here drinking beer, you listen to music I don't like. People are up here just tripping, but you know I'm here; I'm making the most of it, having a good time because I'm here with my friends. Why can't you do that with me?" And then for those ten or fifteen minutes I'm holding my girlfriend's hand: "oh don't leave me!" We go to one of their parties, everybody goes their separate ways, you know, you don't know who ends up where. "Did so and so go home already? I don't know, well this drunk boy can walk me home" or whatever. I just felt like it was offensive. It was offensive to me.

The experiences Raquel describes are what some may call "sins of omission" rather than "sins of commission." For example, in the previous scenario, Raquel related that it was always she who was forced to make compromises in order to appease her White peers and friends by adjusting herself to situations in which she didn't necessarily feel comfortable, so that they would be.

Student #2: Tonya

Tonya considers herself biracial, being of both African American and Filipino ancestry. She has described being perceived as either one or the other, depending on the context. Biracial men and women represent a growing "category" among the racial boxes, and many have to spend time defending one or both sides of their identities, particularly if any part of that identity is African American.

Event #1:

One of my White girlfriends called a fellow African American student a nigger. She was upset at him about something and called him that

under her breath as she glared across the room at him. My response
was definitely reactive and I asked her if she was trying to get socked
in her mouth. She asked me why I was so upset since I was Filipino.
That shocked me for a moment and then I commenced to school her
on why she couldn't pick and choose my ethnicity. I also added that
she shouldn't be using derogatory terms anyway.

Awareness of the realities of race came in various ways for these women; as previously stated, each had a significant encounter with someone of a different
racial background, usually White, who brought the realities of race and the
meaning of difference home to them. While some of the women were taught
either explicitly or implicitly not to trust those of other races or backgrounds,
there were others who were more naive in their understandings of themselves as
racialized beings, and to the meanings that were attached to those understandings. While these stories mark the "encounter" stage of racial identity development, many had been exposed to Whites in some capacity previous to the experiences they described for the study. For each of these women, the encounter
either started them, or aided them in continuing, on the path to examining their
racial identities, which also eventually affected and was affected by, their participation in higher education recruitment/retention programs.

For many students of color in similar situations, living among Whites
means that there are real or perceived invisible boundaries that make them
acceptable in some contexts but not all. Recognizing these unspoken parameters can be disconcerting for students of color, and may have adverse effects
on their self-concepts as well as on the development of a positive racial identity. Fortunately, such an encounter with Whites had the opposite effect on
Tonya, who describes this encounter during a formal interview:

My sister and I were waiting in the car while my mother went into the
grocery store. The kids in the van next to us began calling us niggers,
and telling us that they needed a new maid. The taunting continued
until my mother approached the car. It was interesting to note that
one of the teenagers was apologetic when they realized our mother
was Filipino. It was as if her blood negated any Black blood flowing
through us. Then as we drove away, the kids started smiling and wav-
ing at a Black man who happened to be their neighbor. That basically
got me started early on my "trust no one" theory. It also made me
proud to be a person of color, probably the opposite of the effect the
kids wanted to have on us.

Much like the first story she describes, Tonya's second experience specifically
points out the problem of one aspect of her identity being insulted by some-

one who, in their ignorance, doesn't realize that in addition to whatever they perceive her to be, she also represents the culture they have affronted. Tonya's experiences also illustrate the negative inner feelings that may result when differing identity positions are put in direct conflict with one another. The feelings that each woman possesses about herself as a cultural or racial being greatly affect the ways in which they will or will not be able to congeal within their respective campus communities. For each of these African American women, the ways in which they constructed themselves racially was intricately connected to how they later related to other students, particularly White students.

Dualities of Race

The African American women in the study constructed race and came to identify themselves racially according to their personal background and upbringing. For these women, being taught about race was a "given." That is to say, they had parents, elders, church leaders, or community members who relayed to them ideologies about the value and meaning of race for them as Black people as well as the importance of possessing a strong racial identity. Janet offered the following insight: "The background you grow up in determines how you see the world. And because Black and White was always so rigidly defined, I was always aware of it growing up." While many African Americans are aware of race, they are not necessarily active in pursuing knowledge and history of African American culture. Those women who were reared in predominantly Black environments never had to confront race as an "issue," problem, or especially as a deficiency in their lives, until changing to a racially/ethnically mixed environment. In cases where they did learn about race, however, they learned about race in Black and White. That is to say, they learned either explicitly or implicitly, certain lessons about the nature of race specific to life in the United States.

Unfortunately there are times when even having a parent, friend, or community member to counter the negativity with messages of racial pride, does not preclude encountering a phase, however short, of wanting to be White, or at the least of denying the value of one's own culture. Explaining to adolescents, particularly those of color, that race should be neither rejected, nor embraced without questioning, helps them to develop a stronger sense of racial self. For some, neutral or negative racial experiences can cause a fissure from one's racial self, whereas there are those, as demonstrated by Tonya, for whom having negative interactions causes one to instead cling more vehemently to a sense of racial identity. At the same time, that particular sentiment sometimes produces a sense of paranoia wherein people of color may sometimes be unsure of where to draw the line between racial awareness and hypersensitivity. For example, Janet explains:

> Sometimes I'll see everything through a Black and White lens. And people say "everything is not Black and White," and I know that it's not, so I don't want to overdo that. But my eye is always open for the Black angle, and "is there bias in this", and "am I being treated this way because I'm Black?" But racial identity is ever present for me.

Raquel, on the other hand, feels that education and exposure to various types of people has made her more able to reason situations beyond race. In other words, she is not so quick to think that any given incident is racially motivated but looks instead at what other causes there may be. She mentions having had questionable behavior exhibited toward her in predominantly Black or culturally reflective contexts, in which case she's had to extract other, non-racial explanations. In her words, she doesn't pull what she calls the "race card" unless that is the final card.

Identity and Self Perception

Unlike many of Raquel's peers, having a Black middle-class suburban background allowed her to see African American culture in a wider and deeper range. Her exposure to the Black community ran the gamut from poor to rich: she saw Black men and women in all kinds of professions and walks of life. For example, she always had a Black doctor and dentist; she was exposed to African American professionals and business people just the same as she was exposed to African American garbage men and bus drivers. She was unique in this study, in that she didn't have the problems that many others have had finding positive role models of comparable ethnicity. Interestingly, she never had an issue with Blackness standing out in a negative way until she moved into a predominantly White context as an adolescent girl. It was at this time that she and her family members became, in her opinion, the representation of all things Black, a reality that was more apparent in schooling contexts. In Raquel's assessment, her parents took race for granted when living in predominantly Black contexts, something they could no longer do upon moving into a community where people of color, particularly Black people, were in the minority. Raquel states of her early schooling experience:

> Growing up [in the South], being a light-skinned Black person, I don't know that my parents aggressively taught me anything about race. It

was put forth to me in the environment all the time that there's a difference between White and Black, even though it wasn't really apparent to me in my everyday life. We had very few White people in our school, so it wasn't an outright issue for me, but I can recall as far back as preschool I had a Muslim preschool teacher who wanted to teach us about race.

Starting early teaching Raquel about race provided her with the tools needed to confront the ignorance she often encountered later at the hands of her uninformed White peers.

Navigating Home and School Cultures

While many children may be taught great pride in being Black at home, those attitudes are not necessarily reinforced in elementary and secondary schooling. Instead, school can be a place where there are rarely role models of color to affirm or validate their existence in the academic world. As mentioned, the women described here had a variety of "encounters" with Whites, and almost all of them had at least one event happen within the context of school. These racial experiences happened in subtle ways in the classroom, either with teachers or fellow students, and in the community, as in comments from neighbors or associates. Some experienced specific acts of racism, while others noticed the workings of structural and institutional racism in their lives at an early age. In addition, each actively noticed an inadequate amount of cultural representation of themselves as Black women in their schooling experiences, and a lack of cultural connection with textbooks, teachers, and even with other students. In other words, because many of them were schooled in contexts containing few if any people of color, they found that the information they gained in school also reflected little if any of their cultural history or values. In addition, there were a lack of positive cultural images with which to identify themselves in school, that is, teachers, students, textbooks, and school activities. Most had only the White mainstream against which to model their identity, and in some cases nothing else that would offset the negative effects of that modeling. Unfortunately, the road to racial awareness can be rockier for those who have no balancing influences.

Tatum (1997) posits that schooling is an experience that either perpetuates stereotypes and re-inscribes institutional racism, or that helps students unlearn and explode stereotypes about both themselves and one another. Rather than remaining ignorant to the very real effects of race/class/gender-based oppression in the lives of all students, Tatum (1997) suggests that teachers learn to identify those factors. Tatum further states, as these women personally experienced, that students are better able to recognize and resist the negative impact of oppression when those factors are not ignored or rendered invisible but instead are brought to the forefront of discussion. For example, each of these women excelled in school, yet it was usually not because their teachers, who were often White, challenged or encouraged them. Instead, they felt that neither their White teachers nor their White peers necessarily expected them to be smart. Upon finding that they were indeed intelligent, these women were met with either blank stares or no responses at all, as if they were anomalies. For example, Janet, who relocated from a predominantly Black community to a predominantly White community at a young age, had this recollection and opinion of her schooling experiences:

> I was excelling academically and the teachers didn't know what to do with that. They weren't used to pushing a Black child to succeed, so my mother had to stay on them; and I was the only one in the class who could read at a certain level. Instead of the first grade teacher saying "you know she really does well in reading, she's excelling," as they would for a White student, she said "well, she just goes and goes!" It's like it hurt her to say something positive about a Black child.

In another case, Raquel, who was also moved from a predominantly Black community to a predominantly White community at a young age, had a similar experience:

> It was when we moved to the state of W, where it's kind of a total flip of that, that the race questions were more just out there in my face. Just down to even people on the playground asking me how do I comb my hair, or being surprised that my sister and I were as intelligent as we were. You know, "oh, you placed in this class?" Or just things like that, just the sheer ignorance. That is when I really, really was confronted with the whole issue of race.

Even as undergraduates, these four women found themselves again lacking cultural reflection in their classroom experiences. Fortunately, college proved to be a time for them to take a certain amount of initiative in learning about race and cultural history, and to align themselves with others of similar backgrounds. For many, if not all of them, coming to a university campus as an undergraduate was an important step in developing a positive racial self. For African American students like Raquel, ethnic-based organizations like Black Greek Letter Organizations (BGLO's) provide a means to gain access into the Black campus community and social circles. Raquel found that most of the

African American undergraduate community belonged to one student organization or another, and being acquainted with members of BGLO's allowed her to meet nearly all of the African American students and faculty on her campus.

All of the African American women interviewed for the study experienced being treated as academically inferior to White students, an experience they continued to have even into postsecondary education. Fortunately, the African American women described in the study have had the opportunity to defy Fordham's (1988) theory of a need to adopt a raceless persona in order to succeed. Instead, they prove that African Americans can participate fully as members of various subcultures without sacrificing membership in their/our ethnic culture. In addition, their experiences and development demonstrate that being grounded in ethnic identity provides ammunition for the ignorance sometimes encountered at the hands of others, making it unnecessary to choose one aspect of cultural identity over another, but that academic success can be achieved while preserving ethnic identity.

Current Perceptions of Self and Identity

Consuela, who has grown up in integrated communities all of her life, explains the process of her development in terms of moving from stages of identifying with White culture, to establishing pride in Black culture. Because her father married a White woman, Consuela states that she grew up "intermixing with Whites." As a result, she currently feels that she is more easily adaptable to different racial situations, especially after having attended a predominantly White institution, where she states "you are reminded constantly of your place" as a person of color. Consuela seems to have progressed to what Cross (1995) would call the internalization stage, in which she can identify with and appreciate her racial identity without expressing ill will toward Whites or other non-Blacks:

> I love the fact that I'm Black. I've never thought of it as a shortcoming, or a problem. Of course, when I was a little girl I would watch TV, you know had the blonde Barbie dolls with the blue eyes. I wanted to look like that, you know, all the models on TV have the straight hair. I wanted all that. But I think when you get older and you start to look at yourself and if you have people around you helping you to appreciate yourself and who you are, then you learn to accept and appreciate who you are. And I've had that type of nurturing coming up. And I love being Black, I love who I am, love the culture, and I wouldn't change it for anything.

Janet adds a spiritual twist to her own identity construction:

> Growing up around a lot of White people was good for me in that I am able to deal with a lot of different people, but it is important to me that I am a Black woman, and I don't think it's by accident. You know a lot of people say that color doesn't matter—I don't think that's true. Even in the spiritual sense, people say "well God doesn't see color." I believe that he does, otherwise he's not the God of all creation. If my fingerprints are different than everybody's on the planet, and the hairs on my head are numbered and my DNA is different from every single person on the planet, surely I was designed African American by choice. So that's important, and I don't appreciate when people try to downplay it. I don't want you to see me only as Black because there are different dimensions to me. I'm a human being, and there are some things that transcend race, but being a Black woman is important to my identity.

Janet's perceptions of race also point out the distinctions each individual has by nature of being human, distinctions that may inform race but do not rely on race and are not based on race. As reflected by Janet's comment, many people, even people of color, may come to understand the notion of diversity and unity as tied to characteristics other than race. Finally, Raquel offers this statement:

> I find that I feel pretty comfortable in different cultural situations. I adapt pretty well, but at the same time, always subconsciously perhaps, have my own racial line that certain people can't cross. I mentioned I have my professional friends, you know, and that it's a multiracial group. But certain friends I feel like I can never get as close to as the others because they're White. I think it all goes back to not always wanting to feel like I have to explain myself. Sometimes I don't get what it's like to be White. It's part my ignorance of what it's like to be that, and I don't know that I want to know what it's like to be that. I'm happy being a Black woman. Whatever I have experienced in the past has not made me feel at all remorseful, or regret who I am. It's made me more proud to be who I am, and even more driven to uplift my race because our culture is so rich. And I feel like, because of that, you can't get wit us! You know what I mean? I don't know how to describe it, but it is very significant.

As Raquel implies, being an African American woman, the world has been seen through those eyes, and has been interpreted and translated through those experiences. Dillard (1996) suggests that understanding these influences provides

> a way to not only understand how we have constructed our selves in particular social contexts, but the ways in which those constructions shape ethnic, cultural, gender, and other personal identities . . . it is only through understanding the intricacies of personal histories and identities that we can move past the traditional stereotypes and generalizations that have shaped our perceptions (p. 8).

That is to say, that regardless of how/what we have been taught, either formally or informally, we must always be able to recognize those influences and critically evaluate them in specific contexts. Further, it is necessary in the process of African American female identity development to constantly and critically examine the world in which we live and how events affect us in the context of "African-ness, American-ness, and Woman-ness," because these are the lenses we use to view the world.

Conclusion

Black women have had a variety of lived experiences around issues of race, ethnicity, and culture, all of which helps to shape the people they/we are upon arrival on a college or university campus. This process of development is fluid; the ongoing experience of life can cause further identity development and self-efficacy, or in some cases even regression. A limit to the Cross (1995) model, which has been extended by scholars such as Beverly Tatum (1997), is that none of these women could be considered as having "achieved" racial identity development but may work within or between various stages, dependent upon specific events or experiences. They may also experience regression in regards to these stages, in which an experience may send them back into previous stages, making it necessary to once again examine their racial identity. In other words, racial identity, like many other categories of analysis and difference, is neither fixed nor permanent.

Black women have continually had to reject negative stereotypes and pre-inscribed notions of both Blackness and womanhood based in a system of institutionalized oppression. Because Black women are duly oppressed along the axes of race, class, gender, and sexuality, it is necessary to take on the responsibility of recreating cultural identities and politicized knowledge and theoretical assumptions based on criteria that are important and relevant for them/us. Many Black women have provided models of how this can be done, both within and outside of academia. In either case, Black women constantly work "within and against" White male patriarchy to create spaces in which they/we can comfortably reside. Reclaiming the societal margins to which they/we have been relegated, Black women can then create a vision for liberation that is not only empowering for other Black women, but for all people. Black women have demonstrated throughout history that they/we have been and will continue to be instrumental in the struggle for freedom from oppression, leading the fight from the vanguard.

Bibliography and Suggested Readings

Anzaldúa, G. (Ed.). (1990). *Making face, making soul (haciendo caras): Creative and critical perspectives by feminists of color.* San Francisco: Aunt Lute Books.

Collins, P. H. (1991). *Black feminist thought: Knowledge, consciousness, and the politics of empowerment.* New York: Routledge.

Cross, W. E. (1995). The psychology of Nigrescence. In J. G. Ponterotto, J. M. Casas, L. A. Suzuki, C. M. Alexander (Eds.), *Handbook of multicultural counseling* (pp. 93–122). Thousand Oaks, CA: Sage.

Delpit, L. (1995). *Other people's children: Cultural conflict in the classroom.* New York: The New Press.

Dillard, C. B. (1996). Engaging pedagogy: Writing and reflecting in multicultural teacher education. *Teaching Education, 8*(1), 13–21.

duCille, A. (1996). *Skin trade.* Cambridge, MA: Harvard University Press.

Fordham, S. (1988). Racelessness as a factor in Black students' school success: Pragmatic strategy or Pyrrhic victory? *Harvard Educational Review, 58*(1), 54–83.

Freire, P. (1994). Pedagogy of the oppressed: New revised 20th anniversary edition. New York: Continuum.

Gilmore, A. (1997). It is better to speak. In A. K. Wing (Ed.), *Critical race feminism: A reader* (pp. 51–56). New York: New York University Press.

Guy-Sheftall, B. (Ed.). (1995). *Words of fire: An anthology of African American feminist thought.* New York: The New Press.

hooks, b. (1994). Teaching to transgress: Education as the practice of freedom. New York: Routledge.

hooks, b. (1992). *Black looks: Race and representation.* Boston: South End Press.

hooks, b. (1989). *Talking back: Thinking feminist, thinking Black.* Boston: South End Press.

Ladson-Billings, G. (1996). "Your blues ain't like mine": Keeping issues of race and racism on the multicultural agenda. *Theory into Practice, 35*(4), 248–255.

Ladson-Billings, G. (1994). *The dreamkeepers: Successful teachers of African American children.* San Francisco: Jossey Bass.

Lorde, A. (1984). *Sister outsider.* New York: The Crossing Press.

Maher E. A. & Tetreault M. K. (1997). Learning in the dark: How assumptions of whiteness shape classroom knowledge. *Harvard Educational Review,* 67(2), 321–349.

Markus, H. & Nurius, P. (1986). Possible selves. *American Psychologist,* 41(9), 954–969.

McCarthy, C. & Crichlow, W. (Eds.), (1993). *Race, identity, and representation in education.* New York: Routledge.

Omi, M. & Winant, H. (1993). On the theoretical concept of race. In C. McCarthy & W. Crichlow (Eds.), *Race, identity, and representation in education.* New York: Routledge.

Riggs, M. T. (1992). Unleash the queen. In G. Dent (Ed.), *Black popular culture* (pp. 99–105). Seattle: Bay Press.

Sleeter, C. (1995). An analysis of the critiques of multicultural education. In J. A. Banks & C. M. Banks (Eds.), *Handbook of research on multicultural education.* New York: Macmillan Publishing.

Tatum, B. D. (1997). *"Why are all the Black kids sitting together in the cafeteria?" and other conversations about race.* New York: Basic Books.

Tatum, B. D. (1992). Talking about race, learning about racism: The application of racial identity development theory in the classroom. *Harvard Educational Review,* 62(1), 1–24.

Twine, F. W. (1996). Brown skinned White girls: Class, culture and the construction of White identity in suburban communities. *Gender, Place and Culture,* 3(2), 205–224.

Yamato, G. (1990). Something about the subject makes it hard to name. In G. Anzaldúa, (Ed.), *Making face, making soul (haciendo caras): Creative and critical perspectives by feminists of color* (pp. 20–24). San Francisco: Aunt Lute Books.

Dr. Cynthia A. Tyson

Dr. Cynthia A. Tyson is Assistant Professor of Language, Literacy, and Culture at The Ohio State University, where she is currently teaching social studies, global education, and literacy courses to pre-service and in-service teachers. Her research interests fall within a social-justice framework. She is exploring using children's literature about contemporary events to increase engagement, literate behaviors, and simultaneously move readers toward personal, civic, and communal sociopolitical awareness and action. She received her master's degree in reading from The Ohio State University in 1991 and her bachelor of science in elementary education. For seven years, she has worked in multicultural staff development and is a community social activist. She has published articles in *Education Researcher* and *Theory Into Practice*.

9

FROM THE CLASSROOM
TO THE FIELD
Teacher, Researcher, Activist

Cynthia A. Tyson

I was apprehensive when asked to write this chapter. Writing about my trajectory into the academy before tenure and promotion seemed premature. Moreover, I felt that writing about my "career" might suggest a posture of contention, an assumption that I am not like other women in general and African American women in particular. I was reluctant to write about my personal success or failures, unwilling to render my life as a "how-to case" for success in the academy. There is no one exceptional event in my life that has made me "successful." As I look around at women in my community and my circle of friends, I know that I could be economically fragile, a single parent, homeless, a cell mate, a corpse, or a statistic.

Finally, I decided to lend my story and allow others to "poke and pry with a purpose" into my life as an exemplar of sociopolitical activism, a position that has, over many years, cleared a path leading to the creation of this educator and researcher. Such a critique might serve a very meaningful and pragmatic purpose. There is the possibility that after reading my story, one more sister will understand the struggles and triumphs, and the sacrifices and rewards that allow commitments to teaching, research, and activism to find a place in the academy. Making such critically conscious moves to engage in activist pedagogy and research can be a catalyst for transformation and emancipation (Freire, 1980).

Teacher as Activist

> Teaching is a perfomative act. It is that aspect of our work that offers the space for change, invention, spontaneous shifts, that can serve as a catalyst, drawing out the unique element in each classroom (hooks, 1994, p. 11).

> I wish to engage in this work because I desire the elevation of my race (Lucie Stanton Day, a teacher in Cleveland, Ohio, April 26, 1864, as cited in Sterling, 1984, p. 267).

As an African American elementary school teacher, the roots for activism are deeply entrenched in my history. In the days of segregated schools in the South, many African American teachers' commitment to education evolved from a well of racial pride and the ever-reaching need to help African American children and adults have a better life. Many of these early teachers, like Lucie Stanton Day, were sisters who each day stood before many children to encourage racial pride and academic success from a view of "uplifting the race." In the schools of the segregated South, many students had the circumstances of oppression forced upon them as racism found its reflections in separate but unequal classrooms. My mother often speaks of developing a strong positive identification with African American people, history, and traditions. She attributes her identification to her school years in the South and teachers whose pedagogy reflected the sentiments of Blanche V. Harris, a teacher in Natchez, Mississippi, "money is not the object . . . but we know and feel that there is plenty of work to be done and feel willing to sacrifice much to see our race elevated" (Sterling, 1984, p. 277).

Despite restrictions in the education of African Americans, some African American children completed secondary school and became active citizens in many local and national organizations. Others matriculated to historically Black colleges and universities (HBCUs) to pursue their quest for further knowledge. While enrolled at these institutions, it seemed a natural step in their progression to be part of a mission to educate other African American students and to create environments that nurtured the desire "to give back" to their communities.

As I went into the classroom as an elementary teacher, I stood on the shoulders of these sister teachers. Each and everyday was not just an implementation of plans to get from the first bell to the last, but an opportunity to help "baby" sisters and brothers realize the possibility of academic success while nurturing racial pride. An example that always comes to mind is the day that my administrator (principal) came to my elementary classroom with a query. She stood in the middle of the classroom and pivoted from left to right and back again. As I followed her eyes, it appeared that she was examining every corner of the classroom. She then asked me, "How do you think it feels to be a White child in your classroom?" I didn't answer right away, mostly because that had not been my preoccupation. At the time, I thought that her question was related to me as an African American teacher and it made me remember a school open house, a few years earlier. Caitlin, an eager first grader, walked over to me with father and mother in tow. I made all the proper introductions and held a brief conversation about Caitlin's progress. As they walked away, Caitlin exclaimed, "Now Daddy see, Ms. Tyson is not a nigger." Out of the mouths of children, race matters.

Returning to the administrator's question, I quickly asked, "Why do you ask?" She stated that if you looked around my room, every space, from bulletin boards to bare walls, was covered with pictures and posters of African Americans. Pointing to a bulletin board she exclaimed, "Look at this board for women's history month. There are no White women on this board. How do you think the White girls in your class feel?" It was in that instant that I realized that this, the decoration of my room, was not a "random act of blackness." As I searched the recesses of my mind, I realized that every poster, picture, and bulletin board took hours of searching, researching, and preparation to meet the demands of my commitment. It was teacher activism: my commitment to making sure that the gaps in children's education, with a special focus on African American children, would be filled with stories of successes and triumphs for African Americans in all walks of life. My response to my administrator went something like this, "I have not honestly considered what it feels like to be a White student in my classroom. I bring to my teaching the experiences of what it felt like to be an African American student in the rooms of White teachers, whose classrooms never had a picture of anyone who looked like me. At this moment, the reason why I am a teacher has come full circle. I am an African American who is a teacher, not a teacher who just happens to be African American. The choices I make to integrate and supplement the existing curriculum with African and African American history and contemporary events is part of my commitment to teach. I am here for that purpose and that purpose alone. When I am no longer able to accomplish that goal, then I will leave the classroom for another venue. As for the White children in my classroom who, like the African American children in my classroom, are immersed in a learning environment with Africans and African Americans at the center, they will be just fine. When we juxtapose this one year, 180 days in the life of a student, with the remaining twelve years required by the state for graduation, the scale still tips in favor of the dominant culture. These students will have to be assigned to six more teachers like me just to balance the scale."

As she left my room, she stopped to look at a poster of El Haj Malik El Shabazz (also known as Malcolm X) with the caption, *By Any Means Necessary*, and asked, "Do you believe that too?" My response was, "Yes, education by any means necessary."

As the years progressed in my teaching career, students and their parents came to believe that as well. I became an advocate for African American students and their parents regardless of whether they were in my classroom or not. In school and out, many parents would ask "Ms. Tyson" how to help, not only their child, but with other children in the school and community. I would often receive calls from a friend of a parent who suggested that I could help with a problem. I would encourage them to get involved in the politics of school, to be involved in making change. I went with parents to school board meetings, meetings with teacher colleagues, and social service agencies. When asked why I let the kids and their parents take up so much of my time, my response was the African proverb, *I am because we are*. While I spent countless hours in the library collecting information for teaching, countless hours making copies of material about people of color that was not in our books, countless hours creating teaching materials, countless hours at school board meetings, and countless hours tutoring, I also spent countless hours in the university library reading journal articles related to educational research. I read the *Journal of Reading Research, The Journal of Negro Education, The Journal of Math Education, The Journal of Children's Literature, The Journal of Urban Education*, and *Educational Researcher*, to name a few. Even though I did not belong to the research organizations that published some of these journals, I had a desire to know the latest research in the field. This was a necessary part of my development and growth, and it informed my classroom pedagogy. I wanted to be the best teacher I could be because my community expected and deserved no less. I believed that I personally stood on the shoulders of Mary McLeod Bethune, my role model, whose legacy demanded educational excellence.

My quest for excellence is what moved me to participate in the evaluation of student teachers. A young sister who had been assigned to me as a "problem student in danger of failing," helped me realize that it was time for the next step in my social justice pathway. I added *The Journal of Teacher Education* to my reading. This sister had already failed one student teaching experience and she arrived at my classroom door with a long checklist of things she had to correct and complete successfully before she could be certified. I did not read the list. I put it on my desk, face down, and asked her to tell me what she thought the problems were. She tearfully recounted the story of her daily teaching experiences in a predominantly White elementary school. She attributed some of the problems with her evaluation to racism, but she was also filled with doubt about her ability to teach. I decided to observe her for a few days before I offered my initial assessment. As I watched her with the children, I saw a mirror image of myself as a new teacher trying my hand at what I have come to know as "culturally relevant teaching" (Irvine, 1990; Ladson-Billings, 1995; Lipman, 1995; Gay, 2000). This sister took the time to know her students, to make her teaching relevant, and her assessment authentic. She was really quite masterful as a "novice" teacher.

At the end of a week, we discussed her teaching and I shared my experiences as a new teacher. I offered her some suggestions and gave her copies of some articles about teaching and cultural diversity from the *Journal of Teacher Education* and the *Journal of Negro Education*. She broke down in tears and shared that she was so glad to hear that she was not the problem. She acknowledged her need to improve her teaching in a number of areas, but she was committed to becoming a teacher. She also stated that she was so happy that she had not taken "no" for an answer and left the teacher education program as recommended by some of her other professors. However, if I suggested she did not have the qualifications to be a teacher, she would look for another job in education and not pursue classroom teaching. When I asked her why, she responded, "because you are a sister."

As her statement rang in my head over and over and over again, I remembered my answer to a common set of interview questions for a teaching position: Where do you see yourself in five years? In ten years? I answered that in five years I saw myself as a university professor in teacher education and in ten years as the dean of a school for African American girls. I then decided to pursue my goals to move into teacher education. This move was spurred by an article I read in *Black Issues in Higher Education,* which outlined the poignant need for people of color in universities in general and in teacher education programs in particular. I applied for and was accepted into the doctoral program. I remained in the classroom as a teacher, maintained my active involvement in the community, and started taking classes in the doctoral program. I knew that my classroom teaching was moving into a new arena. The research I was reading in my courses was informative, but it did not satisfy the burning need to actively respond to many needs within my community. For example: Could teacher education programs be designed to help teachers answer a call for culturally responsive teaching? A call for active participation in the lives and the communities of the children they teach? A call to devise ways for children to become participants in personal and public social political action? These questions led to my research, but I found myself wrestling with more epistemological questions.

What happens when the teacher is also a researcher? A person whose methodological moves reflect the cycles of inquiry-based teaching? A person whose epistemological underpinnings are interwoven with being African and American? A person whose research agenda is one of activism? Glesne and Peshkin (1992) state:

> Whether or not researchers should be advocates is a debated topic. Traditionally, if the researcher had a stake in their topic, or took a position on it, then the trustworthiness of their data was suspect. We support action-oriented and advocacy research but urge novice researchers to begin with non-advocacy, non-prescriptive roles. The relationship you and others develop should be marked by reciprocity, trust, and mutual respect, and learning, but at this point not by advocacy and action. If so moved by problems that action must be taken, then complete the research, redefine your relationship with your others and get involved (p. 36).

I, as teacher and activist could not abdicate my responsibilities. In the meantime, the researcher as activist evolved.

Researcher as Activist

> Research is formalized curiosity. It is poking and prying with a purpose (Hurston, 1994, p. 687).

> Activism concretizing ethical ideals in action, allows us to better comprehend a form of thinking unfamiliar in abstract academic thought (James, 1993, p. 128).

> If the presence of increasing numbers of black women within the academy is to have a transformative impact both on the academy and on communities beyond the academy, we have to think seriously about linkages between research and activism, about crossracial and transnational coalitional strategies, and about the importance of linking our work to radical social agendas (Davis, 1989, p. 231).

As a classroom teacher over several school years, I engaged in what I later learned is "action research": gathering data through inquiry to inform my pedagogy for individual students as well as the collective learning community in the classroom. I constantly used the African principles of *Maat* (truth, order, reciprocity, justice) (Asante, 1991) as a part of the fundamental philosophical base of my teaching. In this daily endeavor with my students, the cycle of my own personal inquiry continued to bring me back to a larger picture—pedagogy that is an integral part of activism; that is, a social justice activist framework that is motivated by a sense of urgency. This urgency—the urgency of my house being on fire and in need of immediate action—was explained in an earlier work to help illustrate differences in the motives of collaborative efforts in teacher reform (Tyson, 1997b). The same metaphor could be applied to activist research. The teacher researcher who is an activist, must not only collect data but must act on behalf of, or support participants as they act on their own behalf.

For example, in my earlier work (Tyson, 1997a; Tyson, 1999), I employed a social justice framework, within a critical interpretivist paradigm, to examine a group of five African American boys' perspectives on contemporary children's literature, as well as how children make a difference using literature as a catalyst to social action. In other words, in what ways can the models for culturally relevant pedagogy and multicultural education be expanded to include theoretical models for the development of students' sociopolitical voice? I began by observing African American students in their classrooms and taking general field notes. Soon I was ready to select a few of the African American male participants for the study. Not long after the study began, Paul approached me with a suggestion to include his friend, "He is Black and should come, too." I agreed to include the other student. It was not the qualitative underpinnings of purposeful sampling nor the ethics of reciprocity that moved me to say yes. It was my "teacher sensibility." I was moved to remember the child who wants to participate and is excluded, the child who may need to feel a sense of belonging, and the bonds of friendship between children in the classroom that are often transformed into academic support. Even more importantly, Jay lost a recess playmate (the time our meetings were held) when Paul agreed to join the study. Whatever the reason, the teacher in me would not allow me to say no. The activist in me would not allow me to walk away from a situation where a young African American male student would be turned away from participation just because I had a preconceived number of how many fifth graders to include. He was not a one-too-many participant, he was my little "brother." As a result of my decision, my research was improved in a number of ways. On one level, Paul told me months later that he had decided he would not participate if his best friend could not come, so his participation hinged on the participation of Jay. On another level, Jay's participation added to the data in ways that no other participant did. His participation lead to critical findings and implications for further research; but more importantly, my activist commitment to fight the bankrupting effects of racism and oppression moved me to look at my research as counterfeit if it did not open the door for participation for the very ones I hoped to serve.

As a researcher, my initial plan was to be the participant observer. Nevertheless, I found myself slipping and sliding and often losing ground. Theoretical constraints were intersecting with a school-based epistemology, that is, coming to know in ways that are responsive to the policy, culture, and systemic racism found in schools. It has been argued in early works that research epistemologies are racist (Sheuerich and Young, 1997) and that the specificity of historical interactions (Tyson, 1998) are responses to the endemic ways that racism is systemic in our societies. Researching from an epistemological specificity that was not only operating from the histories of racism in society but racism in schools, I could not just observe and participate on the fringes of a need for intervention. For example, during my research on literacy among African American boys, I observed gaps in their knowledge of literacy and literate behaviors. While some researchers may think that these gaps are emergent themes and collect data to analyze and report them, I found it necessary as a teacher to teach and re-teach the "missing links" in their knowledge. From a social justice framework, my research became an enactment of service to and with the boys as an integral part of the epistemology out of which my methodology emerged.

Teaching, Researching, and Serving

My life belongs to the struggle (Angela Davis, 1989, p. 228).

"Lifting as we climb" is an idea that echoes in the minds of many African Americans. During the civil rights movement, the song *We Shall Overcome* embraced the concept of lifting each other up as we climb in economic ways, in service to individual African American families, in communities, and in society at large. While this may also be true of many other communities, for the purposes of this discussion, I will speak on what has been an influence in my life and the subject of my research, namely, the African American historical context for activism and revolution.

In the context of my work and research, service does not emerge from the concept of filling deficits. Unlike in the criminal system, where "community service" is used as a form of punishment, my understanding of service as activism in research is a far cry from this punitive notion. My understanding of activism in research is tied to reciprocity, not research for the sake of research, but research that is responsive to urgent needs for intervention within the community. For example, imagine you are standing on the deck of a ship and someone yells out "Woman overboard!!" As a researcher, you could choose to collect data by interviewing those standing on deck to find out what they know about the circumstances that led to the person in the deep waters. As a researcher, you could try to form a focus group to gather opinions about the ship's safety drills. As an activist researcher, you instinctively throw a life preserver to the drowning person. You might begin to ask questions, but only while you continue as quickly as possible to help bring this person to safety. As a teacher, researcher, and activist, it is impossible for me to ignore my responsibility to ask the questions, gather the data, and participate in the intervention.

Educational research as service is reflected in an event that occurred during my literacy research with the five African American boys. During one session, Paul asked me what kind of research I was doing and I told him it is called qualitative research. He wanted to know more. I immediately went into the teaching mode to explain the "main" types of research: qualitative and quantitative, interview verses surveys, and so on.

He asked more and more questions and our discussion completely shifted from books to a deep conversation about human subjects review, protocol, rapport, prolonged engagement, and so on. Later, as I listened to the audio tape of our discussion, I realized that I had taught a mini lesson on qualitative research to a fifth grader. For Paul's next scheduled individual interview, I arrived at the room designated for our study. Paul was there, along with the other participants. When I entered the room, the boys announced that Paul had explained the qualitative "research stuff." They thought the research design should be changed. The boys proposed that we meet as a group everyday, rather than individually, so I could get better data; it would also be "more fun that way." I was surprised, yet delighted, that the mini lesson had become a peer teaching opportunity for Paul, something that many teachers hope will happen in the classroom. The "student becoming teacher" added a new dimension of reciprocity to the study. The boys changed the design of the study, the list of books to be read, the location of our meetings, and many other dimensions of the study. I don't know how many researchers have that as a goal in their collection of data; however, I consciously had as a part of my research agenda a place for activism from the participants.

Conclusion

> The drums of Africa beat in my heart. I cannot rest while there is a single Negro boy or girl lacking a chance to prove their worth (Mary McLeod Bethune, 1994, p. 223).

As I was completing my doctorate, a family elder at a reunion pulled me aside for a talk. After the traditional "You still in school girl?" and "When you gon' graduate?", she stated, "Don't matter what you do up there at that university, just make sure you can always come home. Sell your soul and your work will be lifeless. Nobody wants a working stiff." For me, coming home was not limited to my parents' home or my individual community, but it also meant the African American community at large. Historically, to "forget where you came from" has been an attempt at assimilation, at great cost to African American people, into the spaces that leave the normative dominant ideology unchallenged. In my family and community, assimilation is suspect at best, and a recipe for cultural suicide at worst.

As a sister in the academy, the sum of who I am as teacher, researcher, and activist makes it possible for me to continue to breathe a breath of life into my work: A breath of life that sustains pedagogy grounded in critical consciousness, a research agenda grounded in an epistemology of cultural specificity, and an activism grounded in emancipatory action.

Bibliography and Suggested Readings

Asante, M. K.(1991). The Afrocentric idea in education. *Journal of Negro Education, 60*(2), 170–180.

Bethune, M. M. (1994). Winning political equality. In J. L. Papanek (Ed.), *African Americans: Voices of triumph: Leadership* (pp. 205–235). Alexandria, VA: Time Life Books.

Freire, P. (1980). *Education for critical consciousness.* New York: Continuum Publishing Corporation.

Davis, A. (1989). Black women in the academy: Defending our name 1894–1994. In J. James (Ed.), *The Angela Y. Davis reader* (pp. 222–231). Cambridge: Blackwell.

Gay, G. (2000). *Culturally responsive teaching.* New York: Teachers College.

Glesne, C. & Peshkin, A. (1992). *Becoming qualitative researchers: An introduction.* New York: Longman.

hooks, b. (1994). *Teaching to transgress: Education as the practice of freedom.* New York: Routledge.

Hurston, Z. N. & Wall, C. A. (1994). *Folklore, memoirs, and other writings.* New York: The Library of America Literary Classics.

Irvine, J. J. (1990). *Black students and school failure.* New York: Praeger.

James, J. (1993). Teaching theory, talking community. In J. James & R. Farmer (Eds.), *Spirit, space and survival: African American women in (white) academe* (pp. 118–135). New York: Routledge.

Ladson-Billings, G. (1995). Toward a theory of culturally relevant pedagogy. *American Educational Review, 32*(3), 465–491.

Lipman, P. (1995). Bringing out the best in them: The contribution of culturally relevant teachers to school reform. *Theory Into Practice, 34*(3), 203–208.

Sterling, D. (1984). *We are sisters: Black women in the nineteen century.* New York: Norton & Company.

Scheurich, J. & Young, M. (1997). Coloring epistemologies: Are our research epistemologies racially biased? *Educational Researcher, 26*(4), 4–17.

Tyson, C. A. (1999). Shut my mouth wide open: Realistic fiction and social action. *Theory into Practice, 38*(3), 155–159.

Tyson, C. A. (1998). Coloring epistemologies: A response. *Educational Researcher, 27*(9), 21–22.

Tyson, C. A. (1997a). *Shut my mouth wide open: African American fifth grade males respond to contemporary realistic fiction.* Unpublished doctoral dissertation, The Ohio State University.

Tyson, C. A. (1997b). Interlude with a metaphor: My house is on fire. In M. Johnston (Ed.), *Contradictions in school collaboration: New thinking on school/university partnerships* (pp. 81). New York: Teachers College Press.

Dr. Melanie Carter

Dr. Melanie Carter is an assistant professor in the Department of Educational Leadership at Clark Atlanta University, where she teaches the following courses: History of Urban Education, Politics of Urban Education, Society and Education, School and Community Relations, Instructional Leadership, and Qualitative Research. A native of Springfield, Ohio, Dr. Carter was educated in the city's public schools. She earned a bachelor of arts degree in english literature and language at Ohio University; a master of arts degree in english education from Atlanta University; and finally, a doctorate in educational policy and leadership from Ohio State University. While at Ohio State, Dr. Carter held numerous positions in University College, including Coordinator of the Minority Advising Program.

Dr. Carter's research, which is primarily historical, draws upon "family tales" to reconsider mainstream schooling narratives. She argues that these stories trouble the dominant epistemologies, ideologies, and methodologies that interpret the African American educational journey. Dr. Carter's current research projects include exploring the history of the regional accreditation of Black schools in the south; documenting the work of laboratory high schools associated with historically black colleges and universities; and identifying a liberatory research method that illuminates and describes, rather than conceals and distorts, Black schooling experiences.

10

RACE, JACKS, AND JUMP ROPE

Theorizing School through Personal Narratives

Melanie Carter

Most children are born into the world at the top of their game, genius level. The culture that receives them will either nurture and develop the genius in them or silence their minds before they reach the age of six. Most children remain in a learning mode. However, those that truly explode with ideas, creativity and unbounded talent are the ones introduced to knowledge in creative environments by talented and caring people (Madhubuti, 1994, p. 6).

Stories by people of color can counter the stories of the oppressor. Furthermore, the discussion between the teller and the listener can help overcome ethnocentrism and the dysconscious way many scholars view and construct the world (Tate, 1997, p. 220).

Introduction

Childhood memories of school serve as the foundation for mainstream notions about the purpose and process of schooling. It is apparent that these memories, once interpreted and relayed within the dominant narrative, are not reflective of the varied and richly textured experiences of all children who pass through the American school system. Nonetheless, these sanctioned memories often depict schools as neutral sites where deserving children access the knowledge and skills necessary to become full participants in American society.

While much attention has been directed at dispelling this myth (Anderson, 1998; Cochran-Jones 2000; Delpit, 1995; Gordon, 1994; Irvine, 1990), this perspective persists. Unchallenged memories become uncontested truths that are strung together to create a grand schooling narrative. This narrative, then, conceals and trivializes schooling experiences that trouble mainstream notions. For racially marginalized groups, the exclusion of their stories renders their particular challenges and successes invisible (Carter, 1996). This is problematic not only for the marginalized, but for all of us who are committed to making our schools better places for all children.

Our schools have served as battlegrounds for our most pernicious societal challenges. Personal narratives are one way to gain insight into how these struggles play out in the classroom. For example, autobiographical accounts of integration are especially revealing, not because they are concerned with providing a comprehensive objective account of a particular desegregation process, but because the authors' purpose is to offer a perspective that was not, or could not, be relayed in mainstream accounts (Beals 1994). These experiences cannot be detached from their historical, social, and racial context. The stories, their nuances, and their peculiarities can only be understood within their organic framework. Each telling represents an attempt to establish a bond between the teller and the listener as a means to facilitate the acceptance of his or her rendition. Acceptance, however, is predicated upon the existence of a shared perspective, worldview, epistemology. Our challenge is the articulation of this framework. How do we share the story of our stories?

Metastorytelling: Building Theory From Our Lives

> Naw, tain't nothin' lak you might think. So 'taint no use in me telling
> you somethin; unless Ah give you de understandin' to go 'long wid it.
> Unless you see de fur, a mink skin ain't no different from a coon hide
> (Hurston, 1937, p. 19).

In her novel, *Their Eyes Were Watching God* (1937), Zora Neale Hurston provides us with a model for *metastorytelling*. In the above dialogue between the protagonist, Janie Starks, and her neighbor, Phoeby, Janie explains that her life can't be understood from her friend's frame of reference; instead, it must be told within a frame of reference all its own. Janie's rationale for the necessity of historical context illustrates that truth is a shifting construct, defined and redefined each time a story is told and interpreted. Consequently it is imperative that we create safe theoretical sites for our narratives. Since conceptual or epistemological perspectives inform how we know the world, how can we congregate and harmonize competing narratives? The answer to this question lies in understanding that multiple interpretations exist simultaneously and are everchanging. Therefore, we must continuously engage ourselves and others in work that cultivates a theoretical sensibility (Baker, 1991).

Critical Race Theory (CRT) is helpful here as a method of inquiry and analysis. In recent years, CRT, with its emphasis on the use of personal narratives, has provided a platform to name and relay experiences that cannot be understood within a traditional framework. It acknowledges the multidimensional and dynamic nature of reality and our individual and collective interpretation of it (Parker, 1998; Tate, 1997). According to Ladson-Billings (1998) "the primary reason, then, that stories, or narratives, are deemed important among CRT scholars is that they add necessary contextual contours to the seeming 'objectivity' of positivist perspectives" (p. 10). CRT, unlike traditional autobiographical processes, has not been tainted by an imposed structure (Smith, 1987). CRT embraces specificity as necessary for grounded epistemologies—thereby relying upon personal storytelling and narratives to shape ways of knowing. For me, the real strength of CRT is its emphasis on perspective and context and its call for and legitimation of what I call an "epistemology of specificity" that is rare in the academy. In the academy, theories which are specific (in this instance race specific) are viewed as narrow, inferior, or undeveloped interpretive approaches. In short, CRT calls for an acknowledgement that African American experiences cannot be arrived at without a constant reference to the environment that cradles them.

As African American scholars, we have a responsibility to not only tell our stories but to use them as a means to demonstrate the centrality of our experiences in any interpretation of the American schooling system. How then do we bring to the fore those experiences that remain hidden beneath the veneer of a mythical and romanticized common schooling narrative? And even more importantly, how can this knowledge inform our work as scholars in the academy? This essay reflects my ongoing attempts to utilize personal narratives, usually in the form of family tales, to capture and relay varied accounts of schooling.

Neither the grand narrative nor these personal narratives portend to include all stories. Instead, both use stories as mechanisms to speak their own epistemological truths. This essay offers "raced" schooling memories as a means to explore the schooling experiences of three women. These biographical and autobiographical stories are not to be interpreted as representative of all African Americans. Instead, I hope that this telling will inspire larger questions around the construction of public memory about our schools and the way in which those memories are accepted as representative of all of our experiences.

This chapter also reflects my belief in reflective analysis as a way to examine one's epistemological leanings. Some argue that the academy inculcates us with a particular sensibility, one that encourages "free thinking" but within prescribed and closely monitored parameters (hooks, 1994). How then do we protect our culturally grounded perspectives and infuse them into the academy? This is important for at least three reasons. First, it is personally important. As an African American woman, it is important that I can locate my experiences in the dominant narrative. Insisting upon authentic inclusion challenges the validity of a narrative that does not give space and/or voice to people of color. Second, it is collectively important. All of our stories are valuable and lend themselves to a broader understanding of the American schooling experience. Sharing our personal stories is a strategy to identify common experiences. While we are not necessarily seeking personal validation or corroboration, there is a need to refute the universality of the dominant narrative. Our collective stories are self-affirming and are substantive testament to the inadequacy of a supposedly all-encompassing narrative. Third, truth telling is a counterhegemonic strategy. It troubles taken for granted assumptions and long held notions that protect and sustain the status quo.

A Biographical Narrative

> Until every story is heard and responded to, our schools do not fulfill the goals of a democractic society (Paley, 1979/2000, p. xvi).

When I teach history of American education, I often begin with a story about my mother and my paternal grandmother. Their tale encompasses two generations and is but one example of schooling practices that protect and maintain the hegemonic societal structure. Twenty years separated my mother's and my grandmother's high school matriculation. However, both encountered the same guidance counselor. The counselor, a probably well-intentioned White woman, discouraged my grandmother in 1928 and my mother in 1948 from scheduling business education courses, such as typing and bookkeeping. Instead, she enrolled both in domestic science courses. My grandmother acquiesced. She dropped out of high school during her senior year to get married and worked as a seamstress for nearly sixty years. While this work enabled her to support her family, she eventually lost her vision. Decades of threading needles, sleepless nights at her sewing machine, and handiwork, placed undue pressure upon her eyes.

On the other hand, my mother resisted. Unlike my grandmother, she did not follow the guidance counselor's instructions. After querying her White classmates about course meeting times, my mother erased the counselor's entries on her schedule card and replaced the domestic science courses with business education courses. This strategic move provided my mother with the skills necessary to secure a position with a nearby federal government installation upon graduation. As a result, my mother enjoyed a professional career for nearly forty years, retired well before sixty, and is currently enjoying an active retirement. Nonetheless, more than thirty years after her act of resistance, she recalled how afraid she was that she would be caught and reprimanded for this act of disobedience (Carter, 1996). While Woodson's (1933/1977) warning of the perils of Black miseducation continues to be useful in describing the schooling experiences of African Americans, a more apt description of my mother's and grandmother's experiences is "diseducation." Jacob Carruthers (1994) defines diseducation as "pervasive, persistent and disproportionate underachievement in comparison with their white counterparts" (p. 45). However, as evidenced by this family tale, this underachievement has historical origins grounded in racist schooling practices; that is, education that does not foster liberation but instead continues oppression. In this instance, school as an institution fulfilled its historical purpose—to maintain and protect the dominant societal structure (Anderson, 1988).

The purpose of sharing this story with my students is to provide a context for our historical journey. As previously stated, the American schooling experience, though widely depicted as a standardized and universal process, is quite varied. One's interaction with school is shaped by factors that are far too numerous to name. This family tale hopefully encourages my students to come to their study of American educational history with a critical eye, one that considers their own educational story as they explore the dominant schooling narrative. Without this critical eye, the dominant narrative appears one-dimensional and conceals ongoing struggles around very important questions such as What is the purpose of schooling? How do we do this work? How has the way we do our work impacted all of us?

An Autobiographical Narrative

Is this classroom in which I live a fair place for every child who enters? Does every child and family have an equal say in the worlds we invent? (Paley, 1979/2000, xv).

The next tale is structured as an open letter to my fifth grade teacher. Mrs. Jones (a pseudonym), a gray-haired White woman, was an experienced teacher who had taught at my elementary school for many years. Although addressed to Mrs. Jones, this letter is not just about the relationship between a ten-year old Black girl and her White teacher. It represents my efforts to retrospectively make sense of a particular schooling experience.

Dear Mrs. Jones:

You probably don't remember me, but I was one of your fifth grade students in the 1974 through 1975 school year at Highlands Elementary School. I came to your class excited about the school year. Though I had some minor difficulties with my fourth grade teacher, I had high hopes for a great school year. I must say that though I didn't realize it, fifth grade proved to be a pivotal moment in my schooling journey. I don't know if you recall, but I was a vociferous reader even at ten years old. In fact, Mrs. Brown, the assistant librarian, often saved the latest Carolyn Haywood books for Melinda (my twin sister) and me.

I can still remember our classroom. A corner room at the end of the third floor corridor. It was a large airy room, with an extra large coatroom near the front that was a favorite spot for last minute talking and teasing. I can even recall how the desks were arranged and where my classmates sat. The fashions of the day included folded-to-the-knee blue jeans with matching "psychedelic" shirts and socks. Earth shoes were on the horizon, but at Highlands, Converse sneakers still ruled the day.

I wonder what you thought of us. We were a quite a bunch. Highlands was certainly a neighborhood school set in the midst of a working class neighborhood populated by Blacks and Whites. My mother later told me that she gauged the shift in the neighborhood from mostly White to mostly Black by the decreasing number of White children in our classes each year. By fifth grade, though I doubt Blacks were in the majority, Highlands seemed like a "Black" school. Black students were intricately involved with school activities and there was a degree of comfort. Highlands was familiar to us and by and large, we felt like a part of the school; however, there was one area in which Black students were not prominent—high academic achievement. It was in your class, Mrs. Jones, that I learned that though I was "smart," I was not "smart enough."

I don't know why you decided to divide our class into groups, but I'll never forget the day you decided to separate the "smart" students from everyone else. You decided that our class of more than twenty had just two smart students—John Findlay and Mary Smith. In recognition of their intellectual superiority, they were permitted to work independently, at their own pace, and were to ask for help only when necessary. When you announced that only John and Mary would be allowed to work alone, I remember feeling an overwhelming sadness. I certainly knew that Mary and John were smart, but I also believed that I was smart as well. In my other classes, I had always been allowed the same privileges as Mary and John and I couldn't imagine why you were not going to permit me to stay with "my rightful group." Somehow, though I'm not sure where the courage came from, I went to you and asked why I wasn't selected to work independently. I explained that my grades were good, that I had a history of working independently, and that I wanted to be in the group with Mary and John. Surprised by my sudden assertiveness, you begrudgingly agreed to let me work independently. I remember the grimace on your face that day. I was sure that you didn't want to place me in that group, because unlike John and Mary, two White students with stay at home moms who also happened to be our "room mothers," I was the Black child of a widowed mother. It is amazing that more than twenty-five years later, feelings of despair envelope me as I recount this story.

Mary, John, and I occupied the last seats in the row next to the window overlooking the pavement that separated the portables from the main building. I still remember my reluctance to ask questions because you viewed my inquiries as evidence that I should be returned to the larger group. Fearful of your disparaging and discouraging remarks about my work, I spent afternoons gazing out the window, trying to escape from the task of distinguishing participial phrases from gerunds . . .

My attempts to revisit my schooling journey led me to this memory. Recognizing that the way in which we internalize and conceptualize schools differs greatly (Fordham, 1996), I wondered why I held so tightly to memories of my fifth grade year. This reflective account encourages me, as an adult, to confront a childhood memory that has been a source of pain and a source of motivation. However, until I began to write this essay, I had not critically reconsidered my adolescent interpretation. In a strange way, I found some comfort in the knowledge that I had far exceeded Mrs. Smith's low expectations of me. Unlike Vanessa Siddle Walker's (1996) depiction of Caswell County Training School and its staff, my elementary school was not an "institution of caring." Though some teachers were extremely supportive and provided a nurturing environment within their own classrooms, this was the exception rather than the rule.

Mrs. Jones, I'm certain, would tell a very different story. It is likely that we were at the very least, culturally mismatched. I'm certain that this absence of cultural synchronization created or exacerbated unspoken tension between us (Irvine, 1990). Maybe she believed that I was better suited for close monitoring and needed more attention from her. Maybe her many years of experience enabled her to make better instructional decisions than a ten-year-old. Maybe John and Mary were smarter than me. The larger point is that there really is not one story. We interpret our experiences differently. Our individual frame of references demand it.

Conclusion

> The difference lies in distinguishing between theory as a dogma or closed system of ideas to be verified and tested, and theory as a story or narrative operating as an open system of ideas that can be retold and reformulated. How bible stories are used illustrates this process: Everyone knows and shares the same story. However, the changing collectivity constructing such stories—new interpretations, listeners, tellers, and the context itself—changes the meaning of the story with each retelling (Collins, 1998, p. 200).

These stories are liberating—liberating because they problematize common understandings and have the potential to alter our collective public schooling memories. They are also troubling—troubling because they illuminate the insidious ways that individual and institutional practices impact the lives of children, and their children, and their children. Our challenge and responsibility as scholars of color is to interrupt this cycle. Critically reflecting upon our individual and collective stories, we must cultivate and then articulate a dynamic theoretical framework that encourages interpretations that honor individual experiences and particular circumstances. Such a *meta*narrative would provide insight on how race, class, and gender shape a myriad of issues, including teacher student relations, teacher expectations, school and classroom culture, and student resiliency. These challenges cannot be addressed outside of the context from which they emerged. Though sometimes painful and often difficult to adequately capture and relay, our stories speak our truths. We must have the courage to tell them.

Bibliography and Suggested Readings

Anderson, J. D. (1988). *The education of blacks in the south, 1860–1935*. Chapel Hill: University of North Carolina Press.

Baker, H. A. (1991). *Workings of the spirit: The poetics of Afro-American women's writing*. Chicago: University of Chicago Press.

Beals, M. P. (1994). *Warriors don't cry: A searing memoir of the battle to integrate Little Rock's Central High*. New York: Washington Square Press.

Carruthers, J. H. (1994). Black intellectuals and the crisis in black education. In M. Shujaa (Ed.), *Too much schooling, too much education: A paradox of black life in white societies* (pp 37–55). Trenton, NJ: Africa World Press.

Carter, M. D. (1996). *From Jim Crow to inclusion: An historical analysis of the Association of Colleges and Secondary Schools for Negroes, 1934–1965*. Unpublished doctoral dissertation, Ohio State University.

Cochran-Jones, M. (2000). Blind vision: Unlearning racism in teacher education. *Harvard Educational Review,* 70(2), 157–190.

Collins, P. H. (1998). *Fighting words: Black women and the search for justice.* Minneapolis: University of Minnesota Press.

Delpit, L. (1995). *Other people's children: Cultural conflict in the classroom.* New York: The New Press.

Fordham, S. (1996). *Blacked out: Dilemmas of race, identity, and success at Capital High.* Chicago: University of Chicago Press.

Gordon, B. M. (1994). African-American cultural knowledge and liberatory education: Dilemmas, problems and potentials in postmodern American society. In M. Shujaa (Ed.), *Too much schooling, too much education: A paradox of black life in white societies* (pp. 57–78). Trenton, NJ: Africa World Press.

hooks, b. (1994). *Teaching to transgress: Education as the practice of freedom.* New York: Routledge.

Hurston, Z. N. (1937). *Their eyes were watching god.* New York: Negro University Press.

Irvine, J. J. (1990). *Black students and school failure: Politics, practices and prescriptions.* New York: Greenwood Press.

Ladson-Billings, G. (1998). Just what is critical race theory and what's it doing in a *nice* field like education? *Qualitative Studies in Education, II*(1), 7–24.

Madhubuti, H. R. (1994). Cultural work: Planting new trees with new seeds. In M. Shujaa (Ed.), *Too much schooling, too much education: A paradox of black life in white societies* (pp. 1–6). Trenton, NJ: Africa World Press.

Paley, V. G. (1979/2000). *White teacher.* Cambridge: Harvard University Press.

Parker, L. (1998). "Race is . . . race ain't:" An exploration of the utility of critical race theory in qualitative research in education. *Qualitative Studies in Education, II*(1), 43–55.

Smith, V. (1987). *Self-discovery and authority in Afro-American narrative.* Cambridge: Harvard University Press.

Tate, W. F. III (1997). Critical race theory and education: History, theory and implications. In M. W. Apple (Ed.), *Review of research in education.* Washington, DC: American Educational Research Association.

Walker, V. S. (1996). *Their highest potential: An African American school community in the segregated south.* Chapel Hill: University of North Carolina Press.

Woodson, C. G. (1933/1977). *The miseducation of the negro.* New York: AMS Press.

Dr. Lesa Maria Covington Clarkson

Dr. Lesa Maria Covington Clarkson recently completed her dissertation entitled *The Effects of the Connected Mathematics Project on Middle School Mathematics Achievement* for her doctorate in mathematics education from the University of Minnesota. Her research examines the achievement of students in the National Science Foundation–funded standards-based mathematics curricula compared to the achievement of students who participated in a traditional curriculum.

Dr. Clarkson has been a mathematics educator for over twenty years. In 1980 she received her bachelor of science degree with a double major in mathematics and physical education from Concordia University (formerly Concordia Teachers College), Seward, Nebraska. After graduation, she returned to her alma mater, Los Angeles Lutheran High School, and taught math and physical education courses for five and one half years before teaching for the Los Angeles Unified School District for three and one half years. She also served as a mentor teacher and competed for the district's Outstanding Mathematics Teacher Award. Dr. Clarkson has served as an assistant professor of mathematics for the past eleven years at Concordia University–Irvine and Concordia University–St. Paul. Native Californians, Dr. Clarkson and her family moved to St. Paul, Minnesota in January of 1996 when she accepted a position as the Director of Multicultural Affairs at Concordia University.

Dr. Clarkson's professional career has been dedicated to teaching and learning mathematics. Her professional memberships include: the National Council of Teachers of Mathematics, the Minnesota Council of Teachers of Mathematics, the American Evaluation Association, the American Education Research Association, and the National Sorority of Phi Delta Kappa-Beta Theta Chapter. Dr. Clarkson and her family currently live in St. Paul, Minnesota. She is the proud mother of three children: Julian Robert, Cameron Levert, and Morgan Barbara Jivanni.

II

SUFFICIENTLY CHALLENGED

A Family's Pursuit
of a Ph.D.

Lesa M. Covington Clarkson

Introduction

I am a single mother of three energetic children who are six, eight, and ten years old. I have been teaching mathematics, physical education, and mathematics education at the junior high, senior high, and university levels. I am the sole bread winner, hand holder, nose wiper, tear dryer, homework helper, cookie baker, microwave-button-pushing-dinner maker. Succinctly, I am sufficiently challenged. But sufficiently challenged does not *really* begin to represent the day-to-day activities of being a single mother and a full time doctoral student. This chapter briefly describes the last thirty-six months of our lives and the lessons that we learned in *our* pursuit of the Ph.D. In no way can it be assumed that these experiences are typical or representative of every family's experiences. Rather, this chapter shares tips and survival skills that helped us live to tell the *tale of the Ph.D.*

Who Am I?

Who I am at this time in my life is very complicated to describe in just a few sentences. The person I have become is as much a part of my upbringing as it is a result of my experiences and the choices that I've made. The route that I took to the Ph.D., although not unique, is the only one that I could have taken.

I am the second oldest of four girls. I was born and raised in Los Angeles, California, and attended Lutheran schools from kindergarten through college. My father was employed as an electrical engineer and my mother was a stay-home mom who shuttled us to and from school every day for thirteen years. As a one-income family, we struggled to pay the tuition bills and have money left over for "luxury" items like store-bought clothes or a big house. We had little extra money, but our parents provided us with a stable home life and self-confidence. They encouraged our participation in activities like drill team, softball, and choir. My mother sewed our clothes until we learned how to sew our own. We each had four dresses that were rotated during the course of a week, which meant that one dress had to be worn twice in one week. The trick was to wear a different dress each week twice! *My family taught me how to be resourceful.*

We weren't deprived. In fact, we didn't know that we were poor at that time. We had all of the basic (no frills-no thrills) necessities. In fact, my parents took us on family vacations each summer. They wanted to provide us with as many experiences as possible. They wanted to expose us to the beauty of the world accessible to us within the driving distance of our family station wagon. They wanted us to see and experience as much of the western United States as was physically possible. For example, each winter they took us to Mt. Shasta so that we could play in the snow. (I had no idea that I would eventually *live* in the snow!) On weekends, we reconnected as a family. Most Saturdays, we walked to the neighborhood park to play tennis. On the return trip, we walked along the railroad tracks so that we could collect the aluminum cans to redeem for cash and gasoline coupons for the following week. Each Sunday, we went to church and shortly afterwards had a family meal that resembled a Thanksgiving dinner. We were thankful for the blessings that we shared as a family. *My family taught me to be thankful.*

Even though my parents were not college graduates, they valued education and instilled in each of us the importance of education. They never compromised their expectations for any of us; after all, a postsecondary degree had not been available to them. College education was expected. They literally sacrificed their livelihood so that we could attend private schools throughout our elementary and secondary education. This did not go unrecognized. As I watched older students receive scholarships for outstanding academic achievement at the eighth grade graduation ceremonies, I set goals to earn academic scholarships, too. In the end, I only had to pay $100 total to attend college over the course of four years.

At school, my sisters and I were the only African Americans (or one of a few) in our classes. Moreover, I was never taught by an African American teacher in my elementary, secondary, or baccalaureate education, even though the schools we attended were in southern California. (My oldest sister had an African American teacher for typing in high school. She left the school before I had the typing course the following school year.) While I did not have teachers who looked like me, I had parents who had high expectations and teachers who sincerely believed in me. As a result, I decided very early that I, too, wanted to be a teacher. I applied to and was accepted at the same teachers college that the majority of my teachers had attended. One day a teacher took me out of class to talk to me about my decision to attend Concordia Teachers College in Seward, Nebraska. She told me that there were very few "Black" people who lived in Nebraska and even fewer who attended the school. She wanted to warn me before I made my final decision. What she didn't realize was that my parents taught us that the color of our skin did not determine what we could do or where we could go. They also taught us that we could do anything that we set our minds to do. *My family taught me to believe in myself.*

Be resourceful, be thankful, and believe in yourself. These are a few of the lessons that my family taught me. These are the same lessons that I want my children to learn: Set goals, work hard, and don't settle for being ordinary when there is extraordinary. These are the lessons that I gleaned from my experiences. This combination of life lessons and experiences carried me through my pursuit of a Ph.D.

The Pursuit of the Ph.D.

Before I started my Ph.D. program, I had a heart-to-heart talk with Julian, Cameron, and Morgan (my children) to describe the changes that would be occurring in our daily routine and what I expected of them. I told them that I would be going to school to become a "doctor." Morgan then asked me if I would still be their mother. That question, from a three-year-old, was deafening. It was a question that continually surfaced in my mind during this thirty-six-month ordeal. It was certainly a question that I will never forget.

My family and I moved from Irvine, California, to St. Paul, Minnesota, in January of 1996. (When we arrived, the drop in the temperature was 70 degrees.) I was hired as the director of Diversity and Multicultural programming at Concordia University and I also taught two math or math education courses. Two years after our arrival, I made the decision to attend the University of Minnesota to earn a Ph.D. in mathematics education. I was very excited to begin my program, to be a student again. After all, I had previously been successful as a student, but that was before children. I knew that the process would have a tremendous impact on my family, especially since my goal was to complete the degree in three years.

Year One

Although I had arranged to take a two-year leave starting the following fall, I began by taking two classes at the University of Minnesota during that spring quarter. The first day of the spring 1998 quarter, I taught my classes at Concordia University, went home to attend to Julian, Cameron, and Morgan, and dashed off to class each evening. I actually found the classroom on this huge campus for my geometry class, and I really enjoyed the persona of being a student again after an eleven-year hiatus since my masters degree. Shortly after I came home and put the "little people" in the bed, I started experiencing pain that I just couldn't identify. After resting for a short period of time, I got up to start my first assignment. I worked briefly and went back to bed because the pain was agonizing. I woke up at 5 A.M. (I remember the exact time because I am not a morning person) and decided to seek medical attention. I drove myself to the hospital where they performed tests and consequently scheduled gallbladder surgery for me a few hours later. Needless to say, I missed the first day of my second class that was held the same evening of my surgery. In fact, I missed the following week of both classes. I was not off to a very good start. This was not a part of my three-year plan!

My scars healed, but the surgery slowed me down for a few weeks. By the time I returned to my studies after the surgery, I was overwhelmed. I was attending classes two evenings per week and teaching two day classes, as well as an adult class each week. It quickly became a habit for Julian, Cameron, and Morgan to ask each morning if I had class. This became a daily routine for the next three years. Then they wanted to know if I was *teaching the class* or *attending the class*. They were already becoming very concerned.

Before I started the Ph.D. program, I had visions of the kitchen table turning into the "homework table" each evening. I thought my children and I would sit down and work on our respective homework assignments together. That turned out to be a figment of my imagination. I found out very quickly that evenings belonged to them.

At the beginning of the quarter, I sat down to work after dinner and it became very clear that *their* questions and assignments would have to be the priority. There was no such thing as studying at the same time. It was frustrating to even *attempt* doing my work before their work was complete and they were in the bed. In all fairness, the picture of the family "studying together" was lacking the importance of being there for them. It would have worked well for me to study early in the evening, but I forgot that they needed a supportive parent who was available for them. Being available was the most important thing that I could do for my children. They still needed a mother.

I took four courses during my first summer. One sequence of two courses met every morning at 8 A.M. (Remember, I am not a morning person.) I had to return twice a week for an evening course that met during the entire summer. The fourth course met seven hours a day every day for two weeks. I was able to complete seventeen graduate units during my first summer. I felt like I was really making progress now.

I carried my math books with me everywhere we went. We started eating lunch at the park most days after I returned from my morning class. I worked on homework problems while they ate their lunch. When they played outside, I worked. They slept and I worked.

Fall quarter was not much different from the summer except that Julian and Cameron were back in school. Morgan began attending preschool three days per week. I took eighteen graduate credits during the fall quarter. It was more than overwhelming—it was daunting! I questioned my decision to over-load myself in the interest of saving time and money. I had figured that I needed to take sixteen to eighteen credits each quarter in order to finish the course requirements within two years so that I could spend the third year on my dissertation. Well, by the time I finished the first year, I was exhausted. I felt like I had been running a race for months. In fact, my health had suffered from the experience. At the end of my first year of study, I had to have surgery on both feet. I opted for the surgery during the first week of June. Since I had to be completely off my feet for one week, I missed the last day of classes that quarter to allow for time to recuperate the following week. Summer classes would start in one week!

Year Two

The second summer began with two summer school courses and a wheelchair. It was challenging to *wheel* to class, but it was even more difficult to under-stand why people treated me like I was stupid because I was sitting rather than standing. My mother drove me to class everyday and then returned to pick me up, only to return later in the afternoon for another class. Now everything I did became a family effort. We all had to get up early for an 8 A.M. class for two weeks. We all had to go back to the university twice a week for the after-noon class for four weeks.

It was difficult to imagine how life could get more complex. Did I forget to mention the bout of food poisoning? That was a different kind of challenge when you have had surgery on both feet. But I would also be remiss if I didn't mention the emergency trip to the dentist for the removal of a wisdom tooth that hit a nerve. The pain medication for my feet didn't begin to relieve the tooth pain. So I lay in the bed watching the clock and waiting for the sun to rise so that I could call and make an appointment with a local dentist. As I searched the phone book for a dentist at 6 A.M., I made an appointment for 10 A.M. Why did I wait four more hours? I didn't want to wake up my mother and I didn't want to miss class. (It was only a two-week class.)

All in all, it was an interesting summer. It taught me that no matter how strong you think *you* are, the family is even stronger. My children took turns pushing me around in the wheelchair. They brought my books to me, handed my crutches to me, and brought water to me. I was used to being the provider, protector, and transporter. Now I had to depend on everyone else. Now, my classes were a family affair. I originally told them that we would have to work as a team in order to survive the pursuit of my Ph.D. Now, they were proving to me what working together really meant.

During the second summer, I also learned that they were developing into fine human beings. I always loved them, but after that summer I discovered that I also liked the people they were becoming. Sitting down, or maybe it was just slowing down, afforded me the opportunity to see them as they were. It made me sad to discover what I had missed. They were growing up and changing while my head was stuck in a book.

Financing a family is challenging on a private school teacher's salary, but financing a family as a full-time student is something short of a miracle. I could not afford to take my family on a vacation during summer two, so I told Julian, Cameron, and Morgan that we were going to *Camp Clarkson*. This was a two-week period where we were going to forgo chores, textbooks, and assignments in order to do something *fun*—just as they would if they had attended summer camp. We sat down and listed the activity of their dreams. They chose free activities as well as activities with a cost. Organizing the activities into a colorful printed daily schedule, we spent one afternoon watching airplanes takeoff and land at the airport and another day walking through the History Center of Minnesota and exploring a train museum. We played miniature golf at the mall and arcade games at *Circus Pizza*. We watched a movie at the science museum's *Imax Theater.* All in all, it was very successful. It gave our family a chance to reconnect.

Year Three

What a difference a year makes! During summer three, walking became an almost daily activity. I tried to take regular walks at the lake. The problem was that if I left too late, then walking at the lake was not possible. So I moved my walk closer to home. Julian, Cameron, and Morgan would ride their bikes as my mother and I walked in the evenings. (Sometimes we walked to *Dairy Queen*.) This became a more successful plan unless I was distracted and it was too late to walk after dark. One night I started walking around our house while everyone else was inside getting ready for bed. I've continued with this walking program to date. My mother joined me and now the walk has become a time for us to "catch up" on the events of the day while we whittle our waistlines.

Summer three was a good one for us. I didn't have any classes but I did have plans to work on my dissertation all summer. What was I thinking! I was able to transcribe some of the interviews that I had completed during the previous Spring semester but in no way did I accomplish the kind of writing that I had hoped. However, it was a great summer. We spent more time together than we had in a long time. As September approached, I was anxious to return to my dissertation. When they left on the first day of school, instead of Christmas shopping, I sat down and wrote. I think the break allowed me to process the information that I had read and analyzed. I had continued to read throughout the summer despite not being focused enough to write. To prove I was never far from my research, I even took an article to a *Twins* baseball game. Since my children were on different baseball teams, we had games or practice literally six nights a week for eight weeks. I attended most of them but never without an article. They took swimming lessons and I read. Actually, I only read for the first couple of days because I found that I needed the conversation with other moms even more. I finally felt like a "regular" mom whose primary focus was her children. My children were always my primary focus, even in the depth of coursework and exams, but now I didn't have to split my time, even if it was only for two short weeks.

Survival Strategies

As the school year approached during the third year, I had every color pencil, marker, pencil, pen, eraser, highlighter, spiral notebook, and folder (times three students) labeled a week in advance. I simply generated a page of labels for each child and applied the labels to their supplies each evening until the task was complete. This was a totally different experience from the previous year when I had to do them all on Labor Day. I learned several other lessons that made life easier during this experience, too.

Survival Tips

1. McDonald's

2. Maintain balance

3. Be flexible

4. Learn to do more than one thing at a time

5. Schedule time together

6. Develop a network

7. Develop a support system

8. Plan ahead for special occasions

9. Include family when possible

10. Learn to say "NO"

11. Walk

12. Prioritize and downsize

13. Plan for the unexpected

• McDonald's

You can spend time cooking or you can spend the time connecting. We chose "connecting." Periodically, we went to McDonald's to talk while we were having dinner. Leaving the books at home (or in the car) enabled me to listen to them without compromising our time together. Sometimes this time was just an hour between classes. But this hour became a way to maintain my sanity—and to relieve my guilt.

• Maintain Balance

Balancing my children's reality was a constant concern. We continued with their cello lessons at school in addition to a private lesson on the weekend. The cello teacher split the hour between the three of them. They each competed on local baseball or t-ball teams. It was extremely helpful that the park was right across the street from our house. They took swimming lessons for the first time during summer three and participated in a singing/acting/dancing class with a theatrical production at the conclusion of the season.

While maintaining balance in their lives was a priority for me, maintaining balance in my life was a joke. I started staying up late to complete my homework. The boys catch the school bus at 7:40 each morning so we all had to get up early. I was physically exhausted from an average of five (or fewer) hours of sleep. With classes in the evening (in addition to the ones held during the day), I found myself extremely tired and sleepy. My solution for staying awake during class was to snack. Since I had at least one evening class each quarter/semester, it did not take long to accumulate ten to fifteen extra pounds! Lack of sleep, compounded with three different surgeries, made exercise virtually impossible. When I did not take care of myself, I noticed that my confidence diminished and my health deteriorated. Something had to change.

• Be Flexible

Don't be afraid to set goals. I set goals and deadlines for myself that always seemed realistic. I quickly learned that they were subject to change at a moment's notice. Learning that flexibility was not synonymous with failure was a lesson by itself. Flexibility allowed me to focus on my family as purpose instead of a distraction. Sometimes it was simply more important to close my books and join my family than it was to complete my work at that moment.

• Learn to Do More Than One Thing at a Time

Morgan started kindergarten right after summer two. Parents were encouraged to read to their children and record the experiences on a calendar. I knew that she was not going to enjoy listening to the articles that I had to read and I was already wondering how I was ever going to keep up with my required readings. Then the light came on! Julian was now in the fourth grade and Cameron was in the second grade. Students in the St. Paul School District were responsible for reading twenty-five books during the school year. So Julian and Cameron began reading their books to Morgan in the evening. While I was pleased with myself for satisfying requirements for each of them, I also was surprised to learn that Morgan had begun to read, too. She has always been convinced that she could do anything that her brothers could do. They could read so she wanted to learn to read, too. And guess what? She did! She was reading books to me in the car as we were driving. If she didn't know a word, she would spell it and we would sound it out together. I never had to take my eyes off of the road.

It became very important to be able to do at least two things at once! When I combed Morgan's hair, we counted and talked about patterns in numbers. We talked about letter sounds and word families, too.

• Schedule Time Together

Scheduling time together was a priority. One of the things that left a vivid impression on all of us was *Camp Clarkson*. This two-week period, when we did whatever they wanted to do, was filled with activities that were free or low cost. On two different occasions, they traveled with me to California and Hawaii to either attend or to present a paper at a conference. These trips were the highlight of our whole Ph.D. experience. It was worth teaching the extra class so that we could spend the time together. We were able to visit Disneyland and reconnect with family at the same time.

• Develop a Network

I had a colleague who was a semester ahead of me in her coursework. She warned me about certain paperwork or deadlines that she had recently encountered. In fact, she even delivered my papers to the graduate school office after I had completed my oral exam because I had had surgery four days before the exam. Colleagues can also give moral support. It's important to know someone who has experienced the Ph.D. process, a process that can be grueling at times. Giving up is an idea that, if entertained too long, can interfere with successful completion of a dream. It's nice to know that someone understands the frustrations as well as the joys from their own experiences.

• Develop a Support System

I could never have completed my degree in three years without the help of my mother. She cared for Julian, Cameron, and Morgan while I attended classes, conferences, and worked on exams, papers, homework, and my dissertation. She took care of the laundry, transported kids, and prepared meals. On a couple of different occasions when she was not available to help, we had to distinguish what was important from what was not. Life became an even more interesting rendition of survival. We soon accepted the fact that socks did not have to be paired before they went into the drawers.

• Plan Ahead for Special Occasions

Birthdays and holidays seemed to appear out of nowhere. I started shopping for Christmas and birthdays as sales presented themselves. If I had not started a collection of possible gifts, then we would have experienced a few more disasters. The attic and basement closets became treasure chests of future gifts. I made an effort to do the bulk of my Christmas shopping on the first day of school. While we were shopping for school supplies, they would look at the new additions to the toy aisle. I made mental notes and then went to retrieve their "heart's desires" as soon as they got on the bus for school.

• Include Family When Possible

When I had to go to the library on campus, I made it a habit of taking my children with me. I didn't take them because of babysitting concerns, but rather to include them in the process. It was important for them to see what I was going through. It gave them a better appreciation for what I was doing. It also showed them how to use the library and that if you did not know something, there are resources available. I would let the youngest one push the start button of the copy machine while the others held the sorted copies or the books waiting to be copied. It gave them a sense of being helpful.

• Learn to Say "NO"

This was one of the hardest lessons that I had to learn. I was frequently involved in my children's school fieldtrips, church, and community events. I soon downsized my involvement as a matter of survival. I learned to prioritize my time and commitments. My family and my coursework were primary and everything else became secondary—everything else, including cooking, ironing, and socializing. I remember the first time I really said "no." Actually I didn't really say no and mean it until the time commitment got in the way of completing my dissertation on time. (I wish I had said no from the beginning.) If I had to do it all over again, I would have downsized my commitments *before* I started the program. I had to become more creative about my involvement. For instance, instead of going on school field trips, I volunteered to embroider banners for each child in Morgan's kindergarten class. I also embroidered the baptismal banners for my church.

• Walk

I had to walk at least a half a mile from the parking lot to a classroom building during my first year. The morning walk provided me with the opportunity to sort the events of the day or to review the work that I had studied the night before. The afternoon walk afforded me the opportunity to organize the evening's events or to construct a shopping list to be completed on the way home. At first I complained about the length of the walk. Soon I realized that this was my only "free" time during each day. The walk became precious. Walking was a regular time to meditate. Some mornings (before it started snowing), I would stop at the park and walk around the lake before I went to campus. Walking seemed like a luxury so when I was running late or when my schedule was congested, walking was the first thing that was dropped. Any time I skipped walking, it was even easier to skip the next day. When I realized I was overly stressed (as opposed to the regular stress), I felt better after I walked. Walking gave me a chance to cleanse my soul. Sometimes the tears washed my eyes, but walking put things into perspective again. I found that I could accomplish more when walking was a regular part of my week. Walking became my therapy and I truly missed it during the second year. I finally realized the extent of the blessing of walking during the third year. I rewrote outlines, prayed many prayers, worked through tough decisions, and planned the next step for my work. Walking increased my confidence and made me a stronger person physically, mentally, and spiritually.

• Prioritize and Downsize

I went from one fire to the next, for three years. Most times, they were not a result of poor planning but rather trying to do too many things. I was actively involved in my community as an events planner for children's events in my neighborhood. It was a part of a partnership between a local grocery store, restaurant, retailer, and Concordia University. Over the course of three years, we collected school supplies for needy students, held indoor Halloween parties, collected and distributed books for Christmas, and sponsored Easter egg hunts and end of the school year barbeques where children were assisted in making Mother's day cards and presents. We even had Santa Claus arrive by helicopter! The program was valuable for the community but it was also difficult to manage while I was trying to study. After a valiant effort, I decided that I could not keep up with the program after the first year of my program.

We have a computerized embroidery machine for a home-based business that sat idle for the majority of the three years. Prior to my studies, I ran the machine for the business, *Barb's Babes,* which belongs to my mother and me. (We sewed and personalized baby bibs, bath towels, and blankets.) Computerized embroidery is a fascinating business and it was also difficult to downsize this part of my life.

I don't regret downsizing because it was key to my survival. Juggling family and studies was more than enough. Still, I had to constantly remind myself of my priorities and that family and studies were enough.

• Plan for the Unexpected
I sat down to study for my first exam in a mathematics course in approximately twenty years. I was extremely nervous. After studying for less than an hour, I had to take a child (who will remain nameless) to the emergency room to have a piece of a straw removed from the nose. I was concerned about the health and safety of my child, but the timing of this self-inflicted event angered me. I'm sure I appeared callous by bringing my book to the emergency room. I wish I could say that was the only emergency room trip for child-related events, but it was only the first of at least four other trips.

Conclusion

During a recent trip to Washington, D.C., I rode the Metro (underground train). The escalator descended more than 190 feet to the station. It seemed as though the earth swallowed the passengers. Once underground, people scurried around seeking new destinations while others continued about their business above ground, seemingly without missing those who chose to go underground. Upon reaching my destination and then returning back to the original station, I ascended on the same escalator that previously took me down to the lower level. I felt like "life" had continued for the rest of the world while I was trying to reach a new destination. It dawned on me that the Ph.D. experience has been very similar. While I was "underground" for the past thirty-six months, "life" had continued for everyone else. Did anyone miss me? Now, it's time for me to return to "life" as it is right now. I know that I'm a different person from the experience. I can also say that I'm a better person professionally. My family is also different. We're still challenged, but I have high hopes that the juggling act will turn into a balancing act. I survived—no, we survived!

Completing a Ph.D. is somewhat analogous to playing solitaire on the computer. I played to win. I didn't win all of the time but I didn't give up either. I played to win. When I didn't win, I played to prove that I could win. When I won, I continued to play to prove that it wasn't a mistake.

When all has been said and done, I'm still the sole bread winner, hand holder, nose wiper, tear dryer, homework helper, cookie baker, microwave-button-pushing-dinner maker. And yes, I am *still* sufficiently challenged. But with God's help and my family's patience, I earned a Ph.D. and I would not trade being where I am today!

Thank God for what you have. Trust GOD for what you need. *(Author unknown).*

Dr. Brenda "BJ" Jarmon

Dr. Brenda "BJ" Jarmon is an Assistant Professor in the School of Social Work at Florida State University. She received her doctorate from Florida State University in 1992. Her professional experiences include high school teaching, school social work, research design and evaluation, administrative positions, designing early intervention strategies for teen pregnancy prevention, and cultural diversity/cultural competence training. She has publications in refereed journals; has written book chapters, essays, and technical reports; and has given numerous presentations and training sessions at national, state, and local conferences and workshops.

Dr. Jarmon is the recipient of numerous awards, including the University Teaching Award, the Teaching Incentive Award, and Professor of the Year. Tallahassee Community College honored her community involvement with an award entitled, *Putting Her Stamp on Her Community.* Dr. Jarmon is a member of two honor societies: Phi Alpha and Golden Key. *Tallahassee Magazine* recognized her community service efforts in 1996 by listing her as *One of Nine People Who Make a Difference.* The National Association of Social Workers, Big Bend Unit, selected her as Social Worker of the Year. She is a member of Bethel A.M.E. Church, and she currently serves as Vice Chair for the Florida Commission on Responsible Fatherhood. She is an Advisory Board Member of *Your Voice* Talk Show and an Advisory Board Member of the Leon County Sheriff's Drill Academy.

Dr. Jarmon is currently working on two books: *Black in America: When a Ph.D. Is Still Not Enough!* will be published April 2001 and is co-authored with Dr. Lee Jones. The second book, *From Gutting Chickens To . . . Let Me Tell You What the Lord Has Done for Me!* is a personal account of Dr. Jarmon's life story. It will be published September 2001.

12

UNWRITTEN RULES OF THE GAME

Brenda "BJ" Jarmon

Introduction

This chapter examines the important role of mentoring in the early career of a new faculty member. I will draw from personal narratives to illustrate ways in which various mentors have provided guidance and insights to help me navigate the higher education system. By examining the areas of teaching, community service, and research and scholarship (the three criteria used most often to evaluate the progress of junior faculty towards tenure), I will demonstrate the important role of mentors in helping to decipher the unwritten rules within the academy.

I began my academic career at a major research university in the southeast (which I will refer to as Research University in this chapter). My career began with some controversy because I received my doctorate from the same university where I was now teaching. It is highly unusual for universities to hire their own graduates. In fact, there is an "unwritten" rule at most universities that hiring one of their own graduates perpetuates inbreeding. The general preference is that graduates should leave, acquire experiences elsewhere, and perhaps return a few years later. Having lived through this experience, I'm inclined to agree. It is awfully hard to "grow" in one's own backyard. For example, when I assumed a tenure-track position at Research University, I often felt that some of my colleagues (a few of whom taught me), and my former Dean, who had been my major advisor, still viewed me as a "graduate student." This relationship presented challenges (discussed later in this chapter) in the professional relationships we had as colleagues.

When I joined the tenure-track faculty in 1993, I was not formally mentored. There was no formal mentoring system in place at Research University; however, other colleagues had developed informal mentoring relationships. I believe that in my case, because I had been a graduate student at this university, my colleagues assumed that I did not need mentoring because I knew the system. While I had experience as a teaching assistant and an adjunct professor, this assumption was inaccurate. I needed mentoring because as a junior scholar who had never held a full-time faculty position, I knew very little about the academy and the "politics" involved. Therefore, my previous experiences could not adequately inform me in my new role as a tenure-track faculty member. I cannot recall a single incident where someone offered to "formally" mentor me as a junior faculty member, so I had to find alternative strategies to figure out how things worked. I established a good relationship with the departmental secretary, who seemed to know more than most people in my department. I asked my colleagues questions that sometimes got answers and other times did not. I was courteous, friendly, focused, and attended all the social functions in my department; however, I still felt a sense of isolation.

My former dissertation director, who was now my departmental chairperson, mentioned on one or two occasions that I should publish from my dissertation. I began to pave the way to do that, but still without any formal direction. I knew that my "chair" had published with many of her graduate students. I also recalled that we had published an article, a book chapter, and a technical report together when I was her doctoral student. I wondered why did she not ask me to publish with her, particularly because we had related interests? When I asked her, her responses ranged from, "Oh, that wasn't my project," to "I didn't want to overburden you this early in your career," to "You should concentrate on publishing from your dissertation." Since I had never published from a dissertation before and had observed the assistance that my former dissertation chair, and now colleague, offered her other students, I began to ponder what was really going on. First, I was offended by her responses because I knew that she was the principal investigator for many of the research projects she was involved in. Second, how was I supposed to publish from my dissertation without any guidance or support system in place? Third, as for being "overburdened," I thought co-authoring grants and articles, or publishing one's dissertation was supposed to begin *early* in the career of a junior scholar.

As I observed other junior and senior faculty writing articles together, authoring grants together, and cheering each other on, I wondered how I would ever become a part of their world. I often questioned why I was at this research institution when my heart and soul were into teaching and community service. How would I bridge the gap to become a consummate scholar, teacher, and community service person? By sharing with you from whence I have come, I hope to contextualize my journey as a Black woman scholar in the academy.

My Journey to the Academy

In August 1986, I left a job as the director of an alternative school for pregnant and parent teens to pursue my doctoral studies in social work as a McKnight Doctoral Fellow (a prestigious fellowship at this university). This was a major career change for me as I was making a decent salary, owned my home, and had successfully completed a master's degree in social work. Why would I want to leave my job and home, move to another state to live on ten thousand dollars a year and pursue a doctoral degree? The move offered me the opportunity to live on a college campus as a full-time student. This was significant because I had dropped out of high school at fourteen due to pregnancy, and all of my educational pursuits had been on a part-time basis while I worked full-time to support my family. By the age of fifteen, I was the mother of two children without a high school diploma. By the age of nineteen, I had begun to turn my life around. In 1969, after three years working in a poultry processing plant, I joined the Job Corps program located in Charleston, West Virginia. While a student there, I earned my GED and attended the Upward Bound Program at West Virginia State College. Faith, determination, and a positive attitude kept me persevering until I received an associate of arts degree in 1981 and a bachelor of science degree in 1983. It took ten years of night school to earn these degrees. While employed full-time as the director of an alternative school for pregnant and parent teens, I continued my educational pursuits, graduating with a master's degree in social work in 1986. While I prepared and looked forward to this opportunity to be a full-time student, by no means was I the "traditional" college student.

As a former high school dropout and teen parent, I had doubts about my ability to succeed in higher education. I took my first college entrance exam in 1970. While I cannot recall the exact test score on that test, I do remember that it was below the average, and there was much discussion about my ability to do college-level work. Through earlier experiences, I met a counselor who later became my mentor. Unlike others who doubted my ability to succeed, he recognized my persistence, patience, determination, and commitment, and guided me through the sometimes confusing maze of higher education. This counselor was the first of many people who believed in me and gave me the opportunity to prove myself. My test scores may have been low, but my determination, drive, and will to succeed overcame those low scores!

As a young parent, I was determined to emphasize the importance of education to my children. In order to *show* my son and daughter the value of an education, I committed myself to attend night school to obtain my degrees.

The low standardized scores followed me to graduate school. While I had a cumulative GPA of 3.7 for my master's in social work, my scores on the GRE were not very high. These scores again raised questions about my ability to succeed in a doctoral program. While some members of the admissions committee doubted my ability to succeed, others saw beyond the low scores and took into account my persistence and achievement under some extraordinary life situations. Despite these early concerns from some of the faculty members, I began the doctoral program in August 1986 and successfully completed the degree in 1992. A year later, in the Fall of 1993, I accepted a full-time, tenure-track position at Research University. As I began this phase of the journey, once again, I questioned how I would survive in the academy. It was not so much a question of whether I could survive; it was more a question of *whether or not this academic environment would be supportive.*

Teaching Role

Once I became a full-time faculty member, I found it very helpful to have a mentor in the area of teaching, specifically in teaching research methods. As I did not have a formal mentor in my department, I set out to find one who would offer me support in this area. That help came from one of my former professors who had taught me research methods as a doctoral student. He often said, "BJ, the best way to learn something is to teach it." Once he realized my sincere interest, he became my chief advisor. He provided substantive feedback and guidance about my course syllabi, texts and other assigned readings for the class, methods of student evaluation, and various other suggestions to improve my teaching. Initially, we co-taught the research methods course, and in 1995, I began teaching the course on my own. Until I extended myself to my mentor, I found it difficult to "figure out" teaching at the university level.

As I settled into my teaching role and became comfortable with the organization and content of my course, another issue of concern emerged, that is, dealing with students who did not want to be want to be taught by a Black female professor and thus challenged my authority in the classroom. I recall one incident where one graduate student, who was not even enrolled in my class, claimed that he had an "issue with me." Instead of discussing "the issue" with me first, he went straight to the dean to raise his concerns. In turn, the dean called me to inform me about her one-hour long discussion with the student. When I asked the dean why she had allowed this student to discuss the situation without first consulting me, she responded, "He says he's scared to approach you." I bristled at this statement, because I knew this student was very vocal and had never demonstrated any "fear of me" in the past. More perplexing was my dean's attitude and response to this situation. I believe the dean took me to task based on a "White" graduate student's word. Not only did the dean's response compromise my professional integrity, but it also made me more aware of the politics of being a Black woman in higher education.

How did I resolve this situation? I requested a meeting with the student and the dean together, so we could all meet face-to-face. Early into our conversation, the dean discovered that the student had blown the situation completely out of proportion. The student apologized and explained that he did not mean any harm and was certainly "not trying to interfere with my tenure process." When the student made that statement, the dean asked, "How did you know that Dr. Jarmon may be going up for tenure . . . I've never heard of a student keeping check on a professor's tenure clock." Needless to say, the dean was thoroughly embarrassed and ended the meeting. Once the student left, she tried to apologize but it was too late and too placid! It was insulting enough to be called in, but such blatant disrespect from my colleague was more disturbing. But then, I had to remember that in the eyes of the dean, I was still her student and not her colleague.

Community Service

It is critical for junior faculty, especially faculty of color, to find balance between their commitments and interests in the community (within and beyond the university) and the demands of scholarship and research. Community service is important, but as a junior scholar it is imperative to weight it according to the type of institution where one is employed. At major research universities, community service takes a minor role because establishing a research agenda and publication record is paramount. There are high demands on women, and in particular "minority" women, for committee work and other service requirements, and we are generally over-extended. Given our multiple roles, learning to balance is important for our success and sometimes mere survival in the academy. In my case, I refused to give up my activities in the community; therefore, I had to work fourteen to sixteen hours per day to live my passion (community service and teaching) and still try to write, publish, and secure grant dollars. In hindsight, I would not recommend that anyone choose this path. The rationale for my decision was grounded in the fact that I am a product of the community. It was that "village" that helped me in my darkest hours. My community is an integral part of me and I can never give it up—not even for tenure. That, however, is my choice.

Research and Scholarship

Research and pursuit of scholarship are two key areas in the professional lives of faculty, especially at research universities. Early in my academic career, my major professor mentioned on one or two occasions that I needed to publish from my dissertation. I heeded her advice and attempted do so; however, I found myself diverted and caught up in my passion—teaching and community service. By the end of the second year, I still had no clue about how to proceed with my publications. I witnessed other colleagues inviting each other to publish and write grants together but none approached me. To address this situation, I sought out colleagues from other colleges and universities to publish with. This arrangement became my lifeline. Still, I wanted to publish with colleagues in my department. Once again, I found myself "reaching out to" and "asking" my colleagues to include me in their grant proposals and in joint publications. Only two out of a twenty-plus full-time faculty responded positively to my invitations and agreed to work with me. These two faculty members became my surrogate mentors. One invited me to write a chapter for a book he was editing, while the other provided step-by-step guidance on how to parcel out my dissertation for publication. In addition to the support of these two colleagues, I sought out colleagues beyond my department and at other universities and collaborated with them on research projects and publications. Still, I felt the isolation!

One of the critical components in the survival of junior faculty is to concentrate on writing manuscripts for publication. Even in the absence of a mentor, I had to keep my nose to the keyboard, and write, and write, and write. More importantly, once the manuscripts were written, I had to get them off my desk and into the mail. As vulnerable as I might have felt, a manuscript on my desk was absolutely no good.

Grants are similarly important, and it is important that junior faculty acquire and refine their grant-writing skills early in their (our) academic careers. As a new scholar, opportunities to participate in grant activities were slow. I learned early that research funds go to those who have a proven track record of research in a certain area. As such, I had to find and define an area of research interest and develop sufficient experience and expertise in it. Allow me to share a strategy that I employed in this regard.

One of my primary areas of research is designing early intervention strategies for teen pregnancy prevention. In my quest to garner dollars for my research, I periodically (at least once a semester) approached my departmental colleagues who had similar research interests about applying for joint grants. Often, they did not respond. Even though we were working in the same area, they perceived my work as "different." I decided to take the positive approach to their disinterest in my work and conducted workshops, training, seminars, and symposia related to teen pregnancy prevention. As a result of getting my research out into the "real world," funding agencies became familiar with my work and grant opportunities began to flow my way. All of a sudden, my colleagues wanted to collaborate on research grants. Once again, I had to prove myself in an environment that was not used to a Black female scholar teaching research, let alone bringing in grant dollars.

One of the critical issues that many junior faculty have to face is how to prepare a tenure and promotion portfolio. Mentoring is critical in this area. Ideally, finding a mentor within one's department is best; however, in my case, where such relationships had not been well developed, I had to employ an alternative strategy and find colleagues outside my department to guide me through the tenure and promotion process. I took an interdisciplinary approach to my work and established solid relationships with faculty in other departments, who turned out to be great mentors. Although I thought I had followed all the rules—that is, published in refereed journals, secured grant monies, performed community service within and outside of the university, and done all the "right" things—when I submitted my tenure and promotion binder during the 1999–2000 school year, my portfolio was not enough to be granted promotion and tenure. According to the dean (and my former dissertation advisor), the primary explanation was, "None of your articles are in a level one journal; you need to improve your scholarship." This was despite the fact that I had published eight articles in refereed journals, authored four book chapters, authored and co-authored four technical reports, and secured more than $650,000 in grant monies. How else was I supposed to improve my scholarship?

Given the challenges presented in the preceding discussion, how can institutions of higher education provide realistic, holistic, and prolific mentoring to junior faculty? How can institutions of higher education begin to acknowledge the existence and persistence of "isms," which so often place minority women, and specifically, Black women, at the receiving end of oppression and discrimination? This is a difficult task, but until colleges and universities are willing to admit to their own flaws, we will struggle with these questions for years to come.

Dr. Thandeka Joyce F. Kirk

Dr. Thandeka Joyce F. Kirk is an associate professor at the University of Wisconsin–Milwaukee (UWM) in the Department of Africology. The name Thandeka was given to Kirk in March 1999, when she was inducted into the *Magcina* clan at a formal ceremony in Guguletu, an African township near Cape Town, South Africa. Her South African "sister" from the Xhosa-speaking people bestowed the name upon Kirk, which means "lovable." This was the first formal naming ceremony of an African American that anyone from the clan could remember.

Dr. Kirk worked for several years before pursuing undergraduate studies full time at the University of Illinois, Chicago, where she majored in history and Black studies and minored in education. Kirk began graduate school in 1977 at the University of Wisconsin–Madison along with two other African American females. Kirk and her colleagues were the first Black females to complete doctorate degrees in African history at this university. Kirk conducted her field research in South Africa and completed her doctorate in 1987.

In 1988 she spent a year at the University of Michigan, Ann Arbor, as a *Dubois, Mandela, Rodney Post-doctorate Fellow.* Subsequently, in August 1990, she relocated to Milwaukee, Wisconsin, to work in the Department of Afro-American Studies, later changed to the Department of Africology. Kirk was tenured in 1995.

Kirk continues to conduct research or participate in special projects in South Africa. She has published articles on African resistance to segregation in the nineteenth and early twentieth centuries and on African Americans in South Africa in the nineteenth century. In 1999, her book, *Making a Voice: African Resistance to Segregation in South Africa,* was awarded the Kenneth Kingery prize, sponsored by the Council of Wisconsin Writers, for the best scholarly publication in history. She is currently working on three projects: 1) the NTU Rites of Passage Institute program in the United States; 2) the extended family of *Sangomas* (traditional healers) in Cape Town, South Africa, and 3) a study of African Americans in South Africa in the twenty-first century. Kirk recently assumed the position of executive director of the Institute of Race and Ethnicity for the University of Wisconsin system.

13

NOT AN *HONORARY WHITE*

CONDUCTING RESEARCH DURING THE DAYS OF APARTHEID

Thandeka Joyce F. Kirk

Background to Fieldwork in South Africa

This chapter is concerned primarily with my experiences as an African American female graduate student doing field research in South Africa for the first time from October 1981 to January 1983. As I relate throughout the chapter, rather than the *honorary White* status,[1] which historically could exempt foreigners from the apartheid (racial separation) laws as they applied to Black South Africans, I often encountered racial discrimination, segregation, and biased treatment. This was because I share many physical features with Black South African women, for example, skin color, cheekbones, body build, and height (I also wore my hair in a short, natural hairstyle). Thus, until they heard my "American" accent, I faced racial discrimination from Whites. I chose not to display my United States passport, which could have resulted in Whites

---

1. Keto, T. C., "Black Americans and South Africa, 1890–1910," *A Current Bibliography on African Affairs*, 5, 4, July 1972; 382–406. The question was, Were Black Americans to be treated like native Africans and segregated from whites and discriminated against by race, or accorded special privileges that were denied to native Africans and thus allocated an *honorary white* status? Black Americans were required to register at the Consular Agency in Johannesburg and issued with passports. Black Americans in possession of such passports were given the status of "honorary whites" allowing them special privileges such as riding on trains in the same section as whites and using the same hotels as the whites, which were denied to native Africans.

according me special treatment and privileges compared to Black South Africans, for example, sitting in the first-class section on the trains and residing in the same hotels as Whites. I was more interested, however, in understanding the experience of Black South Africans, including the kinds of discrimination they had to navigate in South Africa.

Thinking back over my sixteen months of fieldwork in South Africa during the days of apartheid, I wondered how to explain my everyday life, which included events that had less to do with research in the archives or the library, and much more to do with being Black and living under apartheid. As the editors of *In Pursuit of History: Fieldwork in Africa* indicate, " . . . historical fieldwork in Africa is nothing if not an event in itself" (Adenaike & Vensina, 1996, p. xvii). Yet, my research tenure in South Africa was especially potent because I was among a small number of people of African descent during the entire twentieth century to do field research for a doctorate degree in African history in Africa.

This may sound strange to many who are unaware of the fact that the majority of people doing field research in Africa for a doctorate in history have been of European descent, whether from Europe or America or born in Africa. It is only recently that the number of people of African descent living outside of Africa doing doctoral fieldwork has begun to increase.[2] Why? Primarily because of the history of colonialism, racism, white supremacy, and until recently, Western educational policies and societal practices that discriminated against and prevented most people of African descent from pursuing higher education.

I was anxious about doing fieldwork in urban areas, since most studies heretofore seemed to focus on research in rural settings. Many academics, it seemed to me at the time, thought of fieldwork as living in a rural village with

---

2. At the time I began research in Johannesburg, my friend Keletso Atkins, another African American female graduate student at Wisconsin was doing her research in Natal. Also, Lynda Day, my friend and another African American female graduate student at Madison, was in Sierra Leone doing research. Also, three African American males who did research in Africa come to mind; all were professors at the University of Wisconsin–Madison when I was a graduate student. Following are their names and the areas where they did research: Richard Ralston, South Africa; William B. Brown, Ethiopia; and Tom Shick (deceased), Liberia. Two African American males who completed doctorates in African history were David Anthony and Adell Patton. Among the African graduate students doing doctorate research at the same time as I were Ishmael Abdullah, Mushame Muchambaicham, and Jacob Mohlamme. Jacob was the first African to receive a doctorate in history in all of South Africa. It is noteworthy that Wisconsin is well known for its Africanist program. However, since the time when two other African American women and I completed doctorate degrees in African history, I know of no other African Americans who have completed the program at this university.

the host country's people rather than living in a city with modern amenities as I would be. I also wondered how to go about getting the information I needed from people living in both the city and the rural areas. In any case, when I left for the field, I understood that in doing fieldwork one must locate sources by whatever means necessary, be ethical, not jeopardize one's long-term health, and return home to write the story. In addition, there were no field research classes offered at the University of Wisconsin–Madison; rather, field research methods were developed partly by independent work with individual students. While there were many stories and much discussion about the research done by our professors, no formal courses were offered.

Some might ask why is it so important for historians to do field research, especially for early historical topics, many of which can be researched in the archives and libraries outside of Africa? After all, we are not anthropologists, which is the discipline usually associated with participant observation methods and living with the people in a host society. My answer is that no piece of paper in an archive or library can relate a story in the same way as living in a society and observing and interrelating with its people to learn about the culture. Field research gives life to the stories gleaned from research documents. In particular, because Africa was colonized, the documents often present only the colonial and often racially prejudiced and ethnocentric viewpoint. In order to present a balanced view, it helps to know something about the people and culture. Even if only a small portion of the oral information is used in the study, the experience of observing in the society one is writing about is invaluable.

My desire to travel to South Africa began when I was an undergraduate student at the University of Illinois, Chicago, where I majored in history and Black studies. While taking a course in African and African American literature taught by Sterling Plumpp, a professor in the Department of Black Studies, I first heard about the Limpopo river in Zimbabwe. Limpopo was music to my ears and somehow touched a place deep inside of me: I wanted to go to the area where the river with such a musical name existed. I made up my mind that one day I would go to Southern Africa and find out for myself what was going on there.

The more I learned about South Africa, the more I wanted to go there because I realized that similarities existed between the experiences of African people in South Africa and African Americans under White supremacy in the United States. In general, White supremacy "refers to the attitudes, ideologies, and policies associated with the rise of blatant forms of white or European dominance over 'nonwhite' populations . . . In its fully developed form, White supremacy means color bars, racial segregation, and the restriction of meaningful citizenship rights to a privileged group characterized by its light pigmentation . . . White supremacy suggests systematic and self-conscious efforts to make race or color a qualification for membership in the civil community" (Fredrickson, 1981, p. xi). Under White supremacy, Black peoples faced attacks on their religion, language, physical characteristics, and the denial of civil and human rights. I felt a kinship with the Africans in South Africa based on the knowledge that their skin color, like mine, was used by Whites to justify discriminatory racial practices to insure the subordination of Black peoples. The aim of White supremacy in the United States and in South Africa was to prevent Black people from competing with Whites in every arena: jobs, housing, education, and politics.

Although South Africa was controlled by a White minority and the United States by a White majority, the institutions created to promote Jim Crow segregation in the southern United States and racial segregation and later apartheid in South Africa were essentially the same. A series of laws were created and implemented by the governments, backed by the local military, and administered by Whites to ensure racial separation and the supremacy of Whites over Blacks. In both societies, Blacks were expected to defer to Whites, and personal intimidation and force were tools used to ensure that *Blacks knew their place.* The similar experiences of Blacks in the two places drew me to South Africa. I wanted to go and see for myself what life was like in South Africa, to see the land that I had heard so much about, and to experience how I would be treated by both Blacks and Whites.

I completed my doctorate coursework and passed my preliminary exams in 1980. I applied for a Social Science Research Council (SSRC) Fellowship and a Title IV Language Fellowship to conduct field research in South Africa. I planned to do research on the first Black trade union in South Africa, the Industrial and Commercial Worker's Union (ICU), focusing on the Transvaal (now Gauteng and Mpumalanga) and the eastern Cape region. The ICU functioned from 1916 to 1930 and had branches throughout South Africa. My plan was to conduct archival and library research and to interview people who had been members of the ICU, as well as relatives of members. By examining previous writings, I had identified the specific geographical areas where I could look for individuals who might know something about the ICU.

In 1980 I applied for a research visa to do fieldwork in South Africa. Because research visas were issued for one year, compared to three-month visas for visitors, they were more difficult to obtain. My advisor told me that I might not be issued a research visa and that perhaps I had better think about doing research elsewhere. In general, African Americans were viewed as a threat because they had their "freedom" in America and might be agitators against the apartheid system.[3] The apartheid government, established in 1949 with the election of the Afrikaner Nationalist party, was controlled by a White minority.[4] The Nationalist party strengthened the already existing system of racial segregation with the passage of several laws to entrench White supremacy and Black subordination. These laws, including the *Groups Areas Act*, the *Population Registration Act, Influx Control Laws*, and the *Internal Security Act*, resulted in rampant racial discrimination and suppression in the political and socioeconomic arenas.[5] The objective of the laws was to ensure that Blacks would not be able to compete with Whites for jobs and would remain virtually landless and poor. The apartheid government often justified its stringent security laws and abuse of civil and human rights by claiming that it faced a total onslaught from terrorists engaged in measures to overthrow, undermine, and destabilize the government.

By the early 1980s, Black protest in South Africa, with White liberal support against apartheid laws and practices, resulted in strong government suppression: banning, detention laws, treason trials, roadblocks, and the almost routine murder of Black and White activists by government officials. The African National Congress (ANC), the long-time Black protest organization established in 1912, was banned, and occasionally bombings of soft targets were reported; these bombings were directed at buildings where loss of human life would be minimal, such as magistrate courts and police stations.

Despite the situation in South Africa, I thought my advisor's pessimism was misplaced. Perhaps naively, my fear was not about the apartheid total

---

3. Apparently the idea of Black Americans as a threat is linked to the early contact between them and Black South Africans in the nineteenth and twentieth centuries, in particular, the visit of Bishop Henry McNeal Turner of the African Methodist Episcopal Church (AME) in 1898 to the Cape colony. His activities were viewed by many Whites as both religious and political and a movement to oust the Europeans. See Chapter 7 of Thandeka Joyce F. Kirk (2000), *Making A Voice: African Resistance to Segregation in South Africa.*

4. The Afrikaners are ancestors of the Dutch; the first Whites to settle in South Africa in the Cape area in 1652 and the architects of apartheid. The Dutch intermarried with French settlers and indigenous Africans to create a distinct White group of people who called themselves Afrikaners and their language Afrikaans. The second White group to arrive at the Cape and establish a government in 1806 were the British. The two White groups were at odds with one another for almost a century. Following the South African War from 1899 to 1902, the British slowly came to terms with the conquered Afrikaners. With the establishment of the Republic of South Africa in 1910 and the exclusion of the Africans from the franchise, Whites pursued a policy of racial separation and segregation and White dominance and control.

5. Most of these laws were passed between 1950 and 1952. See William Bigelow (1985), *Strangers in Their Own Country: A Curriculum Guide on South Africa,* for a detailed discussion of these laws.

onslaught, but rather when I would be able to fulfill my dream of traveling to South Africa to live and do fieldwork for my doctoral dissertation. After all, I had studied the Xhosa language for two years and had planned to travel to South Africa for several years. The probable fieldwork was my golden opportunity. In any case, I intended to go to South Africa even if it might be difficult to get a visa. I waited and I waited for my visa: three, six, eight months passed. Then I received a call from the South African Consulate in Chicago, telling me that two consulate officials would be in Madison on business and they would like to meet with me to discuss my proposed research. I agreed. We met. I did not relate the entire truth because I feared they might view my topic on the ICU as too sensitive. Within a month after meeting the officials I received the visa and quickly prepared to depart for South Africa.

South Africa Bound

En route to South Africa I spent one-and-a-half weeks in Oxford, England, to peruse sources relevant to my research and to speak to Colin Bundy (now Vice-Chancellor of the University of the Witwatersrand in South Africa), and William Beinart and Stanley Trapido, who provided useful insights about my research. While I was in England, I sent a telegram to South Africa requesting that my friends, Jacob and Peggy Mohlamme, meet me at the airport. Although there was no time to receive a reply, I assumed they would be there when I arrived. I had met Jacob and Peggy in the late 1970s while a graduate student at the University of Wisconsin–Madison. Jacob and I were both pursuing doctorates in South African history. Peggy was a head nurse at a large hospital in South Africa that served only Blacks.[6] We became friends and they suggested I stay with them my first week in South Africa so I could become acclimated and they could show me around. I agreed. Because they lived relatively close to Johannesburg, this seemed a good way to start my first visit.

I arrived the morning of October 1, 1981, at Jan Smuts Airport in Johannesburg, expecting to meet the Mohlammes. Since this was my first time travelling to South Africa, I was very excited. I was also filled with some trepidation because I was not certain my friends had received the telegram or if they would be at the airport. I encountered no problems with my visa or customs, and after claiming my luggage, I looked for Jacob and Peggy. No familiar faces emerged from the crowd except that of Dr. Neil Maganyi. I had met

---

6. Jacob Mohlamme is presently Professor and Chair of the Department of History at Vista University–Soweto Campus, while Peggy Mohlamme continues to work as head matron at a hospital.

Dr. Maganyi, another passenger going to Johannesburg, in the airport during a brief stopover to refuel at Nairobi, Kenya. He was very polite and well spoken, taught psychology at the University of the Witwatersrand (Wits) and was attached to the African Students Institute. Ironically, this was the institute with which I would be affiliated as a visiting student researcher. We talked about this coincidence, and I told him about expecting to meet my friends at the airport. I found out later that he was the only Western-trained Black psychologist with a doctorate in South Africa. In any case, before we reboarded the airplane, he told me to be sure to let him know if my friends were not at the airport.

Now, here we were at the airport and my friends were nowhere to be seen. Probably noting the distress on my face, Dr. Manganyi approached me, asking, "Is there anything wrong?" I replied, "Well, my friends are not here, so I don't know what to do." Immediately he suggested that we share a taxi to the university. He said he had a flat tire and his car was parked in the university parking lot. Consequently, he had to go to the university and have it repaired and then he could take me where I needed to go. At his office we tried to contact my friends by phone, without success. I was worried. The two people I knew in South Africa had vanished. For all I knew they might be detained by the South African police. I had no idea where I would stay.

The Housing Problem

While Dr. Manganyi tried to get his flat tire fixed, I talked with the secretary and others at the African Studies Institute office. Meanwhile, the director of the Institute, Charles van Onselen, arrived, and welcomed me. Shortly after, his wife, Belinda Bozzoli, a sociology professor teaching at the university, entered. After hearing of my dilemma, Bozzoli offered to call her friend, who was the warden (the dorm director) at Jubilee Hall, a campus dorm for women only, to see if any space was available. The warden said they had a guestroom vacant for one week and I could stay there. Normally these guestrooms were reserved for visiting professors and this particular room had been booked for one week by a professor from the United States. A change of plans led to the room being available. I found out later that the professor was Richard Ralston, an African American from the University of Wisconsin–Madison, whom I knew personally. Apparently he had booked the room far ahead and needed to change his schedule. How fortunate for me!

That day I moved into the guestroom in Jubilee Hall. It included a sitting room, bedroom, and bathroom for R10 per day including meals; in those days, a bargain. As I entered, I spoke to several African students and we exchanged names. To my surprise, I knew the name of one of the students,

Teboho Moja. She was about to leave to attend the University of Wisconsin–Madison to study for a doctorate in education.[7] Coincidentally, she was one of the first people I met at Jubilee Hall; after I returned to Madison, we became good friends, and our friendship continues to this day. That evening she and some of the other African women students came to visit me and began telling me that this was the first year that Jubilee Hall had allowed African women to reside there. At first they were installed in the sick bay rather than given rooms. The sick bay was a separate area with beds for patients, so initially they were all segregated there together. By January 1981 they were allocated rooms. Prior to this, Jubilee Hall had been for Whites only.

Now the White female students were complaining about the Black students and wanted them barred from living at Jubilee. The complaints included, "The Black students are not clean and smell," "They were too loud," and so on: shades of segregation in the United States. I had read about this type of reaction from Whites in the United States to Black people when Blacks began to integrate schools and dorms, so I was not totally surprised.

Once I secured temporary housing, I began trying to locate permanent lodging, which I would need for about six months. I approached the warden, a middle-aged White female, and inquired about staying for a longer period at Jubilee Hall. A few days later the warden told me that, "the Dean of Jubilee Hall said that she had rooms available but she could not rent to me because she had been given strict instructions by the Registrar not to rent to any more Blacks." The warden continued that "if she got the registrar's permission, she would rent me a room." I complained bitterly to Charles Van Onselen and others about my quandary. I wrote a letter to the registrar two days later and he responded the next day, saying I could stay in Jubilee Hall as long as I was in South Africa. During this time, my friends Jacob and Peggy Mohlamme contacted me by phone and came over to pick me up my second weekend in South Africa. They apologized for the confusion and explained that they were not at the airport because they were on vacation when I arrived and did not see my telegram until they returned home, a week later.

Soweto

Meanwhile, I applied to another place for university housing. I spoke to the warden, an African man named Dudu Kunene, and was immediately offered a

---

7. She completed successfully and most recently was advisor to the Minister of Education in South Africa from 1994 to 1999.

room. The room was at Glynn Thomas House in Soweto. Soweto is an acronym for southwest townships. It was established around 1954 near Johannesburg by the apartheid government to residentially segregate Africans. The intent was to create an urban homeland whereby Africans were separated according to ethnic background. This would theoretically prevent African unity and foster ethnic separatism. But Africans, desperate for housing, simply moved into areas regardless of ethnic background and the intended separation did not occur. Among the population of about two million were Zulu, Xhosa, Tswana, Sotho, Shangaan, and Venda.

Glynn Thomas House was situated on the Baragwanath hospital grounds in Soweto. Baragwanath was and still is the largest hospital in all of South Africa for Africans. Glynn Thomas House was the name of student dorms originally constructed for White medical students attending Wits. Since it was constructed for White students, it had all the basic amenities, including a laundromat, and there were tennis and handball courts on the grounds. It turned out that Glynn Thomas House was too far from the university and White students did not like travelling so far or living that close to Soweto. To enter the complex, one passed through a security gate and showed proper identification, so it was relatively safe.

I decided to move into Glynn Thomas House because I was welcomed and because it would be easier to make contact with Soweto residents. I lived there from October 1981 to April 1982. My housing at Glynn Thomas turned out to be an ideal situation because I was able to interact with many diverse students to find out about South African society and culture, as well as political activities. Students taught me specific words and phrases in Zulu, the language spoken most often by Africans in Johannesburg, and how to get from place to place. Students with relatives living in Soweto and Alexandra, another township further away from Johannesburg, invited me to their homes. When I needed an interpreter for interviews, students assisted me. In all cases, I was treated with great care and respect and invited to return. I became very close to several students and their families in Soweto, with whom I continue to correspond and visit when I go to South Africa. They were invaluable friends, always providing help when I needed it. My first weekend living in Soweto, I went home with a female friend. I noted in my diary:

> Soweto had hardly any night lights, very dark. Very little grass or trees. Some people burn fires at night for cooking. The houses are close together, maybe two rooms, made of brick. The streets and yards are very dirty, probably very little garbage collection by the city. It's completely different from the Johannesburg "white" area where there

are beautiful green landscaped areas with trees and grass that is very well cared for. Africans are all crowded into Soweto, which consists of many townships, made up of ethnic zones, e.g. Dube, Meadowlands, and Mofolo North; all classes of people thrown together. My friend's sister and brother-in-law have a two-room flat. Reminds me of our house in Chicago when I was growing up and we had a coal stove. Most people have no electricity and cook with coal fires. At cooking time the whole place is enveloped by smoke. It looks like smog city. It's like a city placed in the middle of nowhere. A suburb without facilities to service it.

I also noted that despite the small size of the house, my friends' sister had a big color television, about twenty-one inches. At this time, South Africa was just getting national television and most people did not have them yet. Programs were broadcast for only six hours a day; three hours in English and three in Afrikaans. The brother-in-law indicated that future plans included offering television in all of the major African languages, which he thought would be a mess. I supposed this was because there are about ten separate languages. Many of the programs were dubbed. I remember standing in the small shopping mall near Baragwanath hospital one evening. I was watching television with other people through the window of a store where they sold televisions. *Ben-Hur* was on and Charleton Heston was dubbed in Afrikaans. It was hilarious, especially since the words did not match the movements of the mouths. Nonetheless, everyone watching was very excited to see the images and talking animatedly.

Race, Color, and Language

When I went to South Africa to do research, and when I returned to the United States in 1983, there was talk about African Americans acquiring an *honorary White* status while they were in South Africa. About six months after I returned to the United States, I gave a presentation on my research. One question was "Were you treated as an honorary White?" My answer was "I am not sure what you mean, but I was treated as any other Black African; that is, judged by my skin color first, and then insulted accordingly by most Whites." Most Black people accepted me as a Black woman who looked like them. Although I could not speak their language fluently, they treated me well, often like a guest or a visiting member of the family.

In fact, initially I was often taken for a South African because I knew the rudiments of Xhosa and Zulu and could extend greetings and carry on a simple conversation.[8] As mentioned, because of my outward appearance, I was often treated by other Black South Africans as a sister or *dade wethu* (Xhosa), especially when I greeted them in an African language.

For my part, I preferred not to advertise that I was from the United States because I was trying to blend in and be a part of the culture. Sometimes this practice could result in interesting scenarios. On one occasion I was driving through an unfamiliar area in Soweto and, after greeting an African woman, I asked for directions in English. She responded in her language and asked why I wanted to speak in English. I replied, "I am not from here and cannot speak the language, so could you speak in English."[9] She thought I was pretending to be from another country and trying to be uppity. Apparently some Africans would pretend they were from the United States and could only speak English or that they were from some other African country. This tended to occur among Africans who liked imitating African Americans, especially Black teenagers and some college students. Some were confused about their identity; others admired "hip" African Americans and claimed not to be South African.

The woman became quite angry and started to talk loudly and berate me. I protested that I was telling the truth. Another African woman walking by overheard us and spoke to me in English. I explained the problem. She spoke to the first woman, explaining that I was from the United States and was telling the truth about not being able to speak her language. The first woman, now convinced, apologized and insisted that I drive her home so she could serve me tea and make up for treating me badly. I drove her home, we went in, she introduced me to all of her relatives, and we had tea. Subsequently, they directed me to my destination.

Similar scenarios unfolded in and around the Black townships near Johannesburg but in reverse. That is, once we had greeted each other, people would often ask me for directions in their language. Since my vocabulary was limited and I would switch to English, they thought I was trying to be uppity. Once the problem was resolved, the Africans always looked amazed, probably thinking, "But she looks so much like us." Clearly my skin color and physical features opened many African doors for me while closing some White ones.

---

8. I studied Xhosa for two years at the University of Wisconsin–Madison with various instructors. My reading and comprehension were good, but speaking was only fair.

9. Tefetso Henry Mothibe's, "Fieldwork Among Neighbors: An African's View of Another African Country," relates that when he interviewed older workers in Zimbabwe and could not speak their language, they said, "You're black: Why can't you speak Shona? Are you too proud to do so?" In C. K. Adenaike & J. Vansina (Eds.) (1996), *In Pursuit of History: Fieldwork in Africa,* (p. 15). Portsmouth: Heinemann.

While I was offered food and housing by Africans, this did not occur as often with Whites. Yet, many of the people who helped me were of different ethnic backgrounds, including White and Black students and ordinary Africans who extended *ubuntu* (hospitality). Certainly the apartheid laws of the country, which separated Whites and Blacks, led many Whites and Blacks to judge me by my skin color. Most Blacks accepted me and viewed me as a sister or auntie. Oftentimes, Whites rejected me on sight, considering me less of a person because of my skin color. Just like South African Blacks, I faced racial discrimination in housing and in public places such as stores, restaurants, theaters, and the archives. I was always involved in negotiating apartheid situations.

For much of the sixteen months of my research in South Africa, I lived in several different areas of the country: about seven months in Soweto near Johannesburg; about three months in Guguletu near Cape Town; about three months in Grahamstown in the eastern Cape; and finally, about three months in Pretoria. At the time, Pretoria was known as the Afrikaner stronghold because it was controlled by the Afrikaners and more of them lived there than English-speaking Whites. Pretoria is located about an hour's drive from Johannesburg. In each of the places I lived, I encountered various degrees and types of racial discrimination.

On one occasion, I went into a store in Johannesburg to buy a cold drink. I was the next to be waited on and a White man entered the store. The White female clerk turned to him and asked him what he wanted. I said to her, "Excuse me, I am next in line." She said, "Wait your turn." I walked out of the store. The man the proprietor was trying to wait on came out of the store after me and apologized for the behavior of the White clerk. He said, "I am sorry, I don't agree with what she did." I was livid. I looked at him and walked away. Similarly, in grocery stores in Cape Town, many of the colored clerks at the delicatessen counter would try to ignore the Black customers and wait on the White or colored ones first. On several occasions I had to speak up to inform the clerk I was next in line. With regard to restaurants and theaters, it was understood that one had to check, and perhaps even call ahead, to see if the restaurant would seat Blacks. When I lived in Grahamstown in the eastern Cape, I shared a house with five White students from Rhodes University. Sometimes if I was with some of my housemates when we traveled to Port Elizabeth, we would stop at a restaurant for dinner and no proprietor ever refused to serve us. I never showed my passport because the American accent, rather than the skin color, won out and I was politely served. In all these places I faced insults because of my skin color. Stories some tell, and that I have read, of the *honorary White* status for African Americans was not something that occurred nor something that I wanted. What I did want was to be treated courteously as a person and not because I carried a United States passport.

Research at the Archives

For the most part, I was the only Black researcher doing archival work at the Pretoria archives, although on one visit, I met an African man doing research. Since the archives were located in the government buildings in Pretoria (about an hour by car from Johannesburg), I often rode with a young White man named Jeremy. We went several days a week with a group of graduate students and visiting professors. Except for me, all were White.

At the government archives, I was treated on the surface as any other researcher, but I began to notice that there was a lot more personal interplay (chatting, discussions about sources, suggestions for sources) between the White archivists and the White researchers. The documents were kept in brown boxes and the number of boxes we could order at one time was limited, but White researchers were able to order a lot more boxes than I was. I began to think the rules were different for Black researchers. When I mentioned this to the archivist, I was able to begin ordering more boxes than was the norm, or perhaps the staff brought them out more quickly. Apparently, while a limited number could be ordered, it was possible to submit the cards earlier and thus receive the boxes sooner. At all times the men bringing out the boxes for the researchers were Black, while the archivists sitting behind the desk were White. Clearly a class hierarchy existed, and White archivists often assumed a superior attitude toward the Black men. In 1982, I lived for almost three months in Pretoria with five housemates, white men and women from diverse backgrounds. They included three Americans and a married couple, an Afrikaner and English woman. Technically this was illegal because it was a White area, but most people in the neighborhood and passersby seemed to think I was the maid.

For the two months of October and November, I was driving to the archives five days a week. Each day I walked past the guard who stood at the bottom of the steps, like a sentinel, to keep out those who did not belong. He was an older White Afrikaner, and although he spoke to everyone else, he refused to speak to me or acknowledge my existence. I intentionally spoke to him every single day to watch his reaction, which resembled a constipated person in pain. By the end of my stay, he was nodding but he never uttered a word.

In contrast to the poor attitudes of the archivists in Pretoria, the archivists in Cape Town were friendly, polite, and helpful. Nonetheless, one day in the Cape Town archives, a White female employee insulted me in the bathroom lounge. There was a couch in the lounge area and since I did not feel well, I decided to lie down. A White female employee entered, looked at me on the couch, and said in a hostile tone, "What do you think you are doing?" I gaped and told her, "I have as much right to be here as you." She walked out. I was furious. I went back to my desk inside the archives, thought about what happened, and told the archivist that I wanted to report how I had been insulted. The archivist recounted what had happened to the Director, who later called me in to apologize and say that the woman was quite ignorant. He assured me that she had been spoken to and this would not happen again. He insisted that she was part of the secretarial staff in the administration building where the archives were housed and not part of the archival staff. He implied that, compared to the better-educated and more liberal White staff, she was uneducated and ignorant. This tendency, for White South Africans to claim their liberalism in opposition to other ignorant Whites, was something I encountered more than once. It was as though they were saying if they had any control or any say, things would be different for the Black people because they were liberals and did not agree with apartheid laws. apartheid was a contradiction for many Whites who said they opposed the racial laws, but were afraid of breaking laws from which they clearly benefited.

Cape Province

I completed my research in the Johannesburg area and drove with a friend to Cape Town. My plan was to spend about six months researching the ICU in the Cape Province, about two months in Cape Town using the archives, and then travelling to the Eastern Cape where I would stay three months or so doing interviews with older people who were ICU members. Thus, I would cover the towns of Port Elizabeth, King Williamstown, and East London, where ICU branches had existed. I decided to make my base in Grahamstown for three reasons. First, I knew Jeff Peires,[10] a graduate of the University of Wisconsin–Madison and now a professor of history at Rhodes University in Grahamstown. Second, there were archives at the university that I thought might be useful. Finally, Grahamstown was situated between Port Elizabeth and East London: I could head in either direction to do interviews. While in

---

10. I met Jeff in Madison when he returned for a semester to defend his dissertation while I was doing graduate work. I found him intellectual, open-minded, and sensitive. He always extended an equal welcome to other scholars and me. Jeff authored the classic book on the Xhosa-speaking people entitled, *The House of Phalo: A History of the Xhosa People in the Days of Their Independence,* Berkeley: University of California Press, 1982. He became a member of Parliament for the ANC in 1994. Currently he works in local government in Queenstown in the eastern Cape of South Africa.

Cape Town, I became affiliated with the Department of History at the University of Cape Town where I got to know some of the faculty and students.

Guguletu

Again the housing situation proved difficult because laws dictated residential segregation. I stayed in Guguletu[11] my first night, a Black township outside of Cape Town established in 1958 as part of the *Group Areas Act* to separate Blacks into residential areas with families consisting of a husband, wife, and about five children in a two-room house. A friend in Johannesburg directed me to a family. This is generally how I found housing; that is, a friend or acquaintance would direct me to someone at the next destination that they knew. In any case, I realized that the family had given up one of the two rooms to me because they felt I was used to and needed some privacy. The room where I slept was used as a common room where the family watched television. At night, the couch became a bed. The rest of the house, which was shaped like a box, was made up of a combination living/dining room. This was the first room one entered and where most meals were eaten. The family had to sleep in every room: the bedroom, the living room, and the kitchen. The house was a typical Black township house provided by the government. It was issued to a family as a four-room house without a ceiling or floor.

After finding out that the family had given up their room for me, I insisted that I find alternative accommodations quickly so I would no longer inconvenience them. By that evening, arrangements were made for me to live with a woman and her son in Guguletu for three months. The woman I stayed with was Lindiwe Mzo, and she and I became like sisters. She was the mother of six children, including fraternal twins. She was divorced and raising her children alone. Only one son was living with her at the time; the others were away at school or working. I paid her for rent and food. Hers was a four-room house with an outside toilet and an outside bathtub. We did not have hot water but we did have electricity so we could heat our water for bathing, cooking, and washing. Those three months were difficult for me because I was used to the

11. The government set up the area for Africans ten years after the Nationalist party came to power in 1948. On November 14, 1958, the South African government issued Notice No. 1697, proclaiming a "Native Village on the outskirts of Cape Town." This came to be known as Guguletu location. In Xhosa, "Guguletu" means "Our Pride." See Lizo Ngcokoto (1989) "Guguletu: A Township is created, Youth Cultures Emerge 1959–1986." B.A. Honours thesis, University of Cape Town, Department of History.

luxury of hot water, showers, and toilets inside the house. I had never bought a washing tub for personal use and did not know where to buy them or the size to buy. Basic needs became problems that needed to be solved. I learned quickly. Previous to this, I had only visited friends living in the same conditions overnight, so it was a novelty. Living in Guguletu, the novelty quickly wore off. The houses were built on sand which got in everything, especially when the wind was blowing: in the house, in your mouth, in your hair, in your shoes. And all the time, in town, and on the way to town, we could see the beautiful homes of the Whites; homes of many different sizes with the toilets inside, hot running water, showers, bathtubs, and attractive green lawns. It was quite infuriating.

Many of the middle-class coloreds (mixed-race people) had these amenities as well. Some of the coloreds benefited from what was called a colored preferential policy, meaning that they were hired before any Africans. The majority of the coloreds reside in Cape Town because this is the place where they originated. Africans were discouraged from settling in Cape Town because it would interfere with the government's creation of the "homeland" policy. Consequently, Xhosa-speaking Africans were said to belong in the Ciskei or Transkei regions of the Eastern Cape, and the Western Cape became the homeland of the coloreds. This was the old divide-and-rule tactic, and it worked relatively well until the 1976 Soweto student uprisings when the coloreds in Cape Town protested in solidarity with the black students being killed and being fired on by the police. Because Cape Town was a colored preferential area and coloreds were designated by government law to be racially superior to Africans and thus higher on the totem pole, some of the coloreds were accorded better housing, with bigger rooms and inside toilets, better schools, and significantly higher skilled jobs and higher pay.

In Cape Town in 1982, I faced discrimination not only from Whites but also from coloreds in the various public facilities because many had absorbed the racial rhetoric and claimed superiority to Black Africans. Although coloreds were privileged over Africans, some of them seemed to lack racial and cultural identity. They did not speak an indigenous African language: they spoke Afrikaans and identified with the culture of their oppressors, the White Afrikaners. Some of the coloreds, however, clearly identified with Blacks and the liberation movement and supported the banned ANC. Nonetheless, my resentment against the apartheid system built up over the three months I was in Cape Town. I think part of the reason was that many of the coloreds looked so much like African Americans that the discrimination I encountered from them was even more painful than from Whites. This was probably because my expectations were based on my cultural background in the United States. In the United States, Blacks were often friendly because of common skin color and common experiences of racial discrimination. Given my increased resentment after a short period, I could only imagine the feelings and thoughts of Africans living under these discriminatory conditions year in and year out.

While I faced racial discrimination from many Whites and coloreds, there were always good people who extended *ubuntu*. For example, I stayed in Grassy Park, a colored area, for a week with two sisters (both teachers), and their "*ouma*" (Afrikaans for grandmother). They had a two-gabled house, three bedrooms, and a beautiful, large bathroom. I was thrilled to take a bath in a tub located inside the house. They cooked everyday and fed me well, for which I was grateful.

The Eastern Cape

In June 1982, I left Guguletu for the eastern Cape where I was affiliated with Rhodes University in Grahamstown. I had noticed in Johannesburg, and also at the Cape, that White academics often had some White foreign professor visiting them from Europe or the United States. In Johannesburg, no White person invited me to visit their home. I believe I was not invited because of apartheid laws and also because I was a graduate student, rather than a professor.

But in Grahamstown, Jeff Peires, and his wife, Mary Louise, offered me their guesthouse for the first weekend, as well as good food and conversations. For the next month I stayed at the university guest flat for visiting scholars, and for two months after that, I shared a house with five White graduate students. Technically this was illegal, since it was a White area, so my housemates and I were breaking the apartheid laws. It is worthwhile noting that I lived with more White students in South Africa during the period of apartheid than I ever did in the United States under the system of residential segregation. Although we never encountered any problems outwardly, we may have been under police surveillance.

Changing My Research Topic

My personal life influenced my research. I started off doing research on the ICU and collected data in the various areas where I lived through oral interviews and at the archives and libraries. Not until I returned home did I realize that I could not tell the story of the ICU as I wanted. In fact, I had great difficulty writing my dissertation on the ICU.[12] Slowly I came to the realization that I would need to change my topic to another, and as I reviewed my sources, I could see the topic taking shape, grounded in my own experience of facing racial and residential segregation. I should emphasize that this was a difficult and agonizing decision that took me several months.

Yet, my new topic was born back in the United States: African resistance to segregation in South Africa during the nineteenth and early twentieth century in Port Elizabeth, South Africa. I began to understand the importance of writing about the African struggle against segregation long before the introduction of apartheid. I wanted to tell the story of African resistance as it unfolded in the nineteenth century, when the government first tried to impose discriminatory racial laws and residential segregation. Because I had faced so many obstacles in finding suitable housing and saw how much residential segregation affected the racial categories of White, Black, colored, and Asian, I wanted to understand how the segregation started. Clearly my personal experiences shaped this new topic. Although my decision to change my topic after fieldwork in South Africa delayed the completion of my dissertation and publication of my book, I have no regrets. In fact, the Council for Wisconsin Writers awarded my book, *Making A Voice: African Resistance to Segregation in South Africa,* the Kenneth Kingery prize for the best scholarly book in Wisconsin for 1998.

The Naming Ceremony

The authors of *In Pursuit of History* write about social and interpersonal relationships during fieldwork. Such relationships certainly characterized my experience. In particular, I developed a sisterly relationship with Lindiwe Mzo, the woman I stayed with in Guguletu in 1982. Lindiwe always looked out for my well being and tried to help me with my research. She would help me find

---

12. I must admit that the problem with the sources was not the only reason I was unable to write my dissertation. When I left for the field in 1981, I was engaged to be married. Upon my return, I found that my prospective mate was involved in another relationship; subsequently the engagement was broken and he married the other woman. The problem of weakening a committed relationship with a mate because of a long absence, whether married or not, is a potential problem for anyone doing research abroad. This problem is mentioned in *Surviving Fieldwork: A Report of the Advisory Panel on Health and Safety in Fieldwork, American Anthropological Association* (AAA Special Publication, No., 26, 1990) by Nancy Howell. Also see Landes, R. (1970) "A Woman Anthropologist in Brazil," in Peggy Golde, (Ed.) *Women in the Field: Anthropological Experiences,* where one researcher doing fieldwork in Brazil relates that her husband could not understand why she had to go off and do research and her marriage eventually ended in divorce.

housing each time I returned to South Africa (never an easy task during the days of apartheid), and if I needed an interpreter or people to interview on a particular topic, she always would help me find them. I contacted Lindiwe and we would meet for dinner or just to talk whenever I traveled to South Africa, whether for research or for some other project.[13]

Not until 1999 was I able to stay more than a few months in South Africa. In 1998 and 1999, I had a one-year sabbatical and spent three months there. By this time, my book had been published and I was starting a new research project. This project was influenced by changes in my personal life, especially my interest in rites of passage among young and adult African Americans in the United States. These personal changes increased my interest in spiritual development and led me to speak to Lindiwe about a naming ceremony and acceptance into her Xhosa clan. She was very excited and immediately began to organize the event. On March 23, 1999, in Guguletu, I was named Thandeka Magcina (Thandeka means lovable and Magcina is the clan name of Lindiwe's father); it was a significant ceremony for me and for all those who attended. Senior male members of the Magcina clan conducted the ceremony; each man made a short speech, and ThathaNcinci Magcina, the senior elder, delivered the main speech. I had studied Xhosa with a tutor for two months so I also made a short speech in Xhosa. It was well received with claps and broad smiles. Ironically, it was translated from Xhosa to English for those attending who did not understand Xhosa. I enjoyed myself thoroughly. A sheep was slaughtered, *umqombothi* (traditional beer, made over two to three days) was brewed, and women friends and relatives of Lindiwe prepared food. We ate, drank beer, and danced. I believe I am the first African American to have a formal naming ceremony in South Africa. It was a joyous occasion and the culmination of my research in South Africa. I am now doing research on some of the other Magcina clan members.

It is noteworthy that a speech made by Mzwamdile Mzamane, the master of ceremonies, included remarks such as the following:

> It is ironic that an African American has come here to South Africa to be among the Xhosas and wants to be an African when many of the Xhosas want to be African Americans. It is sad that an African American values the Xhosa culture more than the Xhosas themselves. Some

---

13. I was in South Africa as co-coordinator of a capacity building project funded by the United States Information Agency in 1994, 1995, and 1996. The objective was to promote capacity building among Black student leaders heading national organizations and administrative staff at historically Black universities in South Africa.

Xhosas want nothing to do with their heritage and pretend they are not Xhosas. Some get all these braids and perms because they want to be Europeans. There is a lesson in this, and we should take heed. I knew an African girl at the University of Cape Town, and she did not want anyone to call her by her African name. Rather, she wanted to be called Cheryl. I could not understand why she preferred Cheryl, rather than her African name.

His words rang true for many Africans and African Americans since in many cases African culture has been so denigrated by Westerners that Africans themselves would rather be Western or American. Yet some African Americans, whose culture has been denigrated in the United States of America, despite being the wealthiest Black people in the world per capita, seek to return to their roots and find their identity in mother Africa. Certainly the identification with Africa and Africans is part mythology, but human societies are built on mythologies and every society needs them. Mr. Mzamane also indicated that he had never been at such an occasion as this, one held to bring an African American into a clan. He thought it was wonderful that I had visited South Africa so much that I wanted to become a permanent part of it.

Conclusion

I am sure that a foreigner designated as an *honorary White* would have never had the experiences that I did in South Africa while doing field research. I rejected this status during the days of apartheid, and I was often treated like a Black South African because of my outward appearance. Most Africans welcomed me, while most Whites insulted me. It is clear from my experiences that not only did race affect the way I was treated, but so did class, gender, and nationality. For example, on occasions when I encountered the police in Soweto or elsewhere, both Black and White, they were respectful, partially because I am a female and partially because of my American accent. Similarly, many people, especially African women who took me home and offered me food and housing or shared their beds, were influenced by my race, gender, nationality, and of course, their own cultural practice of *ubuntu*. Thus, despite my rejection of the honorary White status, being a foreigner, a Black, an American, and a woman, as both Blacks and Whites in different degrees and according to the circumstances viewed me, could be an advantage and disadvantage.

Doing field research during the days of apartheid meant it was difficult, it not impossible, for me not to become involved in the politics of the country. Being Black in South Africa was a political act whether one liked it or not.

While I did not actively seek to protest apartheid, everyday activities brought me up against the laws. For example, when I was in Cape Town in December 1982, I planned to go to the beach with a few friends because this was the day it was to be opened to all races. The police were at the beach and we were not sure if we would be arrested for entering the water. All went well, but imagine being fearful of arrest for enjoying the Atlantic Ocean water.

There were momentous changes in South Africa in the 1990s: the release of Nelson Mandela in 1990, the first democratic elections in 1994, and Mandela as the first Black president of South Africa, all without major bloodshed. In 1999, I was in South Africa doing research as the campaign for the second democratic elections unfolded. Mandela had already retired and Thabo Mbeki was elected president of South Africa.

I was in South Africa as recently as August 2000, and there are some definite changes. For example, it is no longer difficult to find housing for a Black foreigner if you have the resources. Foreigners of various ethnic groups are purchasing property. The number of African Americans and Africans from outside South Africa increases every day. While in South Africa in 1999, I spoke to several African American businessmen who have relocated with their American companies to South Africa or have established their own companies and are doing business in South Africa. Some of my friends have purchased new houses outside of the African townships while others have remodeled and extended their township houses. For the most part, the poor continue to experience hardships, but for many, their psychological condition has improved and hope is still alive.

I find myself being suspicious of comments about how Blacks can use public facilities that were segregated in the past and off limits to them, how Blacks can live wherever they wish and attend any school they want, and how the Black middle class is growing. Somehow these transitions, this availability to Blacks of basic facilities that before were barred to them on one day and open to them the next, makes me ponder the absurdity of racial categories that force the segregation and separation of humans. I wonder how people who have been separated by force and denied their civil and human rights are supposed to simply make the transition, physically and psychologically, and not expect anything concrete except new laws to somehow compensate for the previous apartheid policies and practices. Victims are to forgive and forget. Victims are to understand that they now have equal opportunity with their former oppressors and that they can even live alongside them if they so desire and can afford it. Most Africans remain economically disadvantaged, unemployed, and about 40 percent do not have funds for schooling. Simultaneously, the Black middle class is growing at a fast rate, but like the Black middle class in the United

States, they have one foot in the new class and one in the working class. Perhaps I too, have one foot in South Africa's apartheid past and one foot in the democratic present.

I continue to do research in South Africa, and each time I learn new things about the country and its people. Today, I am accorded *ubuntu,* not only by Africans, but also by coloreds and Whites more so than in the past. As I do in the United States, I still face some racial discrimination. My early identification with Africans, rather than colored and Whites, has shaped my present relationships in South Africa. Each time I visit, the possibilities for extending the boundaries of friendship beyond race, class, and gender improve. I find that, alongside poverty and new wealth, hope still exists. For this, I am glad.

Bibliography and Suggested Readings

Adenaike, C. K. & Vansina, J. (Eds.). (1996). *In pursuit of history: Fieldwork in Africa.* Portsmouth: Heinemann.

Bigelow, W. (1985). *Strangers in their own country: A curriculum guide in South Africa.* Trenton: Africa World Press.

Feierman, S. (1977). *The Shambaa kingdom.* Madison: University of Wisconsin Press.

Fredrickson, G. M. (1981). *White supremacy: A comparative study. An American and South African history.* New York: Oxford University Press.

Howell, N. (1990). *Surviving fieldwork: A report of the advisory panel on health and safety in fieldwork, American Anthropological Society.* AAA Special Publication 26.

Keto, C. T. (1972). Black Americans in South Africa, 1890–1910. *A current bibliography on African affairs.* Volume 5, Series II, (pp. 382–406).

Kirk, T. J. F. (2000). *Making a voice: African resistance to segregation in South Africa.* Boulder: Westview Press.

Landes, R. (1970). A woman anthropologist in Brazil. In P. Golde (Ed.), *Women in the field: Anthropological experiences* (pp. 119–142). Chicago: Aldine Publishing Company.

Mothibe, T. H. (1996). Fieldwork among neighbors: An African's view of another African country. In C. K. Adenaike & J. Vansina (Eds.), *In pursuit of history: Fieldwork in Africa* (p. 15). Portsmouth: Heinemann.

Ngcokoto, L. (1989). *Guguletu: A township is created, youth cultures emerge 1959–1986.* B.A. Honours Thesis. Department of History, University of Cape Town.

Peires, J. (1982). *The house of Phalo: A history of the Xhosa people in the days of their independence.* Berkeley: University of California Press.

Dr. Anna Lucille Green

Dr. Anna Lucille Green is the third child of Ms. Jacquelyn Collins Green and Mr. Murphy Green, Jr. She was reared in Louisiana by a strong hand in faith and family, elements that continue to play an important role in her life. Dr. Green's parents emphasized the importance of education early in her life. She received her bachelor of science degree in psychology from Xavier University in New Orleans, Louisiana. During her undergraduate years, she began to take responsibility for her personal and professional development by pursuing community service opportunities, scholastic opportunities, and the value in becoming a lifelong learner. She received her master of arts degree in educational psychology from Clark Atlanta University in Atlanta. As she focused more on personal goals, Dr. Green diligently worked at building her foundation in the educational arena as a respected scholar and colleague. This foundation supported Dr. Green's determination to obtain her doctorate in educational psychology from Florida State University in Tallahassee. Dr. Green's dissertation examined motivation among African American college students.

Dr. Green's professional background is defined as a process and not a product of her education. This means that with every lesson learned, she learns a little more about herself and seeks to discover her true contribution to others. While a graduate student, she served as an office assistant, teaching assistant, and university adjunct instructor. She is currently an assistant professor at Florida A & M University in the School of Business and Industry.

Dr. Green remains grounded in her early faith and family teachings by staying actively involved in her academic and social community. She is a proud member of Alpha Kappa Alpha Sorority, Inc., the American Educational Research Association, and the National Association for the Advancement of Colored People. Dr. Green makes every attempt to live by the following statement, *Visualize Opportunities, Not Obstacles!*

EPILOGUE

LEAVING A LASTING IMPRESSION

Anna L. Green

The authors in this volume raised poignant issues that relate to and impact the role of Black women scholars at various levels within the education sector from their contributions as teachers at the end of the nineteenth century to their pursuit of education and research in the African diaspora. As an emergent scholar, it has been personally challenging and rewarding to be a part of such an important project. *Sisters of the Academy* provided me the opportunity to reflect concretely about the challenges that continue to influence the professional lives of many scholars of color, but more importantly, this book gave me the opportunity to celebrate the accomplishments, successes, and resilience of Black scholars despite their challenges.

Sisters of the Academy draws its strength from the diverse methodologies and frameworks employed by the authors to capture the essence of the Black woman's experience in higher education. The authors who contributed to this volume (as noted in the introduction), do not claim to have a patent on *how-to-succeed* as a Black woman scholar in the academy, nor do they view their narratives as representative of all Black women scholars; however, they do represent the voices and faces of scholars who have historically been relegated to the fringes of the academy. More importantly, the authors demonstrate the unwounded spirit that drives each and every one of the contributors represented in this volume.

Sisters of the Academy is by no means an end to the many forums and discussions regarding the role and presence of Black women in higher education. There are many questions and issues that require further exploration. It is our hope that this volume will serve as a catalyst for further *positive* dialogue about our contributions to the academy, as well as to the broader African and African American communities. We are here to stay!

In closing, I share the following words of inspiration and celebrate African American women who came before us.

> *It is of no use for us to sit with our hands folded, hanging our heads like bulrushes, lamenting our wretched condition; but let us make a mighty effort, and arise; and if no one will promote or respect us, let us promote and respect ourselves.* (Maria W. Stewart)

> *We need visions for larger things, for the unfolding and reviewing of worthwhile things.* (Mary McLeod Bethune)

> *Education is the jewel casting brilliance into the future.* (Mari Evans)

> *The most rewarding freedom is freedom of the mind.* (Amy Garvey)

> *Knowledge is not power; it is only potential power that becomes real through use.* (Dorothy Riley)

> *One isn't necessarily born with courage, but one is born with potential. Without courage, we cannot practice any other virtue with consistency. We can't be kind, true, merciful, generous, or honest.* (Maya Angelou)

expectations, 66, 67
institutional, 58
school, 131
white male-dominated, 58, 68
Cummings v. County Board of Education, 10, 12

Darwinism, 5
Dual consciousness, 60
Dual status, 49
Duality of Race, 129
DuBois, W.E.B, 12, 49

Education
for liberation, 30, 33, 158
for socialization, 30, 32
Epistemology, 146
Ethnocentrism, 46, 96, 151

Faculty of color, 81
factors affecting, 81
Latina scholars, xx, xix, 81,
82–84, 86–87, 88–90
mentors for, 81, 100, 106, 108,
109–112
teaching role, 178
Fluid Life Structure, 72

GED, 177
Gendered Discrimination, 107

Honorary White, 183, 192, 194, 202
Historically Black Women's
Colleges, 32–33
Bennett College, 32
curriculum, 33
role of missionaries, 32
Spelman College, 32

Identity
and self, 133–135
and self-perception, 130
formation, 122, 124, 128
gender identity, 120

racial identity, 120, 123
and pedagogy, 121
Industrial and Commercial Worker's
Union (ICU), 186, 196, 199
Ivory tower, 57

Knowledge, 64
of academic culture, 64
of culture, 65
of rules, 67
power of, 64

Language
scholarly language, 118
power of, 118
Xhosa, 188, 192, 201
Zulu, 192
Limited-mobility, 49
Loving School, 5

Malcom X, 142
Mandela, Nelson, 203
Marginalization, 93, 97, 99, 106,
112–113, 120, 125, 152
Marginality, 60–62
creative marginality, 58–59
marginal theory, 59
Medary Schools, 9
Mentoring, 98, 100, 108, 109–112
Metastorytelling, 152
Minorities, 49
types of, 49–50
Miscegenation, 3–4, 16–17, 21

Naming Ceremony, 200
Magcina clan, 201
Narratives
autobiographical, 155–157
biographical, 154–155
personal, 153
Non-traditional college student, 177

Oberlin college, 13, 35
African American graduates
of, 35